# Building the Data Warehouse

## Second Edition

# W.H. Inmon

WILEY COMPUTER PUBLISHING

John Wiley & Sons, Inc.
• New York • Chichester • Brisbane
• Toronto • Singapore

Publisher: Katherine Schowalter
Editor: Robert Elliott
Managing Editor: Micheline Frederick
Text Design & Composition: Publishers' Design and Production Services, Inc.

Designations used by companies to distinguish their products are often claimed as trademarks. In all instances where John Wiley & Sons, Inc. is aware of a claim, the product names appear in initial capital or all capital letters. Readers, however, should contact the appropriate companies for more complete information regarding trademarks and registration.

This text is printed on acid-free paper.

This publication is designed to provide accurate and authoritative information in regard to the subject matter covered. It is sold with the understanding that the publisher is not engaged in rendering legal, accounting, or other professional service. If legal advice or other expert assistance is required, the services of a competent professional person should be sought.

*Library of Congress Cataloging-in-Publication Data:*

ISBN No. 0471-14161-5

Printed in the United States of America

10 9 8 7 6 5 4 3 2 1

*For Jeanne Friedman,
a friend for all times*

# Contents

# Preface

**D**atabases and database theory have been around for a long time. Early renditions of databases centered around a single database serving every purpose known to the information processing community—from transaction to batch processing to analytical processing. In most cases, the primary focus of the early database systems was operational—usually transactional processing. In recent years, a more sophisticated notion of database has emerged—one that serves operational needs and another that serves informational or analytical needs. To some extent, this more enlightened notion of database is due to the advent of PCs, 4GL technology, and the empowerment of the end user.

The split of operational and informational databases occurs for many reasons:

- The data serving operational needs is physically different data from that serving informational or analytic needs.
- The supporting technology for operational processing is fundamentally different from the technology used to support informational or analytical needs.
- The user community for operational data is different from the one served by informational or analytical data.

■ The processing characteristics for the operational environment and the informational environment are fundamentally different.

Because of these reasons (and many more!), the modern way to build systems is to separate the operational from the informational or analytical processing and data.

This book is about the analytical [or the DSS (decision support systems)] environment and the structuring of data in that environment. The focus of the book is on what is termed the "data warehouse" (or "information warehouse"), which is at the heart of informational, DSS processing.

The discussions in this book are geared toward the manager and the developer. Where appropriate, some level of discussion will be at the technical level. But for the most part, the book is about issues and techniques. This book is meant to serve as a guideline for the designer and the developer.

What is analytical, informational processing? It is processing that serves the needs of management in the decision-making process. Often known as DSS processing, analytical processing looks across broad vistas of data to detect trends. Instead of looking at one or two records of data (as is the case in operational processing), when the DSS analyst does analytical processing, many records are accessed.

In addition, it is very rare for the DSS analyst to update data. In operational systems, data is constantly being updated at the individual record level. In analytical processing, records are constantly being accessed, and their contents are gathered for analysis, but little or no alteration of individual records occurs.

In analytical processing, the response time requirements are greatly relaxed compared to those of traditional operational processing. Analytical response time is measured from 30 minutes to 24 hours. Response times measured in this range for operational processing would be an unmitigated disaster.

The network that serves the analytical community is much smaller than the one that serves the operational community. Usually there are far fewer users of the analytical network than of the operational network.

Unlike the technology that serves the analytical environment, operational environment technology must concern itself with data and transaction locking, contention for data, deadlock, and so on.

There are, then, many major differences between the operational environment and the analytical environment. This book is about the analytical, DSS environment and addresses the following issues:

- granularity of data
- partitioning of data
- metadata
- lack of credibility of data
- integration of DSS data
- the time basis of DSS data
- identifying the source of DSS data—the system of record
- migration and methodology

This book is for developers, managers, designers, data administrators, database administrators, and others who are building systems in a modern data processing environment. In addition, students of information processing will find this book useful.

This book is the first in a series of books relating to data warehouse. The next book in the series is *USING THE DATA WAREHOUSE. USING THE DATA WAREHOUSE* addresses the issues that arise once you have built the data warehouse. In addition *USING THE DATA WAREHOUSE* introduces the concept of a larger architecture and the notion of an operational data store (ODS). An operational data store is a similar architectural construct to the data warehouse, except the ODS applies only to operational systems, not informational systems. The third book in the series is *BUILDING THE OPERATIONAL DATA STORE*, which addresses the issues of what an ODS is and how an ODS is built.

There are many people who have contributed—directly and indirectly—to this effort. The following list reflects only a few contributors:

- Sue Osterfelt, Nations Bank
- Claudia Imhoff, Intelligent Solutions
- John Zachman, Zachman International

- Jim Kerr, independent consultant
- Ed Young, Prism Solutions
- Jim Ashbrook, Prism Solutions
- Cynthia Schmidt, Prism Solutions
- Peter LaPorte, Tandem Computers
- Edie Conklin, independent consultant
- George Coleman, Prism Solutions
- Jeanne Friedman, Logica
- Cheryl Estep, Chevron Corporation
- Kevin Gould, Sybase
- Chuck Kelley, Pine Cone Systems
- George Comeaux, Bank of Boston
- J.D. Welch, Prism Solutions
- Arnie Barnett, Barnett Data Systems

# Evolution of Decision Support Systems

The world of information systems is an "immature" world. One has to be careful in using that word in public because it normally has a negative connotation. But from a historical perspective it is true. When you compare the history of information processing to that of other professions, there is no contest. We are told that the hieroglyphics in Egypt are primarily the work of an accountant declaring how much grain is owed the pharaoh. We walk down the streets of Rome on paths and structures laid out by a civil engineer over 2,000 years ago. Other professions have roots back to antiquity.

So, the information processing profession is historically immature because it has existed only since the early 1960s.

One of the manifestations of the information processing profession's youth is its tendency to dwell on detail. There is the notion that if we get the details right, the end result will somehow take care of itself and we will achieve success. It's like saying that if we know how to lay concrete, how to drill, and how to install nuts and bolts, we don't have to worry about the shape or the use of the bridge we are building. Such an attitude would drive a more mature civil engineer crazy.

The story of the data warehouse begins with an evolution in

which the larger forces at work in the industry are considered. The larger architecture that is being carved out—of which the data warehouse is the focal piece—is best viewed from a broad, not a detailed, perspective.

## THE EVOLUTION

It is interesting that DSS (decision support system) processing is at the end of a long and complex evolution but continues to evolve. The origins of DSS processing hark back to the very early days of computers.

Figure 1.1 shows the evolution of processing from the early 1960s up to 1980. In the early 1960s, the world of computation consisted of creating individual applications that were run on master files. The applications featured reports and programs, usually COBOL. Punched cards were common. The master files were stored on magnetic tape files, which were good for storing a large volume of data cheaply but had the drawback of needing to be accessed sequentially. Indeed, it is often said that in a given pass of a magnetic tape file where 100 percent of the records have to be accessed, only 5 percent or fewer of the records are actually needed. In addition, accessing an entire tape file may take as long as 20 to 30 minutes, depending on the data on the file and the processing that is being done.

Around the mid-1960s, the growth of master files and magnetic tape exploded. Soon there were master files everywhere. And with that growth came huge amounts of redundant data. The proliferation of master files and massive redundancy of data presented some very insidious problems:

- the need to synchronize data upon update
- the complexity of maintenance of programs
- the complexity of developing new programs
- the amount of hardware required to support all the master files

In short order, the problems of master files that were inherent to the medium itself became stifling. It is an interesting conjecture to speculate what the world of information processing

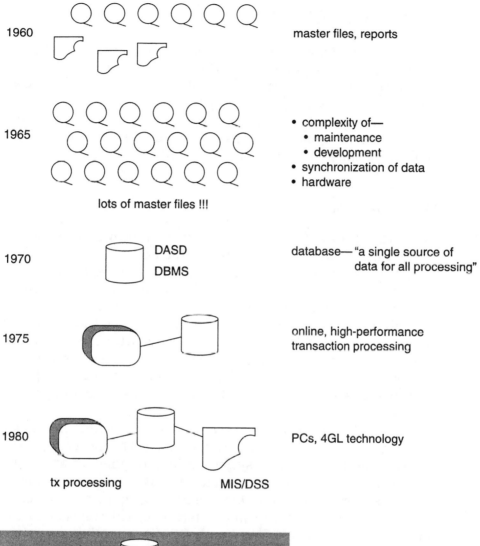

1960 — master files, reports

1965 — lots of master files !!!
- complexity of—
  - maintenance
  - development
- synchronization of data
- hardware

1970 — DASD / DBMS — database— "a single source of data for all processing"

1975 — online, high-performance transaction processing

1980 — PCs, 4GL technology

tx processing          MIS/DSS

the single-database-serving-all-purposes paradigm

**Figure 1.1**   The early evolutionary stages of the architected environment.

would look like if the only medium for storing data had been the magnetic tape.

If there had never been anything to store bulk data on other than magnetic tape files, the world would have never had large, fast reservations systems, ATM systems, and the like. Indeed, the ability to store and manage data on a variety of media other than magnetic tape files opened up the way for a different and more powerful type of processing that brought the technician and the businessperson together as never before.

## THE ADVENT OF DASD

By 1970, the day of a new technology for the storage and access of data had dawned. The 1970s saw the advent of disk storage, or DASD (direct access storage device). Disk storage was fundamentally different from magnetic tape storage in that data could be accessed directly on DASD. There was no need to go through records 1, 2, 3, . . . $n$ to get to record $n + 1$. Once the address of record $n + 1$ was known, it was a simple matter to go to record $n + 1$ directly. Furthermore, the time required to go to record $n + 1$ was significantly less than the time required to scan a tape. In fact, the time to locate a record on DASD was measured in milliseconds.

With DASD came a new piece of system software known as a DBMS or database management system. The purpose of the DBMS was to make it easy for the programmer to store and access data on DASD. In addition, the DBMS took care of such tasks as storing data on DASD, indexing data, and so forth. With DASD and DBMS came a technological solution to the problems of master files. And with DBMS came the notion of a "database." In looking at the mess that was created by master files and the masses of redundant data aggregated on them, it is no wonder that *database* is defined as

a single source of data for all processing.

But the world did not end in 1970. By the mid-1970s, online transaction processing began to take place on databases. With a terminal and the appropriate software, the technician found that quicker access to data was possible—opening whole new vistas. With high-performance online transaction processing, the computer could be used for tasks not previously possible. The computer could now be used to drive reservations systems, bank teller systems, manufacturing control systems, and the like. Had the world remained in a magnetic tape file state, most of the systems that we take for granted today would not have been possible.

## PC/4GL TECHNOLOGY

By the 1980s, more new technologies—such as PCs and 4GLs—began to surface. The end user began to assume a role previously unfathomed—directly controlling data and systems, outside the domain of the classical data processor. With PCs and 4GL technology came the notion that more could be done with data than servicing online high-performance transaction processing. MIS (management information systems)—as it was called in the early days—could also be done. Today known as DSS, MIS was processing that was used to drive management decisions. Previously, data and technology were used exclusively to drive detailed operational decisions. There arose the notion of a paradigm—a single database that could serve both operational, high-performance transaction processing and DSS, analytical processing at the same time. Figure 1.1 shows the single-database paradigm.

## ENTER THE EXTRACT PROGRAM

Shortly after the advent of massive online high-performance transactions, an innocuous program called "extract" processing, began to appear (Figure 1.2).

The extract program is the simplest of all programs. It rummages through a file or database, uses some criteria for selection, and, upon finding qualified data, transports the data over onto another file or database.

Soon the extract program became very popular. It permeated the information processing environment. There are (at least) two reasons for its popularity:

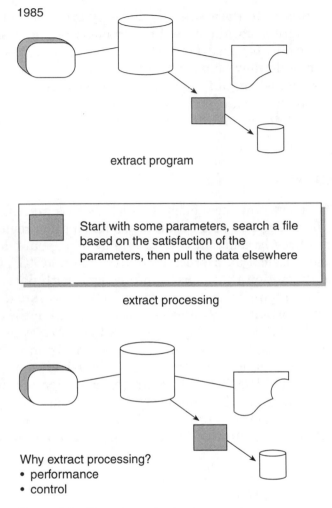

**Figure 1.2** The nature of extract processing.

- ■ Because it can move data out of the way of high-performance online processing with an extract program, there is no conflict in terms of performance when the data needs to be analyzed en masse.
- ■ When data is moved out of the operational, transaction processing domain with an extract program, there is a shift in control of the data. The end user ends up "owning" the data once he or she takes control of it.

The legacy systems environment

1990

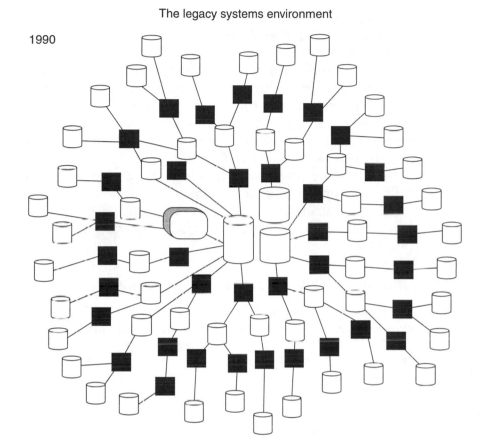

naturally evolving architecture (AKA the "spider web")

**Figure 1.3** Extract processing must have been a good thing based on its widespread proliferation.

For these (and probably a host of other) reasons, extract processing was soon found everywhere. By the 1990s there were many extract programs, as depicted in Figure 1.3.

## THE SPIDER WEB

Figure 1.3 shows that a "spider web" of extract processing began to form. First, there were extracts. Then there were extracts of extracts, then extracts of extracts of extracts, and so forth. It was not unheard of for a large company to be doing as many as 45,000 extracts *per day*.

This pattern of extract processing across the organization became so commonplace that a name was given to it. Extract processing gone out of control produced what can be called the "naturally evolving architecture"—what occurs when an organization handles the whole process of hardware and software architecture with a *laissez-faire* attitude. The larger and more mature the organization, the worse the problems of the naturally evolving architecture become.

Taken collectively, the extract programs form a spider web—just another name for the naturally evolving (or "legacy systems") architecture.

## Problems with the Naturally Evolving Architecture

What exactly are the difficulties associated with the naturally evolving architecture? There are many problems, principally:

- credibility of data
- productivity
- inability to transform data into information

### Lack of Credibility of Data

The first of these problems—the lack of credibility of data—is illustrated in Figure 1.4. Two departments are delivering a report to management. One department states that activity is down 15 percent. The other department says that activity is up 10 percent. Not only are the two departments not in sync with each other, they are off by very large margins. In addition, trying to reconcile the departments is a difficult thing to do. Unless very careful documentation has been done, reconciliation is—for all practical purposes—impossible.

When management receives the two reports, they do not know what to think. Management is faced with the proposition of making decisions based on politics and personalities. This is an example of the crisis in credibility in the naturally evolving architecture.

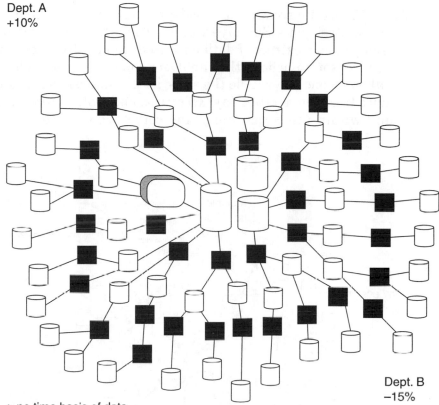

Dept. A
+10%

Dept. B
−15%

- no time basis of data
- algorithmic differential
- levels of extraction
- external data
- no common source of data to begin with

**Figure 1.4**   Lack of credibility in the naturally evolving architecture.

This crisis is widespread and predictable. Why? Five reasons for the predictability of the crisis, as depicted in Figure 1.4, are:

- no time basis of data
- the algorithmic differential of data
- the levels of extraction
- the problem of external data
- no common source of data to begin with

Figure 1.5 shows that one department has extracted its data for analysis on a Sunday evening. The other department doing analysis has extracted data on a Wednesday afternoon. Is there any reason to believe that analysis done on one sample of data taken on one day will be the same as the analysis for a sample of data taken on another day? Of course not! Data is always changing within the corporation. Any correlation between analyzed

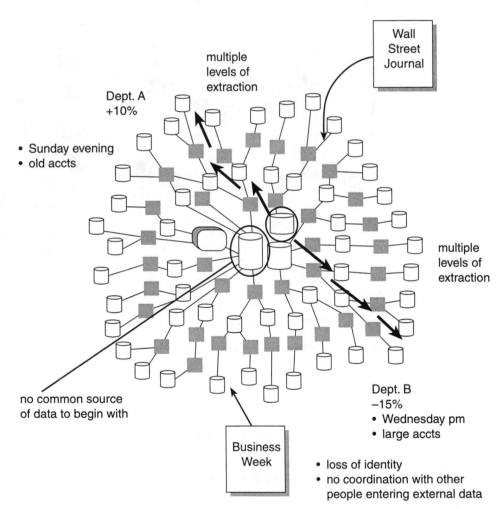

**Figure 1.5**  The reasons for the predictability of the crisis in credibility in the naturally evolving architecture.

sets of data that are taken at different points in time is only coincidental.

The second reason for the predictability of the crisis of credibility of data in the naturally evolving architecture is the algorithmic differential. For example, one department has chosen to analyze all old accounts. Another department has chosen to analyze all large accounts. Is there any necessary correlation between the characteristics of customers who have old accounts and customers who have large accounts? Probably not. So why should a very different result of analysis surprise anyone?

The third reason for predictability of crisis is one that merely magnifies the first two reasons. Every time a new extraction is done, the probabilities of a discrepancy arise because of the timing or the algorithmic differential. And it is not unusual for a corporation to have eight or nine levels of extraction being done from the time the data enters the corporation's system to the time analysis is prepared for management.

The fourth reason for lack of credibility is because of the problem posed by external data. With today's technologies at the PC level, it is very easy to bring in data from outside sources. In the example shown in Figure 1.5, one analyst has brought data into the mainstream of analysis from the *Wall Street Journal*, and another analyst has brought data in from *BusinessWeek*. The first thing the analyst does as he or she brings data in is to strip the external data of its identity. Instead of data originating from the *Wall Street Journal*, once the data is entered into the PC, it simply becomes plain data that could have come from any source.

Furthermore, the analyst who brings in data from the *Wall Street Journal* knows nothing about the data being entered from *BusinessWeek*, and vice versa. No wonder, then, that external data contributes to the lack of credibility of data in the naturally evolving architecture.

The last contributing factor to the lack of credibility is that often there is no common source of data to begin with. Analysis for department A originates from file XYZ. Analysis for department B originates from database ABC. There is no synchronization or sharing of data whatsoever between file XYZ and database ABC.

Given these reasons, it is no small wonder that there is a crisis of credibility brewing in every organization that allows its architecture legacy of hardware, software, and data to evolve naturally into the spider's web.

### The Problems with Productivity

But credibility of data is not the only major problem with the naturally evolving architecture. The productivity (or lack thereof) that is achieved in the naturally evolving architecture, when there is a need to look across the organization, is abysmal.

Consider an organization that has been in business for a while and has built up a large collection of data, as shown in the top of Figure 1.6.

Management desires to produce a corporate report, using the many files and collections of data that have accumulated over the years. The designer assigned the task decides there are three things that must be done to produce the corporate report:

- Locate and analyze the data for the report.
- Compile the data for the report.
- Get programmer/analyst resources to accomplish the above.

In order to locate the data, *many* files and layouts of data must be analyzed. Furthermore, there are complicating factors: One file has an element known as BALANCE; another file has an element with the same name. But the two elements are very different. In another case, one database has a file known as CURRBAL. In another collection of data, there is a file called INVLEVEL that happens to be the same as CURRBAL. This process of having to go through every piece of data—not just by name but by definition and calculation—is a *very* tedious process. But if the corporate report is to be produced, this exercise MUST be done properly. Unless data is analyzed and "rationalized," the report will end up mixing apples and oranges, creating further confusion.

The next task is to compile the data, once located. Certainly the program that must be written to get data from its many sources is a simple one. But it is complicated by the following facts:

**productivity**

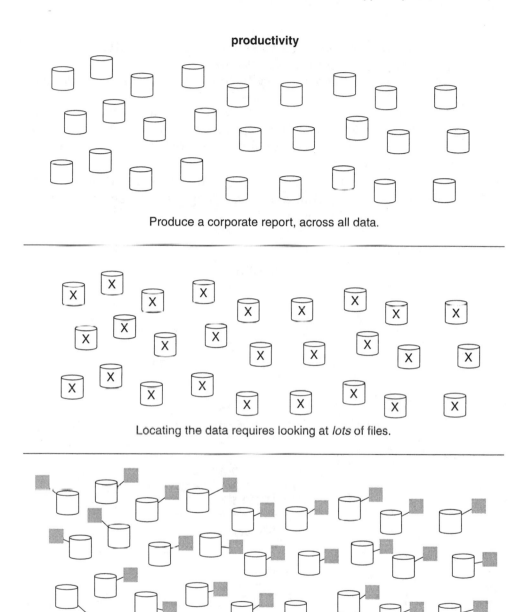

Produce a corporate report, across all data.

Locating the data requires looking at *lots* of files.

Lots of extract programs, each customized, have to cross many technological barriers.

**Figure 1.6**   The naturally evolving architecture is not conducive to productivity.

- There are lots of programs that have to be written.
- Each program must be customized.
- The programs cross every technology that the company has.

In short, even though the report-generation program must be written and appears to be simple to do, because of the above factors, retrieving the data for the corporate report is a very tedious activity.

In a corporation facing exactly the problems described, an analyst recently estimated a *very* long time to accomplish the tasks, as shown in Figure 1.7.

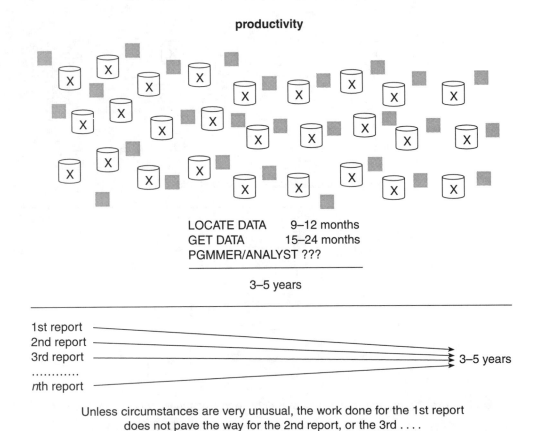

```
LOCATE DATA      9–12 months
GET DATA        15–24 months
PGMMER/ANALYST ???
```

3–5 years

1st report
2nd report
3rd report
............
*n*th report

3–5 years

Unless circumstances are very unusual, the work done for the 1st report
does not pave the way for the 2nd report, or the 3rd . . . .

**Figure 1.7** The requirements for succeeding reports are not known at the time the first report is being written.

If the designer had asked for only two or three man-months of resources, then generating the report might not have required much management attention. But when an analyst requisitions many resources, management must put the request in with all the other requests for resources and must prioritize the requests. So, the analyst estimated a lengthy time to create the desired reports.

But creating the reports using a large amount of resources wouldn't be bad if there were a onetime penalty to be paid. In other words, if the first corporate report generated required a large amount of resources, and all succeeding reports could build on the first report, then it might be worthwhile to bite the bullet and pay the price for generating the first report. But such is not the case.

Unless future corporate reporting requirements are known in advance, and unless those requirements are factored into the building of the first corporate report, then there is every likelihood that *every* new corporate report is going to have to pay the same large overhead! In other words, it is highly unlikely that the first corporate report is going to do anything for future corporate reporting requirements.

Productivity, then, in the corporate environment is a major issue in the face of the naturally evolving architecture and legacy systems.

### From Data to Information

As if productivity and credibility were not problems enough, there is another major fault of the naturally evolving architecture—the inability to go from data to information. At first glance, the notion of going from data to information seems to be an ethereal concept with little substance. But such is not the case at all.

Consider the following request for information, typical in a banking environment: "How has account activity been different this year from each of the past five years?"

Figure 1.8 shows the request for information.

The first thing the DSS analyst discovers in trying to satisfy the request for information is that going to existing systems for the necessary data is about the worst thing to do; there are lots

**going from data to information**

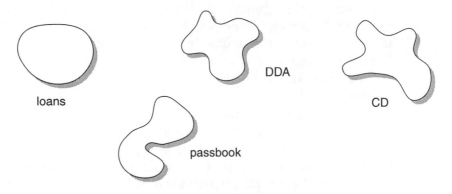

First, you run into lots of applications.

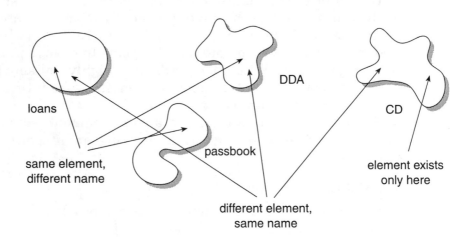

Next, you run into the lack of integration across applications.

**Figure 1.8** "How has account activity been different this year from each of the past five for the financial institution?"

of applications in the legacy environment that will be encountered by the DSS analyst.

Trying to find out what data exists for an account is a difficult thing to do. There are savings applications. There are loan applications. There are DDA applications. There are trust applications. And trying to draw information from them on a common basis is nigh impossible. The applications were never constructed with integration in mind, and they are no easier for the DSS analyst to decipher than they are for anyone else.

But integration is not the only difficulty the analyst meets in trying to satisfy an informational request. A second major obstacle is that there is not enough historical data stored in the applications to meet the needs of the DSS request.

Figure 1.9 shows that the loan department has up to two years' worth of data. Passbook processing has up to one year of data. DDA applications have up to 60 days of data. And CD processing has up to 18 months of data. The applications were built to service the needs of current balance processing (naturally enough!). They were never designed to hold the historical data needed for DSS analysis. It is no wonder, then, that going to existing systems for DSS analysis is a poor choice. But where else is there to go?

The systems found in the naturally evolving architecture are simply inadequate for the task of supporting information needs

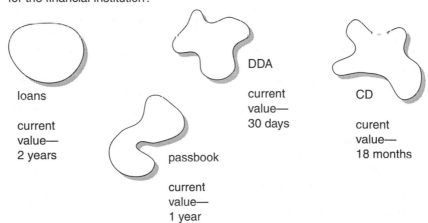

**going from data to information**

an example
"How has account activity been different this year from each of the past five for the financial institution?

loans

current value— 2 years

passbook

current value— 1 year

DDA

current value— 30 days

CD

curent value— 18 months

**Figure 1.9**  Existing applications simply do not have the historical data required to convert data into information.

because of their lack of integration and because of the difference in the time horizon needed for analytical processing and the available time horizon of applications in the spider web environment.

## A Change in Approaches

The status quo of the naturally evolving architecture—where most shops are today—simply is not enough to meet the needs of tomorrow. What is needed is a change in architectures—where the architected data warehouse environment is found.

At the heart of an "architected" environment is the realization that there are fundamentally two kinds of data—primitive data and derived data. Figure 1.10 shows some of the major differences between primitive and derived data.

Primitive data is detailed data used to run the day-to-day

**a change in approaches**

| PRIMITIVE DATA/OPERATIONAL DATA | DERIVED DATA/DSS DATA |
|---|---|
| • application oriented | • subject oriented |
| • detailed | • summarized, otherwise refined |
| • accurate, as of the moment of access | • represents values over time, snapshots |
| • serves the clerical community | • serves the managerial community |
| • can be updated | • is not updated |
| • run repetitively | • run heuristically |
| • requirements for processing understood a priori | • requirements for processing not understood *a priori* |
| • compatible with the SDLC | • completely different life cycle |
| • performance sensitive | • performance relaxed |
| • accessed a unit at a time | • accessed a set at a time |
| • transaction driven | • analysis driven |
| • control of update a major concern in terms of ownership | • control of update no issue |
| • high availability | • relaxed availability |
| • managed in its entirety | • managed by subsets |
| • nonredundancy | • redundancy is a fact of life |
| • static structure; variable contents | • flexible structure |
| • small amount of data used in a process | • large amount of data used in a process |
| • supports day-to-day operations | • supports managerial needs |
| • high probability of access | • low, modest probability of access |

**Figure 1.10** The whole notion of data is changed in the architected environment.

operations of the company. Derived data is data that is summarized or otherwise calculated to meet the needs of the management of the company. Primitive data can be updated. Derived data cannot be updated. Primitive data is primarily current-value data. Derived data is often historical data. Primitive data is operated on by procedures that run in a repetitive fashion. Derived data is operated on by programs that run heuristically, on a nonrepetitive basis. Operational data is primitive; DSS data is derived. Primitive data supports the clerical function. Derived data supports the managerial function.

Thus, there are a host of differences between primitive and derived data. It is a wonder that the information processing community ever thought that *both* primitive and derived data would fit in a single database.

## THE ARCHITECTED ENVIRONMENT

The natural extension of the split in data caused by the difference between primitive and derived data is shown in Figure 1.11.

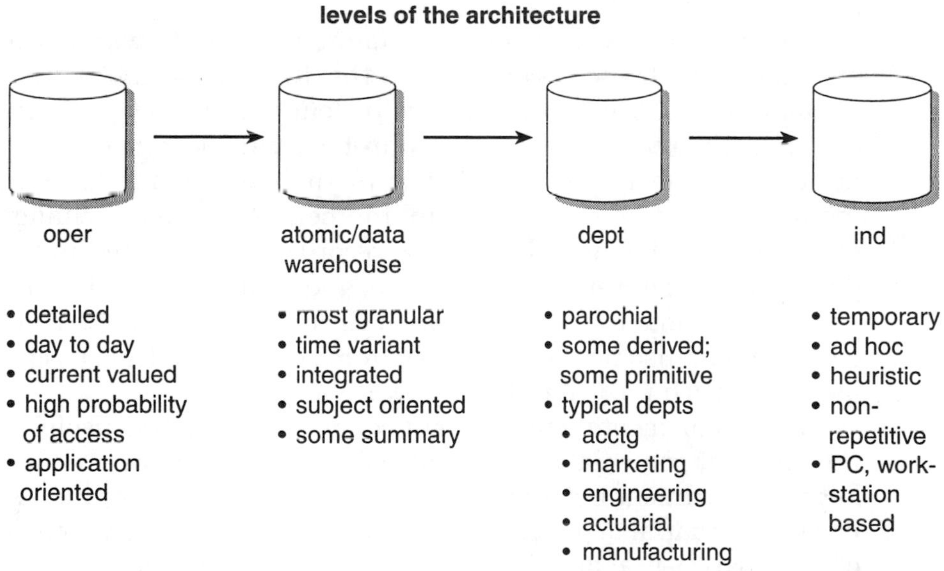

**levels of the architecture**

| oper | atomic/data warehouse | dept | ind |
|---|---|---|---|
| • detailed | • most granular | • parochial | • temporary |
| • day to day | • time variant | • some derived; | • ad hoc |
| • current valued | • integrated | some primitive | • heuristic |
| • high probability | • subject oriented | • typical depts | • non- |
| of access | • some summary | • acctg | repetitive |
| • application | | • marketing | • PC, work- |
| oriented | | • engineering | station |
| | | • actuarial | based |
| | | • manufacturing | |

**Figure 1.11**  Although it is not apparent at first glance, there is very little redundancy of data across the architected environment.

There are four levels in the architected environment—the operational, the atomic or the data warehouse, the departmental, and the individual. The operational level of data holds primitive data only and serves the high-performance transaction processing community. The data warehouse holds primitive data that is not updated. In addition, some derived data is found there. The departmental level of data contains derived data almost exclusively. And the individual level of data is where much heuristic analysis is done.

The immediate reaction to the architecture is that there is much redundant data in the architected environment. Such is not the case at all, although it is not obvious at first glance. Instead, gross amounts of data redundancy are found in the spider's web.

Consider the simple example of data throughout the architecture, as shown in Figure 1.12. At the operational level there is a record for a customer, J Jones. The record at the operational level is the record that contains current value data. To learn the status of the customer right now, the record in the operational level is accessed. Of course, if the information for J Jones changes, the record in the operational level will be changed to reflect the new data that is correct.

Several records for J Jones are found in the data warehouse environment. These records show the history of information about J Jones. To discover where J Jones lived last year, for example, the records in the data warehouse are searched. There is no overlap between the records in the operational environment and the data warehouse environment. If there is a change of address for J Jones, then a new record will be created in the data warehouse, reflecting the *from* and *to* dates that J Jones lived there. Note that the records in the data warehouse are not overlapping. Also note that there is some element of time associated with each record in the data warehouse.

The departmental environment contains information useful to the different parochial departments of a company. There is a marketing departmental database, an accounting departmental database, an actuarial departmental database, and so forth. The source of *all* departmental data is the data warehouse. The departmental level is sometimes called the "datamart" level, the (online analog process ) "OLAP" level, or the "multidimensional DBMS" level.

**a simple example—a customer**

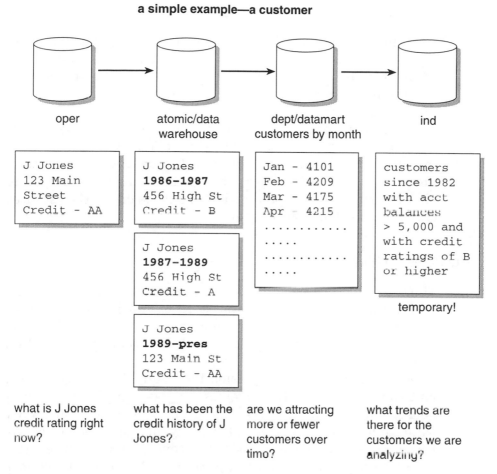

**Figure 1.12** The kinds of queries that the different levels of data can be used for.

Typical of data at the departmental level is a monthly customer file. In the file is a list of all customers by category. J Jones goes into this summary each month. It is a stretch to consider the tallying of information as a form of redundancy.

The final level of data is the individual level. Individual data is usually temporary and small. At the individual level much heuristic analysis is done. As a rule, the individual levels of data are thought of as being supported by the PC. EIS (executive information systems) processing typically runs on the individual levels.

## Integration

One important aspect of the architected environment that is not shown in Figure 1.12 is the integration of data that occurs across the architecture. As data passes from the operational environment to the data warehouse environment, it is integrated, as shown in Figure 1.13.

There is no point in bringing data over from the operational environment into the data warehouse environment *without* integrating it. If the data arrives at the data warehouse in an unintegrated state, it cannot be used to support a corporate view of data. And a corporate view of data is one of the essences of the architected environment.

## WHO IS THE USER?

The user of the data warehouse is a person who can be called the DSS analyst. The DSS analyst is first and foremost a businessperson, and second, a technician. The primary job of the DSS analyst is in the definition and discovery of information used in corporate decision making.

It is important to peer inside the head of the DSS analyst and view how he or she perceives the usage of the data warehouse. The DSS analyst has a mindset of "give me what I say I want, then I can tell you what I really want." In other words, the DSS analyst operates in a mode of discovery. Only upon seeing a report or seeing a screen can the DSS analyst begin to explore the possibilities for DSS.

The attitude of the DSS analyst is important for the following reasons:

■ It is legitimate.
■ It is pervasive.
■ It has a profound effect on the way the data warehouse is developed and on how systems using the data warehouse are developed.

The classical system development life cycle (SDLC) does not work in the world of the DSS analyst. The SDLC assumes that requirements are known at the start of design (or at least can be

**a simple example—a customer**

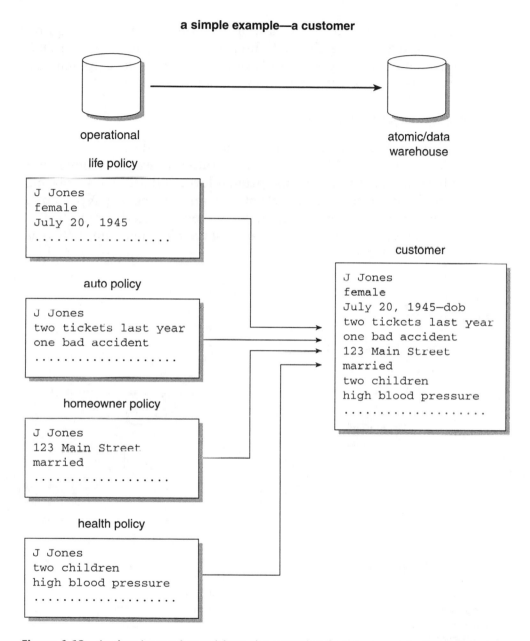

**Figure 1.13**  As data is transformed from the operational environment to the data warehouse environment, it is integrated as well.

discovered). However, in the world of the DSS analyst, requirements usually are the last thing to be discovered in the DSS
development life cycle. There is a very different development life
cycle associated with the data warehouse.

## THE DEVELOPMENT LIFE CYCLE

While operational data is usually unintegrated and, of necessity,
data warehouse data must be integrated, there are other major
differences between the operational level of data and processing
and the data warehouse level of data and processing. A profound
difference between the operational level and the data warehouse level concerns the underlying development life cycles, as
shown in Figure 1.14.

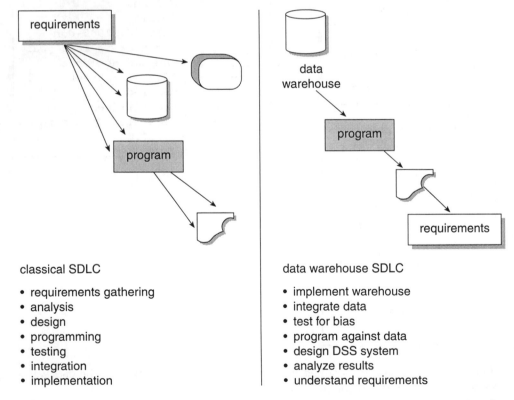

classical SDLC

- requirements gathering
- analysis
- design
- programming
- testing
- integration
- implementation

data warehouse SDLC

- implement warehouse
- integrate data
- test for bias
- program against data
- design DSS system
- analyze results
- understand requirements

**Figure 1.14** The system development life cycle for the data warehouse environment is
almost exactly the opposite of the classical SDLC.

Figure 1.14 shows that the operational environment is supported by the classical systems development life cycle (the SDLC). The data warehouse operates under a very different life cycle, sometimes called the CLDS (the reverse of the SDLC). The classical SDLC is requirements driven. In order to build systems, you must first understand the requirements. Then you go into stages of design and development. The CLDS is almost exactly the reverse. The CLDS starts with data. Once data is in hand, it is integrated, then tested to see what bias there is to the data, if any. Programs are then written against the data. The results of the programs are analyzed, and finally, the requirements of the system are understood.

The CLDS is a classic data-driven development life cycle, while the SDLC is a classic requirements-driven development life cycle. Trying to apply inappropriate tools and techniques of development results only in waste and confusion. For example, the CASE world is dominated by requirements-driven analysis. Trying to apply CASE tools and techniques to the world of data warehouse is not advisable, and vice versa.

## PATTERNS OF HARDWARE UTILIZATION

Yet another major difference between the operational and the data warehouse environments is the patterns of hardware utilization that occur in each environment. Figure 1.15 illustrates this.

The left-hand side of Figure 1.15 shows the classic pattern of hardware utilization for operational processing. There are

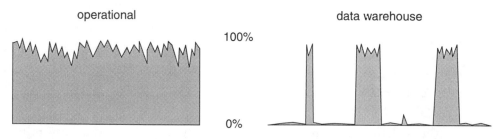

**Figure 1.15** The different patterns of hardware utilization in the different environments.

peaks and valleys in operational processing, but ultimately there is a relatively static pattern of utilization.

There is an essentially different pattern of hardware utilization in the data warehouse environment (shown on the right-hand side of the figure)—a *binary* pattern of utilization. Either the hardware is being utilized fully or not at all. Calculating a mean percentage of utilization for the data warehouse environment is not a meaningful activity.

This fundamental difference is one more reason why trying to mix the two environments on the same machine at the same time does not work. You can either optimize your machine for operational processing, or you can optimize your machine for data warehouse processing, but you cannot do both at the same time on the same piece of equipment.

## SETTING THE STAGE FOR REENGINEERING

Although indirect, there is a very beneficial side effect of going from the production environment to the architected, data warehouse environment. Figure 1.16 shows the progression.

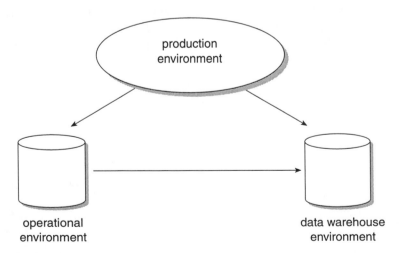

**Figure 1.16** The transformation from the legacy systems environment to the architected, data warehouse–centered environment.

In Figure 1.16, a transformation is made in the production environment. The first effect is the removal of the bulk of data—mostly archival—from the production environment. The removal of massive volumes of data has a beneficial effect in various ways including the following:

- The production environment is easier to correct.
- The production environment is easier to restructure.
- The production environment is easier to monitor.
- The production environment is easier to index.

In short, the mere removal of a significant volume of data makes the production environment a much more malleable one.

Another important effect is the removal of informational processing from the production environment. Informational processing is in the form of reports, screens, extracts, and so forth. The very nature of information processing is constant change. Business conditions change, the organization changes, management changes, accounting practices change, and so on. Each of these changes has an effect on summary and informational processing. When informational processing is included in the production, legacy environment, it appears that maintenance is eternal. But much of what is called maintenance in the production environment in actuality is informational processing going through the normal cycle of changes. By moving most informational processing off to the data warehouse, the maintenance burden in the production environment is greatly alleviated. Figure 1.17 shows the effect of the removal of volumes of data and informational processing from the production environment.

Once the production environment undergoes the changes associated with transformation to the data warehouse–centered, architected environment, the production environment is primed for reengineering because it is:

- smaller
- simpler
- focused

In a word, the single most important step a company can take to make its efforts in reengineering and legacy system

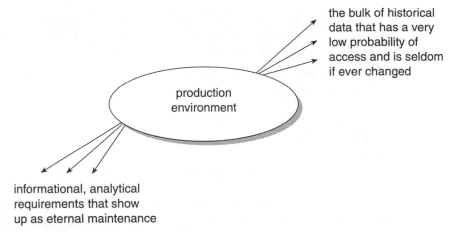

the bulk of historical
data that has a very
low probability of
access and is seldom
if ever changed

production
environment

informational, analytical
requirements that show
up as eternal maintenance

**Figure 1.17**   Removing unneeded data and informational requirements from the production environment—the effects of going to the data warehouse environment.

refurbishment successful is to first go to the data warehouse environment.

## MONITORING THE DATA WAREHOUSE ENVIRONMENT

The two operating components of the data warehouse environment that are monitored on a regular basis are the data residing in the data warehouse and the usage of the data. Monitoring the data that resides in the data warehouse environment is essential to the ability to manage the data warehouse environment. Some of the important results that are achieved by the monitoring of the data in the data warehouse environment include:

- identifying what growth is occurring, where the growth is occurring, and at what rate the growth is occurring
- identifying what data is being used
- calculating what response time the end user is getting
- determining who is actually using the data warehouse
- specifying how much of the data warehouse they are using
- pinpointing when the data warehouse is being used
- recognizing how much of the data warehouse is being used
- examining the level of usage of the data warehouse

When the data architect does not know the answer to these questions, it is impossible to effectively manage the data warehouse environment on an ongoing basis.

As an example of the usefulness of monitoring the data warehouse, consider the importance of knowing what data is being used inside the data warehouse. The nature of a data warehouse is constant growth. History is constantly being added to the warehouse. Summarizations are constantly being added. New extract streams are being created. And the storage and processing technology on which the data warehouse resides is not inexpensive. At some point the question is asked, "Why is all of this data being accumulated? Is there really anyone using all of this?" Whether there is any legitimate user of the data warehouse, there certainly is a growing cost to the data warehouse as data is put into it during its normal operation.

As long as the data architect has no way to ascertain usage of the data inside the warehouse, there is no choice but to continually buy new computer resources—more storage, more processors, and so forth. But with the ability to monitor usage of data in the data warehouse, there is the opportunity to move unused data to another media. When the data architect finds that some data is not being used it makes sense to move that data to less expensive media. With the ability to monitor activity and usage in the data warehouse, the data architect can determine what data is not being used and can actuate the move. There is a very real and immediate payback to monitoring data and activity in the data warehouse environment.

The kinds of profiles of data that can be created during the data monitoring process include:

■ a catalog of all tables in the warehouse
■ a profile of the contents of those tables
■ a profile of the growth of the tables in the data warehouse
■ a catalog of the indexes available for entry to the tables
■ a catalog of the summary tables and the sources for the summary

The need for monitoring activity of the data warehouse is illustrated by the following questions:

- What data is being accessed?
  - □ when?
  - □ by whom?
  - □ how frequently?
  - □ at what level of detail?
- What is the response time for the request?
- At what point in the day is the request submitted?
- How big was the request?
- Was the request terminated or did it end naturally?

The notion of response time in the DSS environment is quite a different notion from response time in the OLTP (online transaction processor) environment. In the OLTP environment response time is almost always mission critical. The business starts to suffer immediately when response time turns bad in OLTP. In the DSS environment there is no such relationship. Response time in the DSS data warehouse environment is always relaxed. There is no mission-critical nature to response time in DSS. Accordingly, response time in the DSS data warehouse environment is measured in minutes and hours, and in some cases, in terms of days.

However, just because response time is relaxed in the DSS data warehouse environment does not mean that response time is not important. In the DSS data warehouse environment, the end user does development iteratively. This means that the next level of investigation of any iterative development depends on the results attained by the current analysis. If the end user does an iterative analysis and the turnaround time is only ten minutes, he or she is going to be able to be much more productive than if turnaround time were to be 24 hours. There is, then, a very important relationship between response time and productivity in the DSS environment. Just because response time in the DSS environment is not mission critical does not mean that it is not important.

The ability to measure response time in the DSS environment is the first step toward being able to manage it. For this reason alone, monitoring DSS activity is a very important procedure that must be put into place.

One of the issues of response time measurement in the DSS environment is "what is being measured?" In an OLTP environment, it is clear what is being measured. A request is sent, serviced, and returned to the end user. In the OLTP environment the measurement of response time is from the moment of submission to the moment of return. But the DSS data warehouse environment varies from the OLTP environment in that there is no clear time for measuring the return of data. In the DSS data warehouse environment there is often a lot of data returned as a result of a query. Some of the data is returned at one moment, other data is returned later. Defining the moment of return of data for the data warehouse environment is no easy matter. One interpretation is the moment of the *first* return of data; another interpretation is the *last* return of data. And there are many other possibilities for the measurement of response time; the DSS data warehouse activity monitor must be able to provide many different interpretations.

One of the fundamental issues of using a monitor on the data warehouse environment is *where* to do the monitoring. One place the monitoring can be done is at the end user terminal. This is a convenient place to do it because there are many free machine cycles here and there is minimal impact on systemwide performance when monitoring is done here. However, to monitor the system at the end user terminal level implies that each terminal that will be monitored will require its own administration. In a world where there are as many as 10,000 terminals in a single DSS network, trying to administer the monitoring of each terminal is nearly impossible.

The alternative is to do the monitoring of the DSS system at the server level. After the query has been formulated and has been passed to the server that manages the data warehouse, the monitoring of activity can occur. Undoubtedly, administration of the monitor is much easier here. But there is a very good possibility of a systemwide performance penalty being incurred. Since the monitor is using resources at the server, the impact on performance is felt throughout the DSS data warehouse environment. The placement of the monitor is an important issue that must be carefully thought out. The tradeoff is between ease of administration and minimization of performance requirements.

One of the most powerful uses of a monitor is to be able to compare today's results against an "average" day. When unusual system conditions occur, it is often useful to be able to ask "How different is today from the average day?" In many cases it will be seen that the variations in performance are not nearly as bad as imagined. But in order to make such a comparison, there needs to be an "average day profile." The average day profile contains the standard important measures that describe a day in the DSS environment. Once the current day is measured, it can then be compared to the average day profile.

Of course, the average day changes over time, and it makes sense to periodically track these changes so that long-term system trends can be measured.

## SUMMARY

This chapter has discussed the architecture into which the data warehouse environment fits. The architecture has evolved throughout the history of the different stages of information processing. There are four levels of data and processing in the architecture—the operational level, the data warehouse level, the departmental level, and the individual level.

# 2

# The Data Warehouse Environment

At the heart of the architected environment is the data warehouse. The data warehouse is the foundation of DSS processing. Because there is a single integrated source of data in the data warehouse, and because the data is accessible, the job of the DSS analyst in the data warehouse environment is immeasurably easier than in the classical environment.

This chapter will describe some of the more important aspects of the data warehouse.

A data warehouse is a *subject oriented, integrated, nonvolatile*, and *time variant* collection of data in support of management's decisions.

The subject orientation of the data warehouse is shown in Figure 2.1.

Classical operations systems are organized around the applications of the company. For an insurance company, the applications may be auto, health, life, and casualty. The major subject areas of the corporation might be customer, policy, premium, and claim.

The second salient characteristic of the data warehouse is that *it is integrated*. Of all the aspects of a data warehouse, this is the most important. Figure 2.2 illustrates the integration that

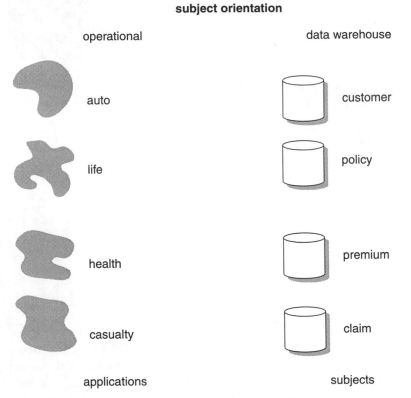

**Figure 2.1**  An example of a subject orientation of data.

occurs when data passes from the application-oriented operational environment to the data warehouse.

The different design decisions the applications designers have made over the years show up in a thousand different ways. There is no application consistency in encoding, naming conventions, physical attributes, measurement of attributes, and so forth. Each application designer has had free rein to make his or her own design decisions.

As data is entered into the data warehouse, it is done in a way so that the many inconsistencies at the application are undone. For example, in Figure 2.2, as far as encoding of gender is concerned, it matters little whether data in the warehouse is encoded as m/f or 1/0. What does matter is that however ware-

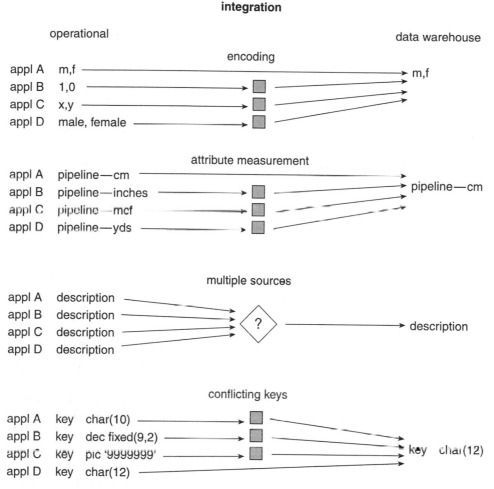

**Figure 2.2**   The issue of integration.

house encoding is done, it should be done consistently, whatever the source application. If application data is encoded as X/Y, it is converted as it is moved to the warehouse. The same consideration of consistency goes for all of the application design issues, such as naming conventions, key structure, measurement of attributes, and physical characteristics of data.

The third important characteristic of a data warehouse is that *it is nonvolatile*. Figure 2.3 illustrates nonvolatility of data.

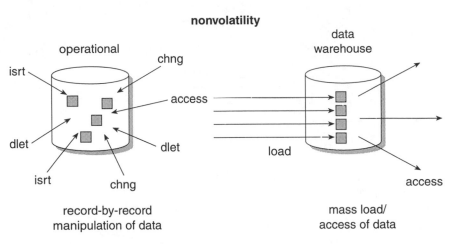

**Figure 2.3** The issue of nonvolatility.

Figure 2.3 shows that operational data is regularly accessed and manipulated a record at a time. Update is done to data in the operational environment. But data warehouse data exhibits a very different set of characteristics. Data warehouse data is loaded (usually en masse), and is accessed. But update of data (in the general sense) does not occur in the data warehouse environment.

The last salient characteristic of the data warehouse is that *it is time variant*. Figure 2.4 illustrates how time variancy of data warehouse data shows up in several ways:

■ The time horizon for the data warehouse is significantly longer than that of operational systems. A 60-to-90-day time horizon is normal for operational systems; a 5-to-10-year time horizon of data is normal for the data warehouse.

■ Operational databases contain "current value" data—data whose accuracy is valid as of the moment of access. As such, current value data can be updated. Data warehouse data is nothing more than a sophisticated series of snapshots, taken at one moment in time.

■ The key structure of operational data may or may not contain some element of time, such as year, month, day, etc. The key structure of the data warehouse always contains some element of time.

**time variancy**

operational

data warehouse

- time horizon—current to 60–90 days
- update of records
- key structure may/may not contain an element of time

- time horizon—5–10 years
- sophisticated snapshots of data
- key structure contains an element of time

**Figure 2.4**   The issue of time variancy.

## THE STRUCTURE OF THE DATA WAREHOUSE

The data warehouse is structured as shown in Figure 2.5.

Figure 2.5 shows that there are different levels of detail in the data warehouse. There is an older level of detail (usually an alternate, bulk storage), a current level of detail, a level of lightly summarized data (the datamart), and a level of highly summarized data. Data flows into the data warehouse from the operational environment. Usually a significant amount of transformation of data occurs at the passage from the operational level to the data warehouse level.

Once the data ages, it passes from current detail to older detail. As the data is summarized, it passes from current detail to lightly summarized data, then from lightly summarized data to highly summarized data.

## SUBJECT ORIENTATION

The data warehouse is oriented to the major subject areas of the corporation that have been defined in the data model. Typical subject areas include:

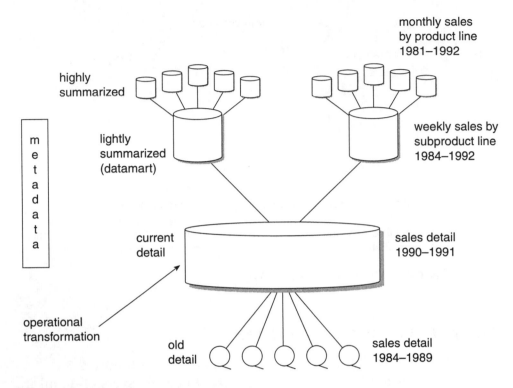

**Figure 2.5** The structure of the data warehouse.

- customer
- product
- transaction or activity
- policy
- claim
- account

The major subject area ends up being physically implemented as a series of related tables in the data warehouse. For example, a customer implementation might look like that shown in Figure 2.6.

There are five related tables in Figure 2.6, each of which has been designed to implement a part of a major subject area—customer. There is a base table for customer information as defined from 1985 to 1987. There is another for the definition of customer data between 1988 and 1990. There is a cumulative cus-

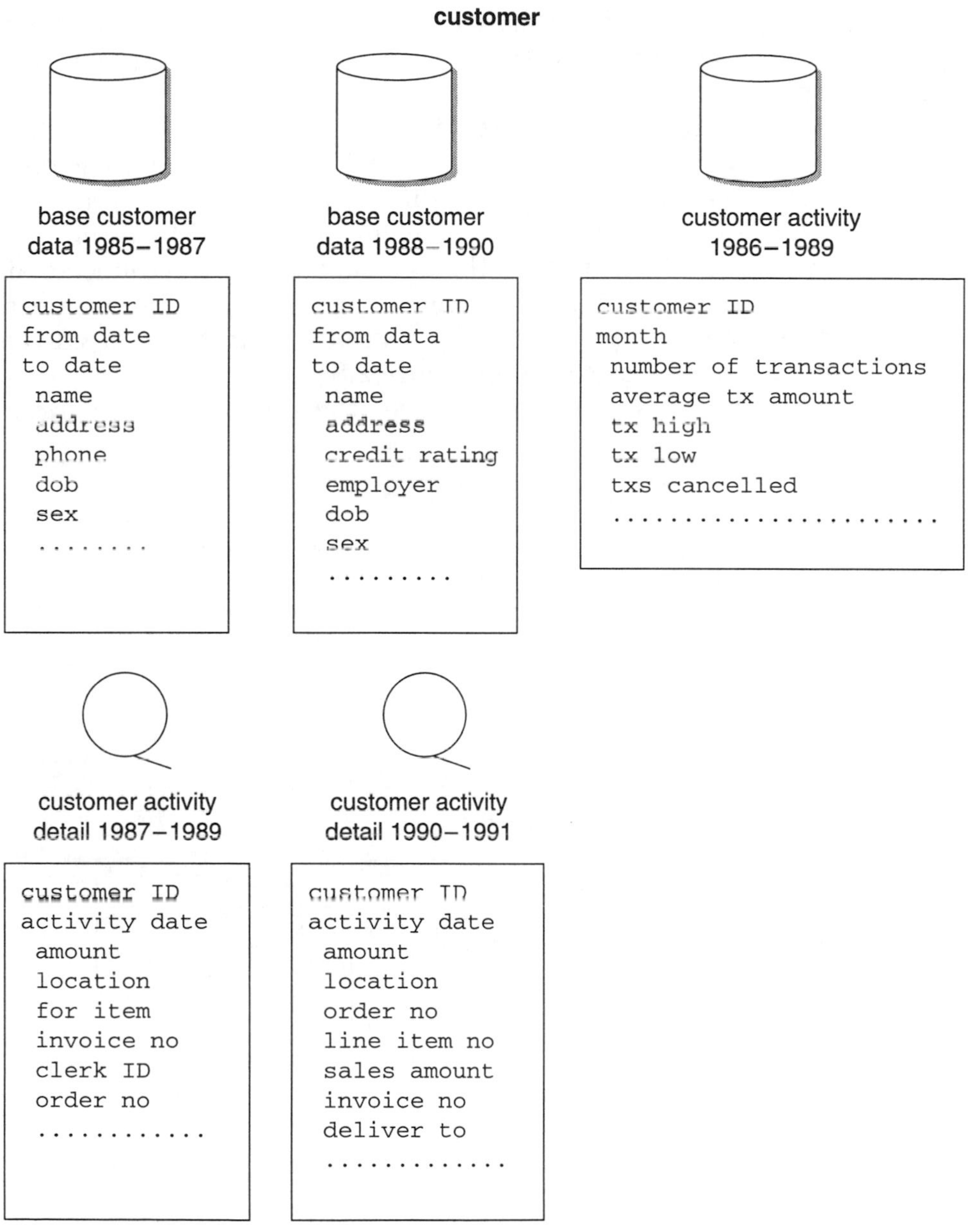

**customer**

| base customer data 1985–1987 | base customer data 1988–1990 | customer activity 1986–1989 |
|---|---|---|
| customer ID<br>from date<br>to date<br> name<br> address<br> phone<br> dob<br> sex<br> . . . . . . . . | customer ID<br>from data<br>to date<br> name<br> address<br> credit rating<br> employer<br> dob<br> sex<br> . . . . . . . . . | customer ID<br>month<br> number of transactions<br> average tx amount<br> tx high<br> tx low<br> txs cancelled<br> . . . . . . . . . . . . . . . . . . . . . . |

| customer activity detail 1987–1989 | customer activity detail 1990–1991 |
|---|---|
| customer ID<br>activity date<br> amount<br> location<br> for item<br> invoice no<br> clerk ID<br> order no<br> . . . . . . . . . . . | customer ID<br>activity date<br> amount<br> location<br> order no<br> line item no<br> sales amount<br> invoice no<br> deliver to<br> . . . . . . . . . . . |

**Figure 2.6**   Data warehouse data is organized by major subject area—in this case by customer.

tomer activity table for activities between 1986 and 1989. Each month a summary record is written for each customer record based upon customer activity for the month.

There are detailed activity files by customer for 1987 through 1989 and another one for 1990 through 1991. The definition of the data in the files is different, based on the year.

All of the tables for one customer are related by a common key. Figure 2.7 shows that the key—customer ID—connects all of the data found in the customer subject area. Another interesting aspect of the customer subject area is that it may reside on different media, as shown in Figure 2.8.

Figure 2.8 shows that some of the data reside on direct

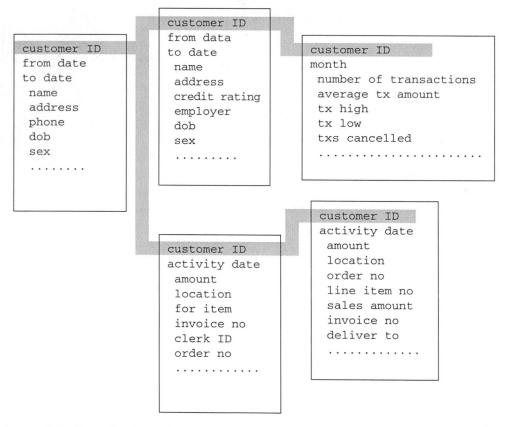

**Figure 2.7** The collections of data that belong to the same subject area are tied together by a common key.

**customer**

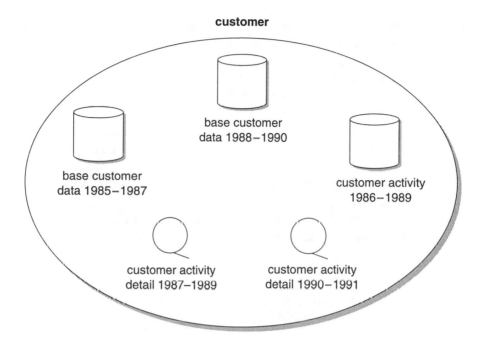

**Figure 2.8**   The subject area may contain data on different media in the data warehouse.

access storage device (DASD) and some reside on magnetic tape. One implication of data residing on different media is that there may be more than one DBMS managing the data in a warehouse, or that some data may not be managed by a DBMS at all. Just because data resides on magnetic tape does not mean it is not a part of the data warehouse.

Data that has a high probability of access and a low volume of storage resides on a medium that is fast and relatively expensive. Data that has a low probability of access and is bulky resides on a medium that is cheaper and slower to access.

As a rule DASD and magnetic tape are the two most popular media on which to store data in a data warehouse. But they are not the only media; two others that should not be overlooked are fiche and optical disk. Fiche is good for storing detailed records that never have to be reproduced in an electronic medium again. Legal records are often stored on fiche for an indefinite period of time. Optical disk storage is especially good for data warehouse storage because it is cheap, relatively fast, and able to hold a mass of data. Another reason why optical disk is useful is because data warehouse data, once written, is seldom, if ever, updated. This last characteristic makes optical disk storage a very desirable choice for data warehouses.

Another interesting aspect of the files (shown in Figure 2.8) is that there is both a level of summary and a level of detail for the same data. Activity by month is summarized. The detail that supports activity by month is stored at the magnetic tape level of data. This is a form of a "shift in granularity," which will be discussed later.

When data is organized around the subject—the customer— each key has an element of time, as shown in Figure 2.9.

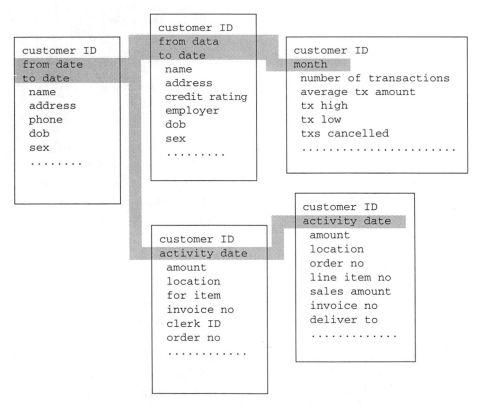

**Figure 2.9** Each table in the data warehouse has an element of time as a part of the key structure, usually the lower part.

Some tables are organized on a from-date-to-date basis. This is called a continuous organization of data. Other tables are organized on a cumulative monthly basis, and others on an individual date of record or activity basis. But all records have some form of date attached to the key, usually the lower part of the key.

## DAY 1–DAY *N* PHENOMENON

Data warehouses are not built all at once. Instead, they are designed and populated a step at a time, and as such are evolutionary, not revolutionary. The costs of building a data warehouse all at once, the resources required, and the disruption to the environment, all dictate that the data warehouse be built in an orderly iterative, step-at-a-time fashion.

Figure 2.10 shows the typical process of building a data warehouse. On day one there is a polyglot of systems essentially doing operational processing. On day two, the first few tables of the first subject area of the data warehouse are populated. At this point a certain amount of curiosity is raised, and the users start to discover data warehouses and analytical processing.

On day three, more of the data warehouse is populated, and with the population of more data comes more users. Once users find there is an integrated source of data that is easy to get to and has a historical basis that is made for looking at data over the spectrum of time, there is more than curiosity. At about this time, the serious DSS analyst becomes attracted to the data warehouse.

On day four, as more of the warehouse becomes populated, some of the data that had resided in the operational environment become properly placed in the data warehouse. And the data warehouse is now "discovered" as a source for doing analytical processing. All sorts of DSS applications spring up. Indeed, there start to appear so many users and so many requests for processing, coupled with a rather large volume of data that now resides in the warehouse, that some users begin to be put off by the work and effort required to get to the data warehouse. The competition to get at the warehouse becomes an obstacle to its usage.

On day five, departmental databases (datamart, or OLAP)

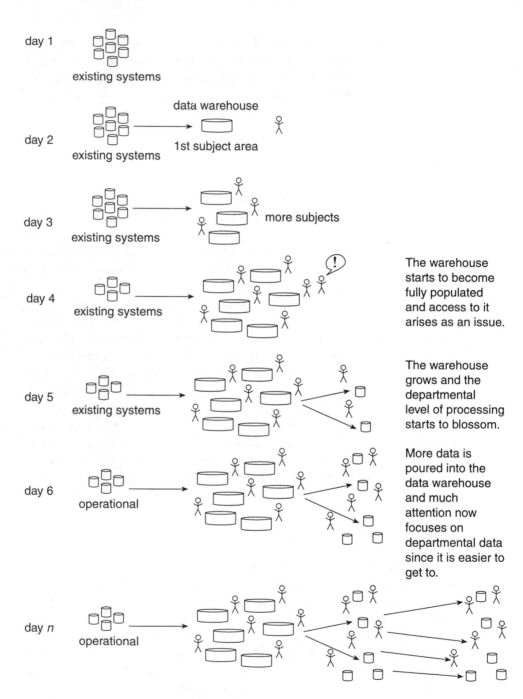

day 1

existing systems

data warehouse

day 2

existing systems  1st subject area

day 3

existing systems  more subjects

day 4

existing systems

The warehouse starts to become fully populated and access to it arises as an issue.

day 5

existing systems

The warehouse grows and the departmental level of processing starts to blossom.

day 6

operational

More data is poured into the data warehouse and much attention now focuses on departmental data since it is easier to get to.

day n

operational

**Figure 2.10**  Day 1–day *n* phenomenon.

start to blossom. Departments find that it is cheaper and easier to get their processing done by bringing data from the data warehouse into their own departmental processing environment. As data goes to the departmental level, a few DSS analysts are attracted.

On day six, the landrush to departmental systems takes place. It is cheaper, faster, and easier to get departmental data than it is to get data from the data warehouse. Soon end users are weaned from the detail of data warehouse to departmental processing.

On day *n*, the architecture is fully developed. All that is left of the original set of production systems is operational processing. The warehouse is full of data. There are a few direct users of the data warehouse. There are a lot of departmental databases. Most of the DSS analytical processing occurs at the departmental level because it is easier and cheaper to get the data needed for processing there.

Of course, evolution from day one to day *n* takes a long time. Several years is the norm. And all during the process of moving from day one to day *n* the DSS environment is up and functional.

(It is normal at this time to observe that the spider web appears to be developed in a larger, more grandiose form. Such is not the case at all, although the explanation is rather complex. Refer to "The cabinet effect," May 1991, *Data Base Programming Design*, for an in-depth explanation.)

## GRANULARITY

The single most important aspect of design of a data warehouse is the issue of granularity. Granularity refers to the level of detail or summarization held in the units of data in the data warehouse. The more detail there is, the lower the level of granularity. The less detail there is, the higher the level of granularity.

Granularity of data has always been a design issue. In the early operational systems that were built, granularity was taken for granted. When detailed data is being updated, it is almost a given that data be stored at the lowest level of granularity. But in the data warehouse environment, granularity is *not* assumed. Figure 2.11 illustrates the issues of granularity.

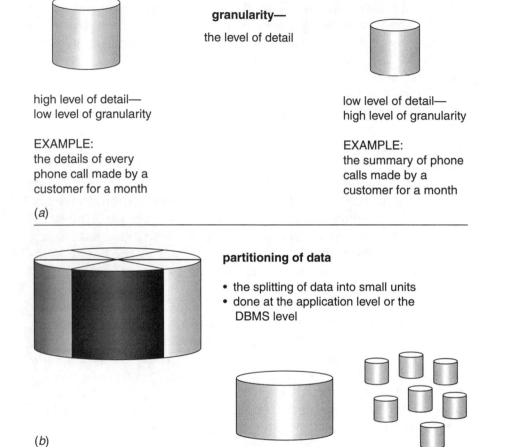

**granularity—**

the level of detail

high level of detail—
low level of granularity

low level of detail—
high level of granularity

EXAMPLE:
the details of every
phone call made by a
customer for a month

EXAMPLE:
the summary of phone
calls made by a
customer for a month

(a)

**partitioning of data**

- the splitting of data into small units
- done at the application level or the
  DBMS level

difficult to manage

easy to manage

(b)

**Figure 2.11** Major design issues of the data warehouse: granularity, partioning, and proper design.

The reason why granularity is *the* major design issue in the data warehouse environment is that it profoundly affects the volume of data that resides in the data warehouse and at the same time affects the type of query that can be answered. The volume of data in a warehouse is traded off against the level of detail of a query.

## An Example of Granularity

Figure 2.12 shows an example of the issues of granularity. On the left-hand side there is a low level of granularity. Each activity—in this case, a phone call—is recorded in detail. The layout of the data is shown. At the end of the month, each customer has on the average 200 records (one for each recorded phone call throughout the month) that require about 40,000 bytes collectively.

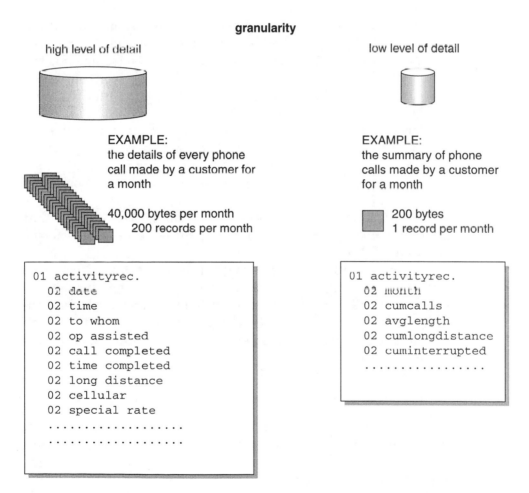

**granularity**

high level of detail

low level of detail

EXAMPLE:
the details of every phone call made by a customer for a month

40,000 bytes per month
200 records per month

EXAMPLE:
the summary of phone calls made by a customer for a month

200 bytes
1 record per month

```
01 activityrec.
  02 date
  02 time
  02 to whom
  02 op assisted
  02 call completed
  02 time completed
  02 long distance
  02 cellular
  02 special rate
  ..................
  ..................
```

```
01 activityrec.
  02 month
  02 cumcalls
  02 avglength
  02 cumlongdistance
  02 cuminterrupted
  ................
```

**Figure 2.12** Determining the level of granularity is the most important design issue in the data warehouse environment.

On the right-hand side of the figure is a higher level of granularity. The data represent the summary information for a customer for a month. There is one record for each customer for a month, and that record requires about 200 bytes. The layout of the record is shown.

It is obvious that if space is a problem in a data warehouse (and volume of data is *always* the first and major issue in the data warehouse), a high level of granularity is a much more efficient way of representing data than a representation using a low level of granularity.

Not only are many fewer bytes of data required with a higher level of granularity, but fewer index entries are needed. But the volume of data and the issue of raw space are not the only relevant issues. The amount of processing power that needs to be used in the face of a large volume of data in order to access the data is a factor as well.

There is, then, a very good case for the compaction of data in a data warehouse. When data is compacted there are nontrivial savings in the amount of DASD used, the number of index entries required, and the processor resources required to manipulate data.

But there is another aspect to the compaction of data that occurs when the level of granularity is raised. Figure 2.13 shows the tradeoff that is made.

In Figure 2.13, as the level of granularity of data rises, there is a corresponding loss in the capability of using the data to answer queries. Put another way, with a very low level of granularity, you can answer practically any query. But with a high level of granularity, the number of questions that the data can handle is limited.

In Figure 2.13 the following query is made:

"Did Cass Squire call his girlfriend in Boston last week?"

With a low level of granularity, the query can be answered. It may take a lot of resources to thumb through a lot of records, but at the end of the day, whether or not Cass called his girlfriend in Boston last week can be determined.

But with a high level of detail, there is no way to definitively answer the question. If all that is kept about Cass Squire in the

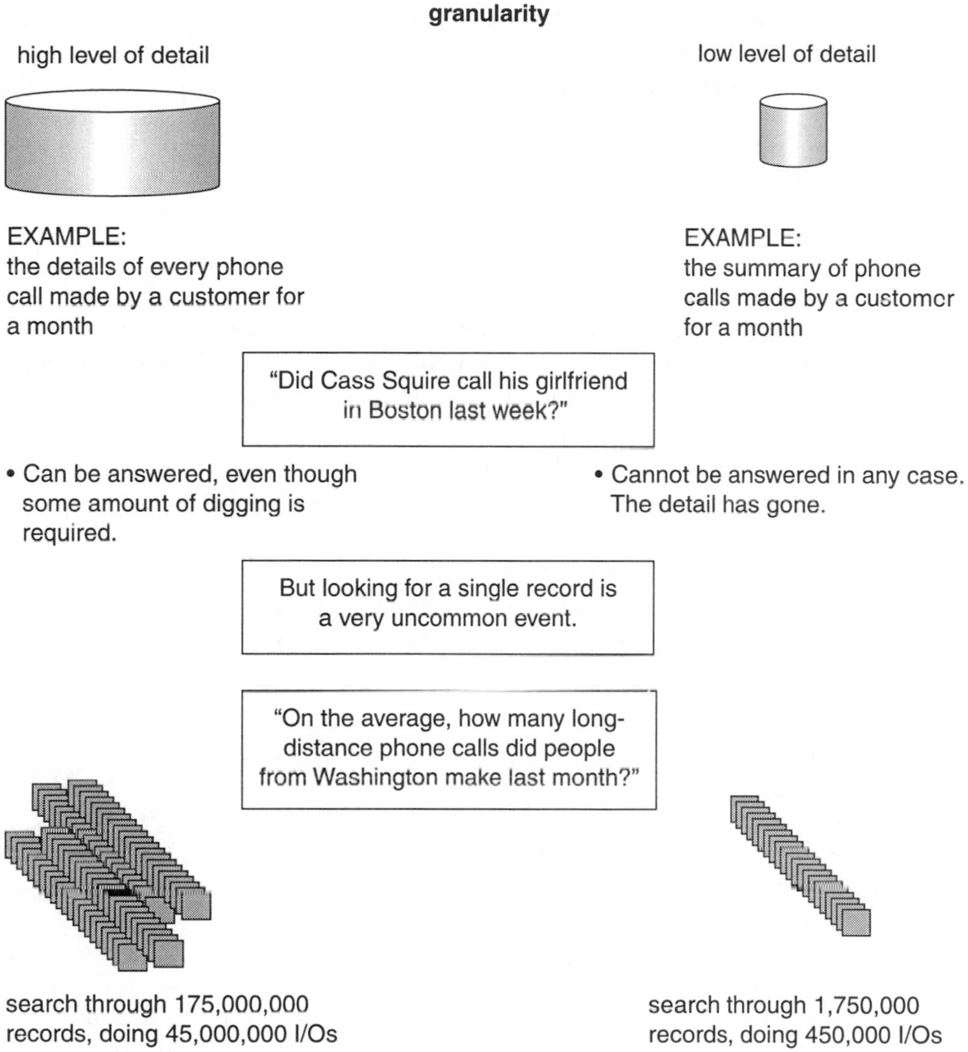

**granularity**

high level of detail                                        low level of detail

EXAMPLE:                                                    EXAMPLE:
the details of every phone                                 the summary of phone
call made by a customer for                                calls made by a customer
a month                                                    for a month

> "Did Cass Squire call his girlfriend
> in Boston last week?"

• Can be answered, even though          • Cannot be answered in any case.
  some amount of digging is               The detail has gone.
  required.

> But looking for a single record is
> a very uncommon event.

> "On the average, how many long-
> distance phone calls did people
> from Washington make last month?"

search through 175,000,000                          search through 1,750,000
records, doing 45,000,000 I/Os                      records, doing 450,000 I/Os

**Figure 2.13**  The level of granularity has a profound effect both on what questions can be answered and on what resources are required to answer a question.

data warehouse is the total number of calls that he made, no determination can be made whether one of those calls went to Boston.

But when doing DSS processing, as is common in the data warehouse environment, it is rare that only a single event is examined. It is much more common that a collective view of data is taken. This means looking at a large number of records.

For example, suppose the following collective query is made:

On the average, how many long-distance phone calls did people from Washington make last month?

This type of query is very normal in a DSS environment. Of course, it can be answered by both the high level and the low level of granularity. But in answering it, there is a tremendous difference in the resources used. To answer this query in the low level of granularity case requires going through every record. Many resources are required to answer this question.

But using the high level of granularity, the data is much more compact and able to provide an answer. It is *much more* efficient to use the high level of granularity data if it contains sufficient detail.

The tradeoff in managing the issue of granularity of data is shown in Figure 2.14. This tradeoff must be considered very carefully at the outset in the design and the construction of the data warehouse.

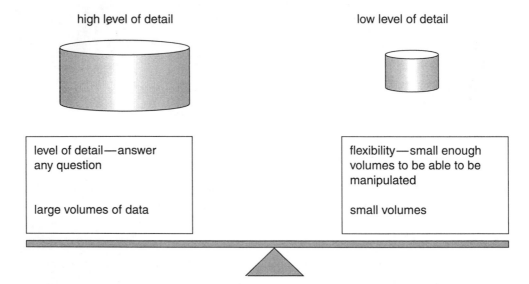

high level of detail

low level of detail

| level of detail—answer any question<br><br>large volumes of data | flexibility—small enough volumes to be able to be manipulated<br><br>small volumes |

**Figure 2.14** The tradeoff with granularity is so stark that for most organizations the best solution is some form of multiple levels of granularity.

## Dual Levels of Granularity

Most of the time, there is a great need for efficiency in storing data and its access *and* for the ability to analyze data in great detail. (In other words, the organization wants to have its cake and eat it, too!) When an organization has lots of data in the warehouse, it makes eminent sense to consider two (or more) levels of granularity in the detailed portion of the data warehouse. In fact, the need for more than one level of granularity is such that the dual level of granularity design option should be the default for almost every shop. Figure 2.15 shows two levels of granularity at the detailed level of the data warehouse.

Called a "dual" level of granularity, the design shown in Figure 2.15—a phone company—fits the needs of most shops. At

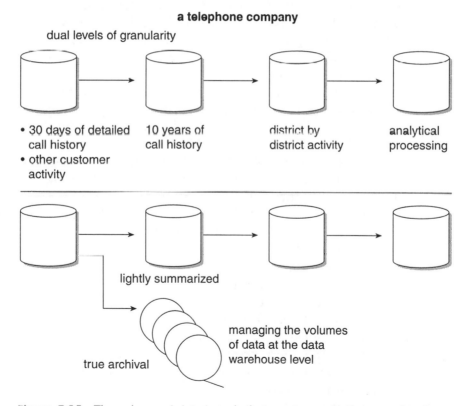

**a telephone company**

dual levels of granularity

- 30 days of detailed call history
- other customer activity

10 years of call history

district by district activity

analytical processing

lightly summarized

true archival

managing the volumes of data at the data warehouse level

**Figure 2.15** The volume of data is such that most organizations need to have two levels of granularity in the data warehouse.

the operational level is a tremendous amount of detail. Most of this detail is needed for the billing systems. Up to 30 days of detail is stored in the operational level.

The data warehouse in this example contains two types of data—lightly summarized data and "true archival" detail data. The data in the data warehouse can go back 10 years. The data that emanates from the data warehouse is "district" data that flows to the different districts of the telephone company. Each district then analyzes its data independently from other districts. At the individual level much heuristic analytical processing occurs.

It may not be immediately obvious what is meant by a light level of summarization. Figure 2.16 shows such a summarization.

As data is passed from the operational, 30-day store of data, it is summarized, by customer, into fields that are likely to be used for DSS analysis. The record for J Jones shows the number of calls made per month, the average length of each call, the number of long-distance calls made, the number of operator-assisted calls, and so forth.

There is significantly less volume of data in the lightly summarized database than there is in the detailed database. Of course, there is a limit to the level of detail that can be accessed in the lightly summarized database.

The second tier of data in the data warehouse—the lowest level of granularity—is stored in the true archival level of data, as shown in Figure 2.17.

At the true archival level of data, *all* the detail coming from the operational environment is stored. There is truly a multitude of data at this level. For that reason, it makes sense to store the data on a medium such as magnetic tape because the volume of data is so large.

By creating two levels of granularity in the detailed level of the data warehouse, the DSS architect has killed two birds with one stone—most DSS processing goes against the lightly summarized data where the data is compact and efficiently accessed. But on those occasions where some greater level of detail must be delved into—5 percent of the time or less—there is the true archival level of data. It is expensive, cumbersome, and complex

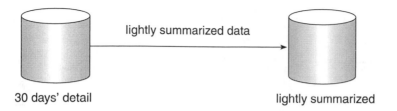

30 days' detail                                     lightly summarized

```
J Jones
April 12 6:01 pm to 6:12 pm
415-566-9982 operator assisted
April 12 6:15 pm to 6:16 pm
415-334-8847 long distance
April 12 6:23 pm to 6:38 pm
408-223-7745
April 13 9:12 am to 9:23 am
408-223-7745
April 13 10:15 am to 10:21 am
408-223-7745 operator assisted
April 15 11:01 am to 11:21 am
415-964-4738
April 15 11:39 am to 12:01 pm
703-570-5770 incomplete
April 15 12:10 pm to 12:46 pm
703-841-5770 wrong number
April 16 12:34 pm to 12:56 pm
415-964-3130
.............................
.............................
```

```
April
J Jones
number of calls - 45
avg length of call - 14 minutes
number of long distance calls - 18
number of operator assisted calls - 2
number of incomplete calls - 1
```

number of bytes required to house a
record—225

For a single customer for a month, an
average of 45,000 bytes are required
to house 200 records.

**Figure 2.16**   With light summarization of data, large quantities of data can be compactly represented.

to access data at the true archival level of granularity. But if there is a necessity to go to that level of detail, it is there.

Over time, should there develop a pattern of searching the true archival level of data, the designer may want to create some new fields of data at the lightly summarized level.

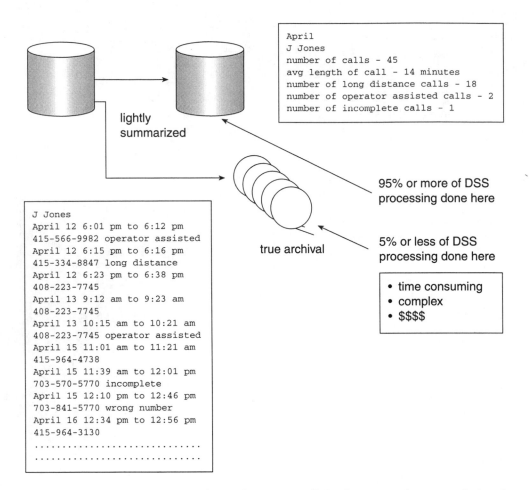

**Figure 2.17** Dual levels of granularity allow you to efficiently process the vast majority of requests and answer any question that can be answered. It is the best of all worlds and should be the default design choice.

Because of the costs, efficiencies, ease of access, and ability to answer any query that can be answered, the dual level of data is the best architectural choice for the detailed level of the data warehouse for most shops. Only when a shop has a relatively small amount of data in the data warehouse environment should a single level of data be attempted.

## PARTITIONING

A second major design issue of data in the warehouse (after that of granularity) is that of partitioning (Figure 2.11b). Partitioning of data refers to the breakup of data into separate physical units that can be handled independently. In the data warehouse, the issues surrounding partitioning do not focus on whether partitioning should be done but how it should be done.

It is often said that if both granularity and partitioning are done properly, then almost all other aspects of the data warehouse design and implementation come easily. But if granularity is not handled properly and if partitioning is not designed and implemented carefully, then no other aspects of design really matter.

Of course, there are other design aspects of the data warehouse that will be discussed in later chapters.

## LIVING SAMPLE DATABASE

An interesting hybrid form of a data warehouse is the "living sample" database. This is merely a subset of either true archival data or lightly summarized data. The term "living sample" stems from the fact that it is a subset—a sample—of a larger database, and that it needs to be periodically refreshed. Figure 2.18 shows a living sample database.

In some circumstances (for example, statistical analysis of a population), a living sample database can be very useful. But there are some severe restrictions with a living sample database, and the designer should not build such a database as part of the data warehouse unless he or she is aware of the limitations.

A living sample database is *not* a general-purpose database. If you wanted to find out whether J Jones is a customer, you would not look into a living sample database for that information. It is absolutely possible for J Jones to be a customer but not be on record in the living sample. Living sample databases are good for statistical analysis and looking at trends. Where data must be looked at collectively, living sample databases can offer

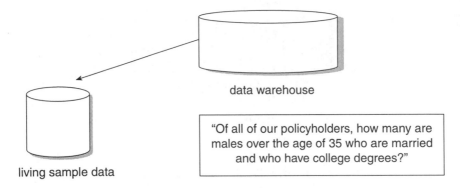

data warehouse

"Of all of our policyholders, how many are males over the age of 35 who are married and who have college degrees?"

living sample data

- a fraction of data in the warehouse
- used for very efficient formulation of a query
- *cannot be used for general purpose analysis— can only be used for statistical analysis*

**Figure 2.18**   Living sample data—another way of changing the granularity of data.

some very promising results, but they are not at all good for dealing with individual records of data.

Consider how a living sample database is typically loaded. A program rummages through a large database selecting every one hundredth or every one thousandth record. The record is then shipped to the living sample. The resulting living sample database, then, is 1/100 or 1/1000 the size of the original database.

The selection of records of the living sample is usually random. On occasion, a "judgment sample" is taken—one where a record must meet certain criteria in order to be selected. The problem with judgment samples is that they almost always introduce bias into the living sample data. The problem with a random selection of data is that it may not produce statistical significance. In any case, data is selected for the living sample. The fact that any given record is not found in the living sample database means nothing.

The greatest asset of a living sample database is that it is very efficient to access. Given that it is a fraction of the size of the larger database from which it was derived, it is correspondingly much more efficient to access and analyze.

Put another way, suppose an analyst takes 24 hours to scan

and analyze a large database. It may take as little as 10 minutes to scan and analyze a living sample database. In doing heuristic analysis, the turnaround time is crucial to the analysis that can be done. In heuristic analysis, the analyst runs a program, studies the results, reformulates the program, and runs it again. If it takes 24 hours to execute the program, the process of analysis and reformulation is greatly impaired (not to mention the resources required to do the reformulation).

But with a living sample database that is small enough to be scanned in 10 minutes, the analyst can go through the iterative process very quickly. In short, the productivity of the DSS analyst depends on the speed of turning around the analysis being done.

There is the argument that doing statistical analysis yields incorrect answers. Consider the case where an analyst runs against a large file using 25,000,000 records to determine that 56.7 percent of the drivers on the road are men. Using a living sample database, the analyst uses 25,000 records to determine that 55.9 percent of the drivers on the road are men. One analysis has required vastly more resources than the other. Yet, the difference between the answers that have been calculated is very, very small. Undoubtedly, the analysis against the large database was more accurate, but the cost of that accuracy is exorbitant, especially in the face of heuristic processing where iterations of processing are the norm.

If very high degrees of accuracy are desired, a useful technique is to formulate the request and go through the iterative processing on the living sample database. In doing so, the DSS analyst quickly formulates the request. Then, when the request is understood, it is run one final time against the large database.

Living sample data is just one more way of changing the level of granularity in the data warehouse to accommodate DSS processing.

## PARTITIONING OF DATA

In the data warehouse environment, the question is not *whether* current detail data will be partitioned but *how* current detail data will be partitioned. Figure 2.19 illustrates partitioning.

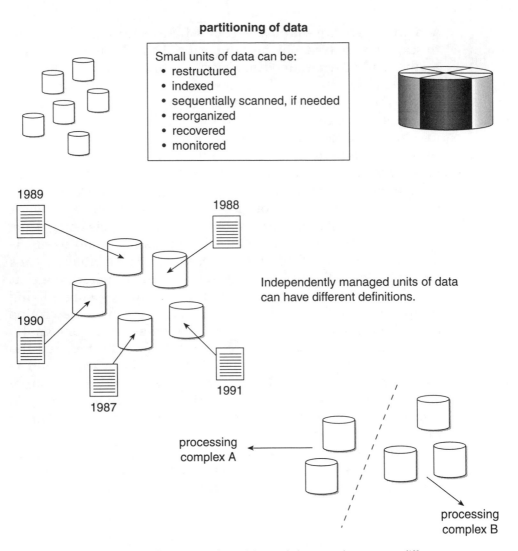

**Figure 2.19** Independently managed partitions of data can be sent to different processing complexes with no other system considerations.

The whole purpose of partitioning of current detail data is to break data up into small physical units. Why is this so important? Small physical units afford the operations staff and the designer much more flexibility in the management of data than do large physical units.

When data resides in large physical units, among other things it cannot be:

- restructured easily
- indexed freely
- sequentially scanned, if needed
- reorganized easily
- recovered easily
- monitored easily

In short, one of the essences of the data warehouse is the flexible access of data. Having a big mass of data defeats much of the purpose of the data warehouse. Therefore, *all current detail data warehouse data will be partitioned.*

What exactly does it mean to partition data? Data is partitioned when data of a like structure is divided into more than one physical unit of data. In addition, any given unit of data belongs to one and only one partition.

There are many criteria by which data can be divided, for example:

- by date
- by line of business
- by geography
- by organizational unit
- by all of the above

The choices for partitioning data are strictly up to the developer. However, in the data warehouse environment it is almost mandatory that one of the criteria for partitioning be by date.

As an example of how a life insurance company may choose to partition its data, consider the following physical units of data:

- 1988 health claims
- 1989 health claims
- 1990 health claims
- 1987 life claims
- 1988 life claims
- 1989 life claims
- 1990 life claims

- 1988 casualty claims
- 1989 casualty claims
- 1990 casualty claims

The insurance company has used the criteria of date—that is, year—and type of claim to partition the data.

One of the major issues facing the data warehouse developer is whether to do partitioning at the system level or at the application level. Partitioning at the system level is a function of the DBMS and the operating system to some extent. Partitioning at the application level is done by application code and is solely and strictly controlled by the developer and the programmer. The DBMS and the system know of no relation between one partition and the other when data is partitioned at the application level.

As a rule, it makes sense to partition data warehouse data at the application level. There are some important reasons for this. The most important is that at the application level there can be a different definition of data for each year. There can be 1988's definition of data and there can be 1989's definition of data, which may or may not be the same thing. The nature of data in a warehouse is the collection of data over a long period of time.

When the partitioning is done at the system level, the DBMS inevitably wants a single definition of data. Given that the data warehouse holds data for a long period of time—up to 10 years—and given that the definition regularly changes, it does not make sense to allow the DBMS or the operating system to dictate that there should be a single definition of data.

Another important feature of allowing the partitioning of data to be managed at the application level is that it can be moved from one processing complex to another with impunity. When the workload and volume of data become a real burden in the data warehouse environment, this feature may be a real advantage.

The acid test for partitioning of data is to ask the question "Can an index be added to a partition with no discernible interruption to other operations?" If an index can be added at will, then the partition is fine enough. If an index cannot be added easily, then the partition needs to be broken down more finely.

## STRUCTURING DATA IN THE DATA WAREHOUSE

So far, we haven't gone into what the data structures found in the data warehouse really look like. There are many kinds of structures found in the data warehouse. We will look at some of the more common ones now.

Perhaps the simplest and most common data structure found in the data warehouse is the simple cumulative structure, shown in Figure 2.20.

Figure 2.20 shows that the daily transactions are transported from the operational environment. After being transported, they are summarized into data warehouse records. The summarization may be by customer, account, or whatever subject area the data warehouse is organized into. The transactions are summarized by day. In other words, all daily activity for a customer for an account are totaled and passed into the data warehouse on a day-by-day basis.

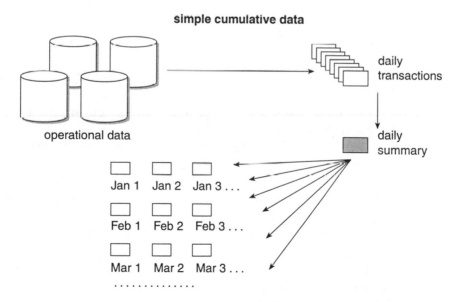

**Figure 2.20** The simplest form of data in the data warehouse is that of data that has been accumulated on a record-by-record basis—called simple cumulative data.

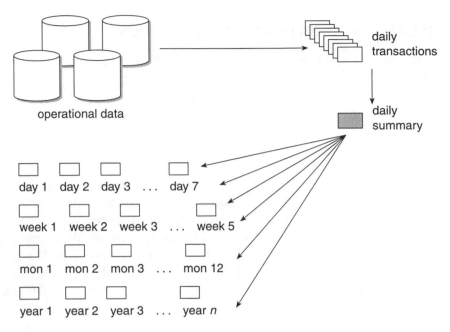

**Figure 2.21** A variation of the cumulative file is the rolling summary file.

Figure 2.21 shows a variation of the simple daily cumulation called the *storage of rolling summary data*.

The data passes from the operational environment to the data warehouse environment as it did previously. Only in rolling summary data, the data is entered into a very different structure. For the first seven days of the week, activity is summarized into seven daily slots. On the eighth day, the seven daily slots are added together and placed into the first weekly slot. Then the daily totals are added into the first daily slot.

At the end of the month, the weekly slots are added together and placed in the first monthly slot. Then the weekly slots are reset to zero. At the end of the year, the monthly slots are added together, and the first yearly slot is loaded. Then the monthly slots are reset to zero.

A rolling summary data structure handles many fewer units of data than does a simple cumulative structuring of data. A comparison of the advantages and the disadvantages of rolling summary versus simple cumulative structuring of data is shown in Figure 2.22.

Another possibility for the structuring of data warehouse data is the simple direct file, shown in Figure 2.23.

Figure 2.23 shows that data is merely pulled from the operational environment to the data warehouse environment; there is no accumulation. In addition, the simple direct file is not done on a daily basis. Instead, it is done over a longer period of time, such as a week or a month. As such, the simple direct file represents a snapshot of operational data taken as of one instant in time.

From two or more simple direct files can be created a continuous file, as shown in Figure 2.24. Two snapshots—one from January and one from February—are merged together to create

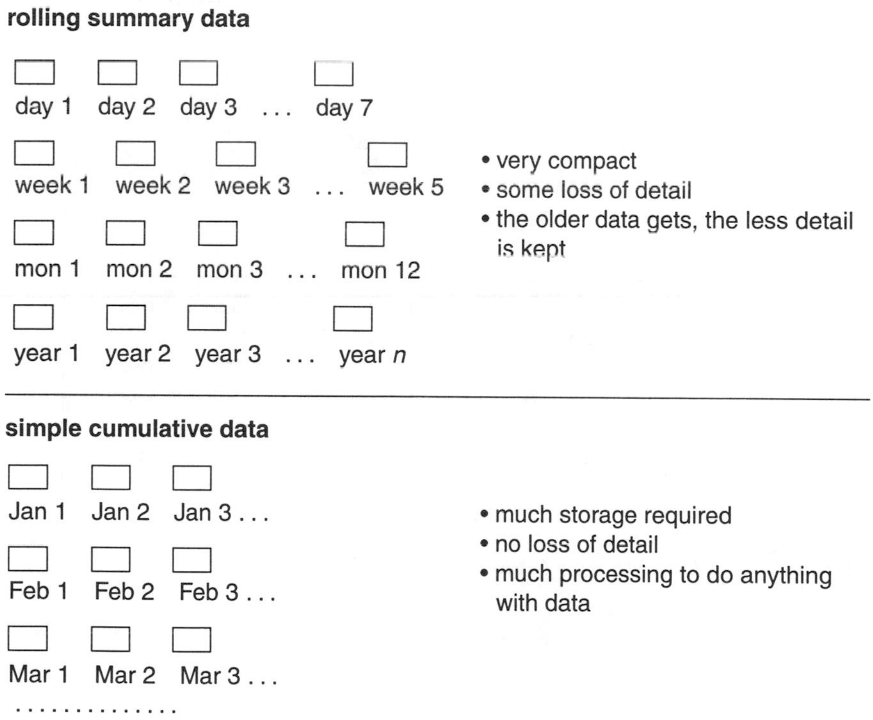

**rolling summary data**

day 1   day 2   day 3   . . .   day 7

week 1   week 2   week 3   . . .   week 5

mon 1   mon 2   mon 3   . . .   mon 12

year 1   year 2   year 3   . . .   year *n*

- very compact
- some loss of detail
- the older data gets, the less detail is kept

**simple cumulative data**

Jan 1   Jan 2   Jan 3 . . .

Feb 1   Feb 2   Feb 3 . . .

Mar 1   Mar 2   Mar 3 . . .

. . . . . . . . . . . . .

- much storage required
- no loss of detail
- much processing to do anything with data

**Figure 2.22**   Comparing simple cumulative data with rolling summary data.

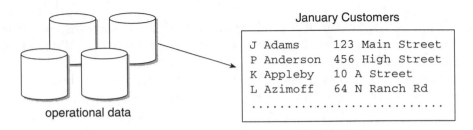

**Figure 2.23** A simple direct file, another data warehouse structure.

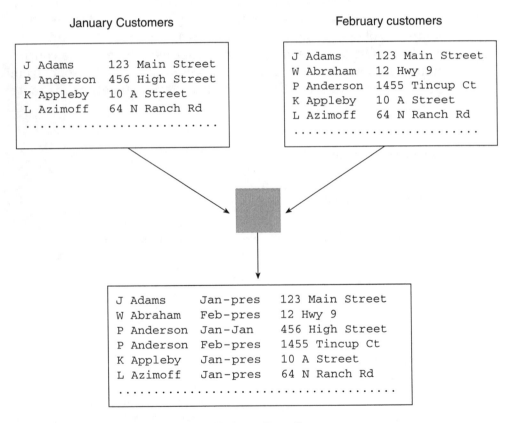

**Figure 2.24** Creating a continuous file from direct files.

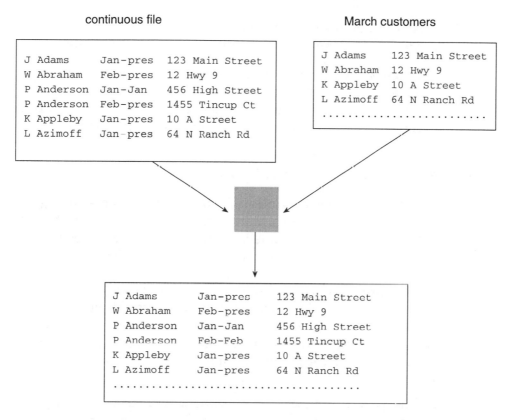

**Figure 2.25**   Continuous files can be created from simple direct files, or may have simple direct files appended onto them.

a continuous file of data. The data in the continuous file represents the data continuously from the first month to the last.

Of course, a continuous file can be created by appending a snapshot of data onto a previous version of the continuous file, as shown in Figure 2.25.

There are *many* more structurings of data within the data warehouse. The most common are:

- simple cumulative
- rolling summary
- simple direct
- continuous

At the key level, data warehouse keys are inevitably compounded keys. There are two compelling reasons for this.

- Date—year, year/month, year/month/day, and so on, is almost always a part of the key.
- Because data warehouse data is partitioned, the different components of the partitioning show up as part of the key.

## DATA WAREHOUSE—THE STANDARDS MANUAL

The data warehouse is relevant to many people—managers, DSS analysts, developers, planners, and so forth. In most organizations, data warehouse is new. Accordingly, there needs to be an official organizational explanation and description of the data warehouse.

It is probably deadly to call the warehouse explanation a "standards manual." Standards manuals have a dreary connotation and are famous for being ignored and gathering dust. Yet, some form of internal publication is a very worthwhile endeavor.

The kinds of things the publication should contain are the following:

- a description of what a data warehouse is
- a description of source systems feeding the warehouse
- how to use the data warehouse
- how to get help if there is a problem
- who is responsible for what
- the migration plan for the warehouse
- how warehouse data relates to operational data
- how to use warehouse data for DSS
- when not to add data to the warehouse
- what kind of data is not in the warehouse
- a guide to the metadata that is available
- what the system of record is

## AUDITING AND THE DATA WAREHOUSE

An interesting issue that arises with data warehouses is whether auditing can be or should be done from them. Auditing can be done from the data warehouse; there are a few examples of detailed audits being performed there. But there are many more reasons why auditing—even if it can be done from the data warehouse—should *not* be done from there. The primary reasons for not doing so are the following:

- Data that otherwise would not find its way into the warehouse suddenly has to be there.
- The timing of data entry into the warehouse changes dramatically when auditing capability is required.
- The backup and recovery restrictions for data warehouse change drastically when auditing capability is required.
- Auditing data at the warehouse forces the granularity of data in the warehouse to be at the very lowest level.

In short, it is possible to do auditing from the data warehouse environment. However, the complications associated with auditing are such that it makes much more sense to do auditing elsewhere.

## COST JUSTIFICATION

One of the interesting aspects of the data warehouse is that cost justification for the warehouse is normally not done on an a priori, return-on-investment (ROI) basis. To do such an analysis requires that the benefits of a data warehouse be known prior to the building of the data warehouse.

In most cases, the real benefits of the data warehouse are not known or even anticipated at the moment of construction because the warehouse is used in a way entirely different from other data and systems built by information systems. The usage of the data warehouse occurs in a mode different from the rest of information processing—something like a "Tell me what I say I want, then I can tell you what I really want" mode. The DSS analyst really cannot say what the possibilities and potentials of the data warehouse are until the first iteration of the data warehouse is built and becomes available. Then, once the DSS analyst gets his or her hands on the warehouse, the analyst can start to unlock the potential of DSS processing.

Thus it is that classical ROI techniques simply are not applicable to the data warehouse environment. Fortunately, data warehouses are built incrementally. The first iteration can be done quickly and for a relatively small amount of money. Once the first portion of the data warehouse is built and populated, the analyst can start to explore the possibilities. It is at this point that the analyst can start to justify the development costs of the warehouse.

As a rule of thumb, the first iteration of the data warehouse should be small enough to be built and large enough to be meaningful. For these reasons, the data warehouse is best built a small iteration at a time, with a direct feedback loop between the warehouse developer and the DSS analyst in place, and quickly.

In addition, these reasons explain why it is said that if the initial design of the data warehouse is 50 percent accurate as initially designed, then the design is a success. The feedback loop between the warehouse developer and the DSS analyst is constantly modifying the existing warehouse data and adding other data to the warehouse.

Typically the first cut at the data warehouse focuses on one of these subject areas:

- finance
- marketing
- sales

Occasionally the data warehouse first subject area will focus on:

- engineering/manufacturing
- actuarial interests

## PURGING WAREHOUSE DATA

Data does not just pour into a data warehouse. It has its own life cycle within the warehouse as well. At some point in time, data is purged from the warehouse. The issue of purging data is one of the fundamental design issues that must not escape the data warehouse designer.

In some senses, data is not purged from the warehouse at all. It is simply rolled up to higher levels of summary. There are several ways in which data is purged or the detail of data is transformed, including the following:

- Data is added to a rolling summary file where detail is lost.
- Data is transferred to a bulk medium from a high-performance medium such as DASD.
- Data is actually purged from the system.
- Data is transferred from one level of the architecture to another, such as from the operational level to the data warehouse level.

There are, then, a variety of ways in which data is purged or otherwise transformed inside the data warehouse environment. The life cycle of data—including its purge or final archival dissemination—should be an active part of the design process for the data warehouse.

## REPORTING AND THE ARCHITECTED ENVIRONMENT

It is a temptation to say that once the data warehouse has been constructed *all* reporting and informational processing will be done from there. That is simply not the case. There is a legitimate class of processing that rightfully belongs in the domain of operational systems. Figure 2.26 shows where the different styles of processing should be located.

Figure 2.26 shows that operational reporting is for the clerical level and focuses primarily on the line item. Data warehouse or informational processing focuses on management and contains summary or otherwise calculated information. In the data warehouse style of reporting little use is made of line item, detailed information, once the basic calculation of data is made.

## THE OPERATIONAL WINDOW OF OPPORTUNITY

The foundation of DSS processing—the data warehouse—contains nothing but archival information, most of it at least 24

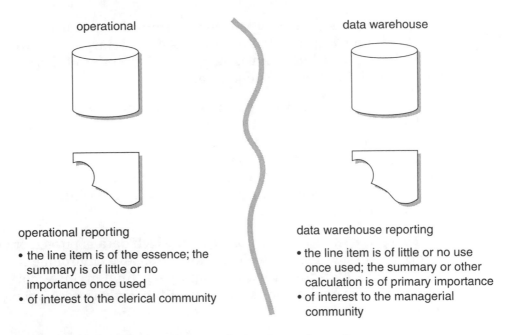

operational

data warehouse

operational reporting

• the line item is of the essence; the
  summary is of little or no
  importance once used
• of interest to the clerical community

data warehouse reporting

• the line item is of little or no use
  once used; the summary or other
  calculation is of primary importance
• of interest to the managerial
  community

**Figure 2.26** The differences between the two types of reporting.

hours old. But archival data is found elsewhere throughout the architected environment. In particular archival data is also found in the operational environment.

In the data warehouse it is normal for there to be a lengthy amount of archival data—from five to ten years is common. Because of the time horizon, there is a massive amount of data there.

The time horizon of archival data found in the operational environment—the "operational window" of data—is not nearly so long. It can be anywhere from one week to up to two years. But the time horizon of archival data in the operational environment is not the only difference between archival data in the data warehouse and in the operational environment. Unlike the data warehouse, the operational environment's archival data is nonvoluminous and has a high probability of access.

In order to understand the role of fresh, nonvoluminous, high-probability-of-access archival data in the operational environment, consider the way a bank works. In a bank environment, the customer can reasonably expect to find information about this month's transactions. Did this month's rent check clear? When was the deposit of a paycheck made? What was the low balance for the month? Did the bank take out money for the electricity bill last week?

Very detailed, very current transactions (which are still archival) can be expected to be contained in the operational environment of a bank. But is it reasonable to expect the bank to tell the customer whether a check was made out to the grocery store five years ago? or whether a check to a political campaign was cashed ten years ago? These transactions would hardly be in the domain of the operational systems of the bank. Not only are these transactions very old, but they contain data that has a very low probability of access.

The operational window of time varies from industry to industry and even in type of data and activity within an industry.

For example, an insurance company would have a very lengthy operational window—from two to three years. The rate of transactions in an insurance company is very low, at least compared to other types of industries. There are relatively few direct interactions between the customer and the insurance company. The operational window for the activities of a bank, on the other hand, is very short—from 0 to 60 days. A bank has many direct interactions with its customers.

The operational window of a company depends on what industry the company is in. In the case of a large company, there may be more than one operational window, depending on the particulars of the business being conducted. For example, in a telephone company, customer usage data may have an operational window of 30 to 60 days, while vendor/supplier activity may have a window of two to three years.

The following are some suggestions as to how the operational window of archival data may look in different industries:

- insurance—2 to 3 years
- bank trust processing—2 to 5 years
- telephone
    - customer usage—30 to 60 days
    - supplier/vendor activity—2 to 3 years

- retail banking
    - customer account activity—30 days
    - vendor activity—1 year
    - loans—2 to 5 years
- retailing
    - SKU activity—1 to 14 days
    - vendor activity—1 week to 1 month
- airlines
    - flight seat activity— 30 to 90 days
    - vendor/supplier activity—1 to 2 years
- public utility
    - customer utilization—60 to 90 days
    - supplier activity—1 to 5 years

The length of the operational window is very important to the DSS analyst, because it determines where the analyst goes in order to do different kinds of analysis and what kinds of analysis can be done. For example, the DSS analyst can do individual-item analysis on data found within the operational window, but cannot do massive trend analysis. Data within the operational window is geared for efficient individual access. Only when the data passes out of the operational window is it geared for mass data storage and access.

On the other hand, the DSS analyst can do sweeping trend analysis on data found outside the operational window. Data out there can be accessed and processed en masse, whereas access to any one individual unit of data is not optimal.

## SUMMARY

This chapter described subject orientation, the time variant of each record of data, and linkage by a common key in the data warehouse.

The two most important design decisions that can be made concern the granularity of data and the partitioning of data. For most organizations, a dual level of granularity makes the most sense. Partitioning of data is done to break it down into small physical units. As a rule, partitioning is done at the application level rather than at the system level.

# The Data Warehouse and Design

**3**

There are two major aspects to the building of the data warehouse—the design of the interface coming from operational systems and the design of the data warehouse itself. In a way, "design" is not an accurate description for what happens in the building of the data warehouse, which is constructed in a heuristic manner. First, one portion of data is populated. It is then used and scrutinized by the DSS analyst. Then, based on the feedback of the end user, the data is modified and/or other data is added to the data warehouse.

The feedback loop continues throughout the entire life of the data warehouse. It is a mistake to think that design approaches that have worked in the past will suffice in building the data warehouse. The requirements for the data warehouse *cannot be known* until it is partially populated and being used by the DSS analyst. So, it cannot be designed in the same way that the classical requirements-driven system is designed. On the other hand, it is also a mistake to think that not anticipating requirements is a good idea. Reality lies somewhere in between.

## BEGINNING WITH OPERATIONAL DATA

At the outset, there is operational data locked up in existing systems. It is a temptation to think that all there is to creating the data warehouse is extracting operational data and entering it into the data warehouse. Nothing could be further from the truth.

Figure 3.1 shows a simple depiction of pulling data from the existing systems environment over to the data warehouse. We see here that multiple applications will contribute to the data warehouse.

There are a multitude of reasons why Figure 3.1 is overly simplistic. The primary fault in thinking that building a data warehouse is merely an extraction process is that the data in the operational environment is unintegrated. Figure 3.2 shows the lack of integration that is normal in the existing systems environment.

When the existing applications were constructed, no thought was given to their possible future integration. Each application had its own set of unique and private requirements, and there was no consideration of other applications during the development process. It is no surprise, then, that some of the *same* data exists in various places with different names; some data is labeled the same way in different places but it is still the same data; and some data is all in the same place with the same name but reflects a different measurement, and so on. Trying to extract data from the many places it exists is a very complex problem.

This issue of lack of integration is the extract programmer's nightmare. There are a thousand and one details that have to be

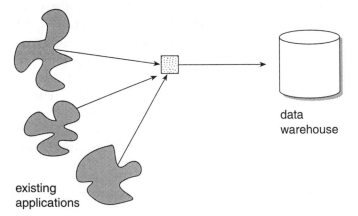

**Figure 3.1** Moving data from the operational to the data warehouse environment is not as simple as mere extraction.

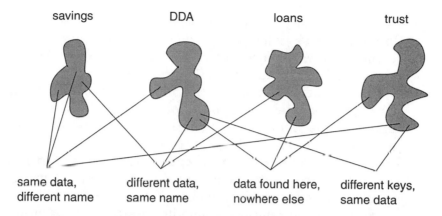

**Figure 3.2** Data across the different applications are terribly unintegrated.

programmed just to bring the data from the operational environment properly, as illustrated in Figure 3.3.

As a simple example of lack of integration, data may not be encoded consistently, as shown by the encoding of gender. In one application, gender is encoded as "m/f". In another, it is encoded

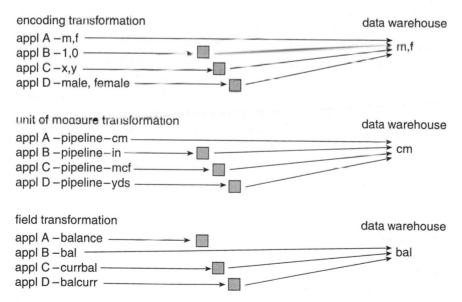

**Figure 3.3** In order to properly move data from the existing systems environment to the data warehouse environment, it must be integrated.

as "0/1". It really doesn't matter how gender is encoded in the data warehouse as long as it is done consistently. As data passes to the data warehouse, the different values must be correctly deciphered and recoded with the proper value.

As another example of the integration issues facing the developer, consider four applications that have the same field—pipeline. The field, however, is measured differently in each application. In one application, pipeline is measured in inches. In another, it is measured in centimeters, and so forth. It does not particularly matter how pipeline is measured in the data warehouse, as long as it is measured consistently.

Field transformation is another issue of integration. The same field exists in four applications in four names. In order to transform the data to the data warehouse properly, there must be a mapping from the different source fields to the data warehouse fields.

These simple examples hardly scratch the surface of integration, and they are not complex in themselves. But when they are multiplied by the thousands of existing systems and files, the issue of integration becomes very complex and burdensome.

But integration (or lack thereof) of existing systems is not the only difficulty in the transformation of data from the operational, existing systems environment to the data warehouse environment. Another major problem is that of the efficiency of accessing existing systems data. How does the program that scans existing systems know whether a file has been scanned previously? There is a lot of data in the existing systems environment and attempting to scan all of it every time a data warehouse scan is done is wasteful and unrealistic.

There are three types of loads to be made into the data warehouse from the operational environment:

■ the loading of archival data
■ the loading of data currently contained in the operational environment
■ the loading of ongoing changes to the data warehouse environment from the changes (updates) that have occurred in the operational environment since the last refreshment of the data warehouse

As a rule, the loading of archival data presents a minimal challenge because it often is not done. Organizations find the use of old data not to be cost effective in many environments.

The loading of data from the existing operational environment likewise presents a minimal challenge because it only needs to be done once. Usually the existing systems environment can be downloaded to a sequential file and the sequential file can be downloaded into the warehouse with no disruption to the online environment.

The loading of data on an ongoing basis—as changes are made to the operational environment—presents the largest challenge to the data architect. Efficiently trapping those changes and manipulating them is not easy to do. Scanning existing files, then, is a major issue facing the data warehouse architect.

There are five common techniques used to limit the amount of data scanned, as shown in Figure 3.4. The first technique is to scan data that has been timestamped. When an application happens to stamp the time of last change or update on a record, the data warehouse scan can run quite efficiently, because data with a date other than that applicable does not have to be touched. However, it usually is only by happenstance that existing data has been timestamped.

The second technique of limiting the data to be scanned for data warehouse extraction is to scan a "delta" file. A delta file is one that is created by an application that contains only the changes made to an application. When there is a delta file, the scan process is very efficient because data that is not a candidate for scanning is never touched. But not many applications build delta files.

The third technique is that of scanning an audit or log file. The log file or the audit file contain essentially the same data as a delta file. However, there are some major differences. Many times, operations protects the log files because they are needed in the recovery process. Computer operations is not particularly thrilled by having its log file used for something other than its primary purpose. Another difficulty with a log tape is that the internal format is built for systems purposes, not applications purposes. It may require a technological guru to interface the contents of data on the log tape. Another shortcoming of a log

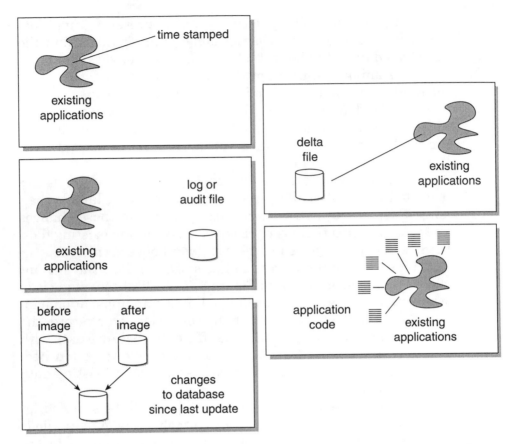

**Figure 3.4** How do you know what source data to scan? Do you scan every record every day? every week?

file is that it usually contains much more information than that desired by the data warehouse developer. Audit files have many of the same shortcomings as log files.

The fourth technique for managing the amount of data scanned as data warehouse extraction occurs is to modify application code. This is never a popular option, as much application code is old and fragile.

The last option (in most respects, a hideous option, the primary purpose of which is to convince people that there must be a better way) is that of rubbing a "before" and an "after" image file together. In this option, a snapshot of a database is taken at the moment of extraction. When it comes time to do another extraction, another snapshot is taken. The two snapshots are serially compared to each other to determine the activity that has transpired. This approach is cumbersome, complex, and requires an inordinate amount of resources. It is simply a last resort.

But integration and performance are not the only major discrepancies that prevent a simple extract process from being used to construct the data warehouse. A third major difficulty is that of a time basis shift, as shown in Figure 3.5.

Existing operational data is almost always current value data. Current value data is data whose accuracy is valid as of the moment of access, and it can be updated. But data that goes into the data warehouse cannot be updated. This data must have an element of time attached to it. There needs to be a major shift in data, then, as data passes from the existing systems environment to the data warehouse environment.

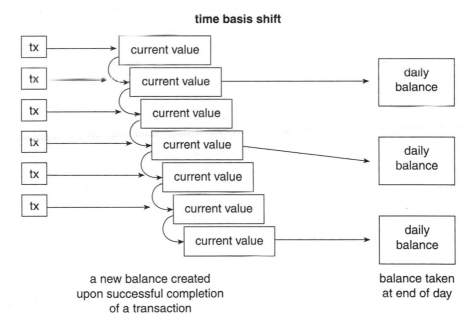

**Figure 3.5**  A shift in time basis is required as data is moved over from the operational to the data warehouse environment.

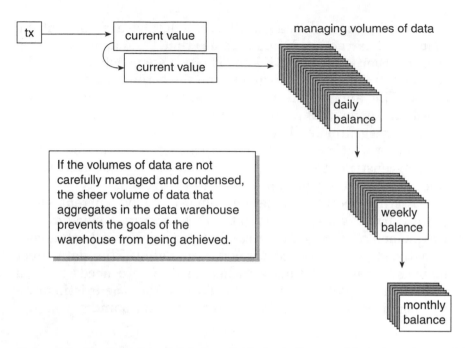

**Figure 3.6**  Condensation of data is a vital factor in the managing of warehouse data.

Yet another major consideration when data is passed from the existing systems environment to the data warehouse environment is that of the need to manage the volume of data. Condensation of data needs to be done; otherwise, the volume of data in the data warehouse will grow out of control in rapid order. Condensation of data needs to begin at the moment of extraction. Figure 3.6 shows a simple form of condensation of data warehouse data.

## DATA/PROCESS MODELS AND THE ARCHITECTED ENVIRONMENT

Before any attempt is made to apply conventional design techniques, the designer *must* understand the applicability and the limits of those techniques. Figure 3.7 shows the relationship between the levels of the architecture and the disciplines of data modeling and process modeling. The process model applies to *only* the operational environment. The data model applies to

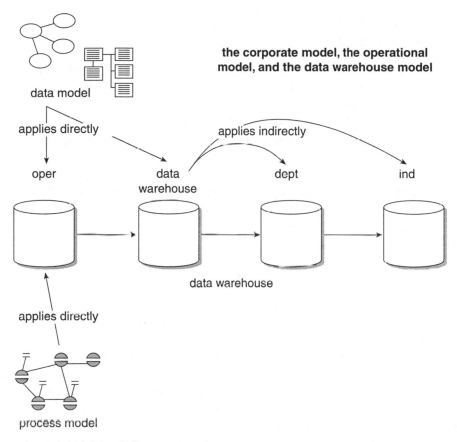

**Figure 3.7** How the different types of models apply to the architected environment.

both the operational environment and the data warehouse environment. Trying to use a data or process model in the wrong place will produce nothing but frustration.

Data models will be discussed in depth later in this chapter. What is a process model? A process model typically consists of the following (in whole or in part):

- a functional decomposition
- a context level zero diagram
- a data flow diagram
- a structure chart
- a state transition diagram

- an HIPO chart
- pseudocode

There are many contexts and many environments where a process model is invaluable. But in building the data warehouse, a process model is a hindrance. The process model is requirements based. This assumes that there is a set of requirements that is known—a priori—before the details of the design are established. In dealing with processes such an assumption can be made. But those assumptions do not hold for the data warehouse. Indeed, many development tools, such as CASE tools, have the same orientation and as such are not applicable to the data warehouse environment.

## THE DATA WAREHOUSE AND DATA MODELS

The data model is shown as being applicable to both the existing systems environment and the data warehouse environment. A more lucid explanation is depicted in Figure 3.8.

Figure 3.8 shows that there is an overall corporate data model that has been constructed with no regard for a distinction between existing, operational systems and data warehouse. The corporate data model contains only primitive data. In order to construct a separate existing data model, the beginning point is the corporate model, as shown. However, performance factors are added into the corporate data model as the model is transported to the existing systems environment. All in all, very few changes are made to the corporate data model as it is used operationally.

However, there are a fair number of changes that are made to the corporate data model as it is applied to the data warehouse. The first thing done is data that is used purely in the operational environment is removed. Next, the key structures of the corporate data model are enhanced with an element of time. Derived data is added to the corporate data model where the derived data is publicly used and calculated once, not repeatedly. And, finally, data relationships in the operational environment are turned into "artifacts" in the data warehouse.

A final design activity in going from the enterprise data model to the data warehouse data model is to perform "stability"

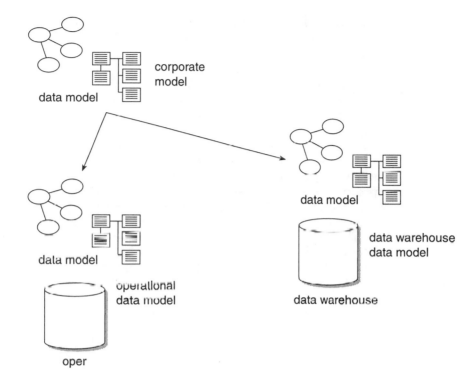

corporate
model

data model

data model

data warehouse
data model

data model

operational
data model

data warehouse

oper

- operational data model equals corporate data model
- performance factors are added prior to database design

- remove pure operational data
- add element of time to key
- add derived data where appropriate
- create artifacts of relationships

**Figure 3.8**   How the different levels of modeling relate.

analysis. Stability analysis is the act of grouping attributes of data together based on their propensity for change. Figure 3.9 illustrates stability analysis.

In Figure 3.9, it is seen that data that seldom changes is grouped with other like data, data that sometimes changes is grouped with other data that sometimes changes, and data that frequently changes is grouped with other data that frequently changes. The net result of stability analysis (which usually is the last step of data modeling before going onto physical database design) is to create groups of data with similar characteristics.

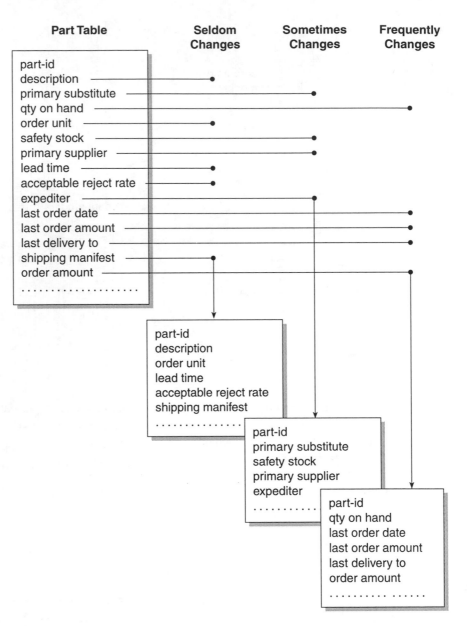

**Figure 3.9** An example of stability analysis for the manufacturing environment, showing how three tables are created from one large, general-purpose table based on the stability requirements of the data contained in the tables.

There is, then, a common genesis of data models. Using an analogy, the corporate data model is Adam, the operational data model is Cain, and the data warehouse data model is Abel. They are all from the same lineage but, at the same time, they are all different.

## The Data Model

(Other books have been written on data modeling. There are a wide number of approaches to choose from. Any number of the approaches can be used successfully in the building of a data warehouse. The approach that will be discussed here, in a summary fashion, can be further explored in *Information Systems Architecture*, Wiley.)

There are three levels of data modeling: high-level modeling (called the ERD, entity relationship level), midlevel modeling (called the DIS, data item set), and low-level modeling (called the physical model).

The high level of modeling features entities and relationships, as shown in Figure 3.10. The name of the entity is sur-

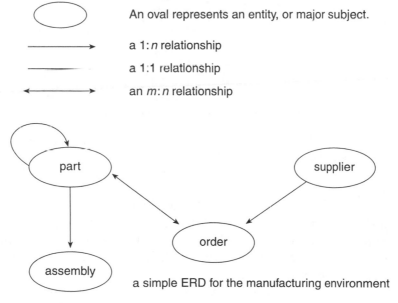

**Figure 3.10**   Representing entities and relationships.

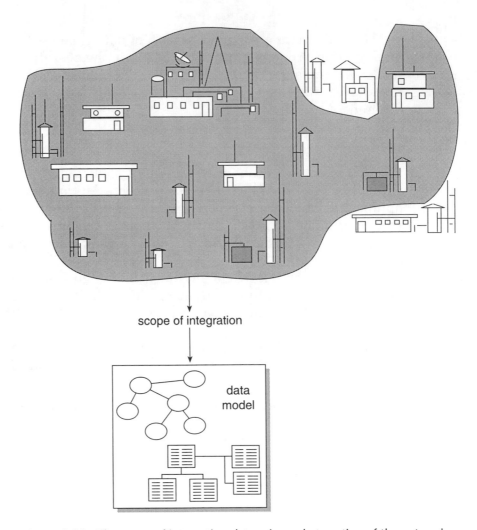

**Figure 3.11** The scope of integration determines what portion of the enterprise will be reflected in the data model.

rounded by an oval. Relationships between entities are depicted with arrows. The direction and number of the arrowheads indicate the cardinality of the relationship, and only direct relationships are indicated. In doing so, transitive dependencies are minimized.

The entities that are shown in the ERD level are at the highest level of abstraction. The determination of what entities belong in the scope of the model and what entities do not is determined by what is termed the "scope of integration," as shown in Figure 3.11.

The scope of integration defines the boundaries of the data model and needs to be defined before the modeling process commences. The scope is agreed upon by the modeler, management, and the ultimate user of the system. If the scope is not predetermined, there is the great chance that the modeling process will continue forever. The definition of the scope of integration should be written in no more than five pages and written in language understandable to the businessperson.

The corporate ERD is a composite of many individual ERDs that reflect the different views of people across the corporation, as seen in Figure 3.12. Separate high-level data models have been created for different communities within the corporation. Collectively they comprise the corporate ERD.

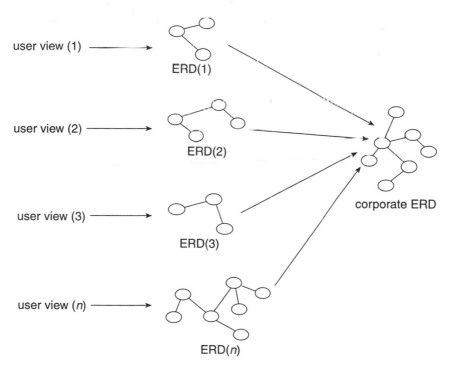

**Figure 3.12** The construction of the corporate ERD from the different user view ERDs.

The community ERDs are created by means of user view sessions, which are interview sessions with the appropriate personnel in the various departments.

### The Midlevel Data Model

After the high-level data model is created, the next level is established—the midlevel model, or the DIS. For each major subject area, or entity, identified in the high-level data model, a midlevel model is created, as seen in Figure 3.13. The high-level data model has identified four entities, or major subject areas. Each of the major subject areas is subsequently developed into its own midlevel model.

Interestingly, only very rarely are all of the midlevel models developed at once. The midlevel data model for one major subject area is expanded, then the midlevel model is fleshed out while other parts of the model remain static, and so forth.

The constructs of data modeling that are found at midlevel modeling are shown in Figure 3.14. There are four basic constructs for the midlevel model:

- a primary grouping of data
- a secondary grouping of data

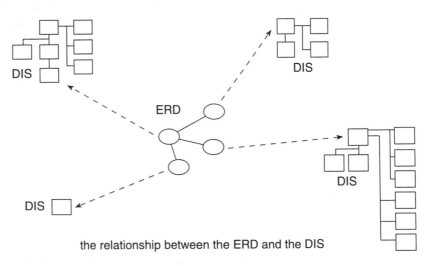

the relationship between the ERD and the DIS

**Figure 3.13**   Each entity in the ERD is further defined by its own DIS.

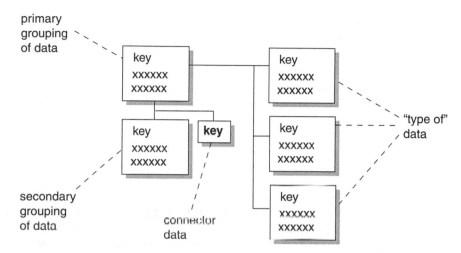

**Figure 3.14** The four constructs that make up the midlevel data model.

- a connector, signifying the relationships of data between major subject areas
- "type of" data

The primary grouping exists once, and only once, for each major subject area. It holds attributes that exist only once for each major subject area. As with all groupings of data, the primary grouping of data contains attributes and keys.

The secondary grouping of data holds data attributes that can exist multiple times for each major subject area. The secondary grouping is indicated by a line emanating downward from the primary grouping of data. There may be as many secondary groupings as there are distinct groups of data that can occur multiple times.

The third construct is the connector. The connector relates data from one grouping to that of another. A relationship identified at the ERD level results in an acknowledgment at the DIS level. The convention used to indicate a connector is an underlining of a foreign key.

The fourth construct in the data model is that of "type of" data. "Type of" data is indicated by a line leading to the right of

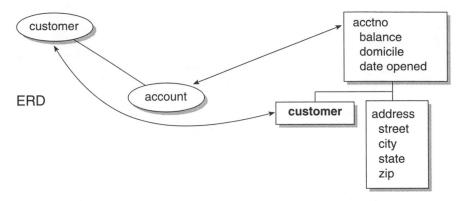

**Figure 3.15** The relationships identified in the ERD are reflected by connectors in the DIS. Note that only one connector—from acctno to customer—is shown in this diagram. In reality, another connector from customer to acctno would be shown elsewhere in the DIS for customer.

a grouping of data. The grouping of data to the left is the super type. The grouping of data to the right is the subtype of data.

These four data modeling constructs are used to identify the attributes of data in a data model and the relationship between those attributes. When a relationship is identified at the ERD level, it is manifested by a pair of connector relationships at the DIS level. Figure 3.15 shows one of those pairs.

At the ERD, a relationship between customer and account has been identified. At the DIS level for account, there exists a connector beneath account. This indicates that an account may have multiple customers attached to it. Not shown is the corresponding relationship beneath the customer in the customer DIS. In the customer DIS, there will be a connector to account, indicating that a customer can have an account or accounts.

As an example of what a full-blown DIS might look like, consider the example shown in Figure 3.16. There is a DIS for an account for a financial institution. All of the different constructs are shown in the DIS.

Of particular interest is the case where a grouping of data has two "type of" lines emanating from it, as seen in Figure 3.17. The two lines leading to the right indicate that there are two "type of" criteria. One type of criteria is by activity type—either

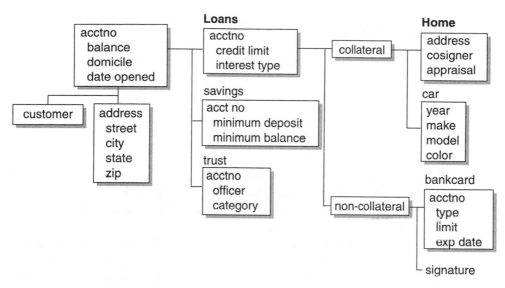

**Figure 3.16** An expanded DIS showing the different types of loans that a bank may support.

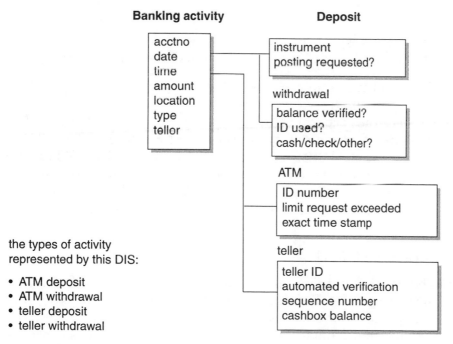

the types of activity represented by this DIS:

- ATM deposit
- ATM withdrawal
- teller deposit
- teller withdrawal

**Figure 3.17** A DIS showing different subcategorization criteria.

a deposit or a withdrawal. The other line indicates another—either an ATM activity or a teller activity. Collectively, the two types of activity encompass the following transactions:

- ATM deposit
- ATM withdrawal
- teller deposit
- teller withdrawal

Another feature of the diagram is that all common data is to the left, and all unique data is to the right. For example, the attributes date and time are common to all transactions. But cashbox balance relates only to teller activity.

The relationship between the data model and physical tables that result from the data model is shown in Figure 3.18. In general, each grouping of data in the data model results in a table being defined in the database design process. Assuming that to be the case, two transactions result in several table entries, as seen in the figure. The physical table entries that resulted came from the following two transactions:

- an ATM withdrawal that occurred at 1:31 P.M. on January 2
- a teller deposit that occurred at 3:15 P.M. on January 5

The two transactions caused six entries in five separate tables to be generated.

Like the corporate ERD that is created from different ERDs reflecting the community of users, the corporate DIS is created from multiple DISs, as illustrated by Figure 3.19. When the interviews or JAD sessions are done for a particular user, a DIS, as well as an ERD, are created. The parochial DIS is then merged with all other DISs to form the corporate view of a DIS.

## The Physical Data Model

The physical data model is created from the midlevel data model merely by extending the midlevel data model to include keys and physical characteristics of the model. At this point, the physical data model looks like a series of tables, sometimes called relational tables.

the different types of data that would exist in separate tables as a result of the DIS

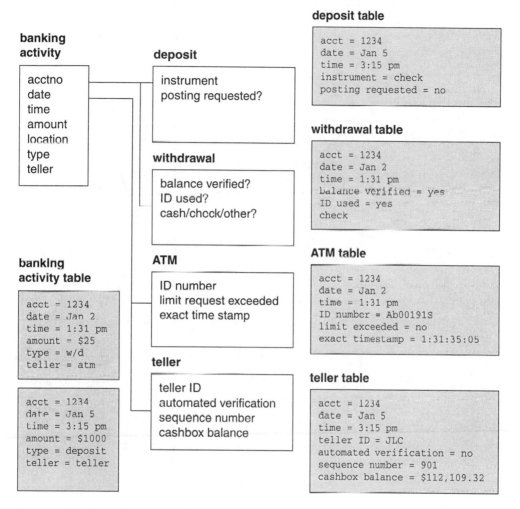

**Figure 3.18** The table entries that are represented by the two transactions.

It is a temptation to say that the tables are ready to be cast into the concrete of physical database design. However, one last design step remains—factoring in the performance characteristics.

In the case of the data warehouse, the first step in factoring in performance characteristics means deciding on the granular-

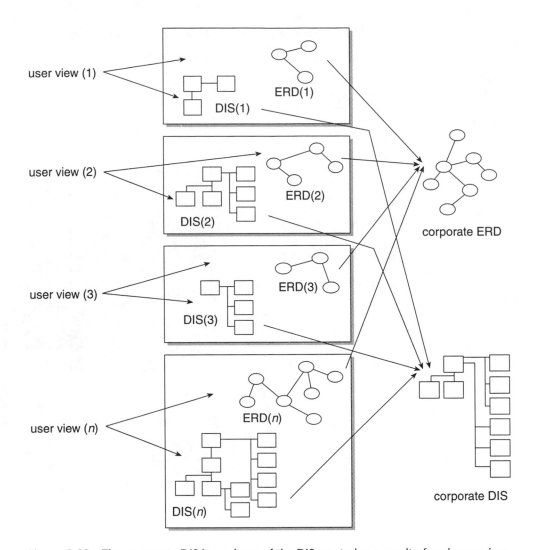

**Figure 3.19** The corporate DIS is made up of the DIS created as a result of each user view session.

ity and partitioning of the data. This must be done. (Of course, the key structure is changed to add the element of time, to which each unit of data is relevant.)

After granularity and partitioning are factored in, a variety of other physical design activities are embedded into the design.

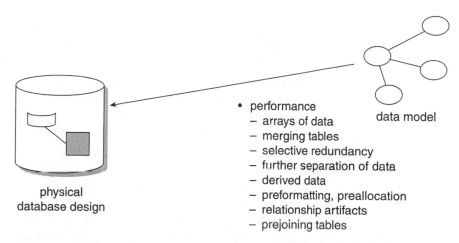

**Figure 3.20**   Getting good performance out of the data warehouse environment.

These other physical design considerations are outlined in Figure 3.20. At the heart of the physical design considerations is the usage of physical I/O (input/output). Physical I/O is the activity that brings data into the computer from storage or sends data to storage from the computer. Figure 3.21 shows a simple case of I/O.

Data is transferred to and from the computer to storage in terms of blocks. The reason that the I/O event is so important to performance is that the transfer of data to and from storage to the computer occurs at roughly two to three orders of magnitude slower than the speeds at which the computer runs. The computer runs internally in terms of nanosecond speed. Transfer of data to and from storage occurs in terms of milliseconds. Thus, physical I/O is the main impediment to performance.

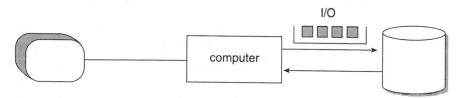

**Figure 3.21**   Getting the most out of the physical I/Os that have to be done.

The job of the data warehouse designer is to physically organize data for the return of the maximum number of records that will be returned from the execution of a physical I/O. (Note: This is not an issue of blindly transferring a large number of records from DASD to main storage. This is a more sophisticated issue of transferring a bulk of records that have a high probability of being accessed.)

For example, suppose a programmer must fetch five records. If those records are organized into different blocks of data on storage, then five I/Os will be required. But if the designer can anticipate that the records will be needed as a group and can physically juxtapose those records into the same physical block, then only one I/O will be required, thus making the program run much more efficiently.

There is another mitigating factor regarding physical placement of data in the data warehouse: Data in the warehouse normally is not updated. This frees the designer to use physical design techniques that otherwise would not be acceptable if it were regularly updated.

## THE DATA MODEL AND ITERATIVE DEVELOPMENT

In all cases the data warehouse is best built iteratively. The following are some of the many reasons why iterative development of the data warehouse is important:

- The industry track record of success strongly suggests it.
- The end user is unable to articulate requirements until the first iteration is done.
- Management will not make a full commitment until actual results are tangible and obvious.
- There is a need to see visible results quickly.

What may not be obvious is the role of the data model in iterative development. In order to explain the role of the data model during iterative development, consider the typical iterative development suggested by Figure 3.22. First one development effort is undertaken, then another, and so forth. The data ware-

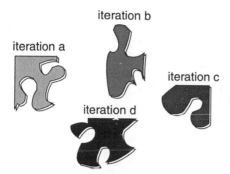

**Figure 3.22** The different iterations of data warehouse development.

house serves as a roadmap for each of the development efforts, as seen in Figure 3.23.

When the second development effort ensues, the developer is confident that he or she will intersect his or her effort with the first development effort because all development efforts are being driven from the data model. Each succeeding development effort builds on the preceding one. The result is that the different development efforts are done under a unifying data model. And because they are built under a single data model, the individual iterative efforts produce a cohesive and tightly orchestrated whole, as seen in Figure 3.24.

When the different iterations of development are done with no unifying data model, there is much overlap of effort and much

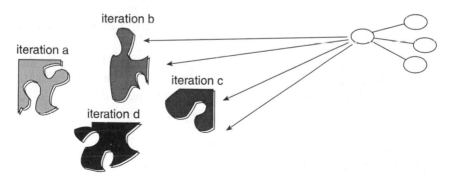

**Figure 3.23** The data model allows the different iterations of development to be built in a cohesive manner.

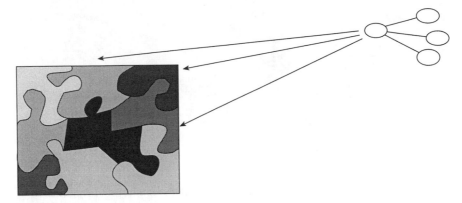

**Figure 3.24** At the end of the development effort all the iterations fit together.

**Figure 3.25** When there is no data model the iterations do not form a cohesive pattern. There is much overlap and lack of uniformity.

separate disjoint development. Figure 3.25 suggests this cacophonous result.

There is, then, an indirect, yet important, correlation between the data model and the ability to achieve long-term integration and a harmonious effort in the incremental and iterative development of a data warehouse.

## NORMALIZATION/DENORMALIZATION

The output of the data model process is a series of tables, each of which contains keys and attributes. The normal output of the data model process is *lots* of tables, each of which contains only a modicum of data.

While there is nothing wrong—per se—with lots of little tables, from a performance perspective there is a problem. Consider the work the program has to do in order to interconnect the tables dynamically, as shown in Figure 3.26.

In Figure 3.26, a program goes into execution. First, one table is accessed, then another table is accessed. In order to successfully execute, the program has to jump around many tables. Each time the program jumps from one table to the next, I/O is consumed, both in terms of accessing the data and in terms of accessing the index to find the data. If there were only one or two programs that had to pay the price of I/O, there would be no problem. But when *all* programs have to pay a stiff price for I/O, then performance in general suffers, and that is precisely what happens when many small tables, each containing a limited amount of data, are created as a physical design.

A more rational approach is to merge the tables together so that only a minimum of I/O is consumed, as seen in Figure 3.27, where many small tables have been physically merged together.

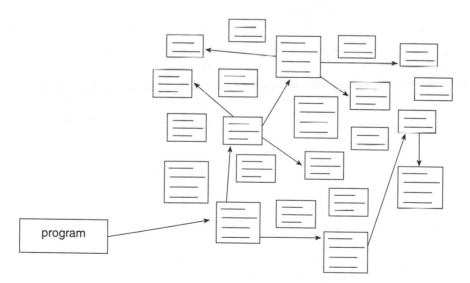

**Figure 3.26**  When there are many tables, much I/O is required for dynamic interconnectability.

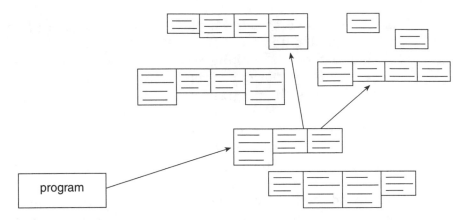

**Figure 3.27** When tables are physically merged, much less I/O is required.

In doing so, the same program operates as before, only it now needs much less I/O to accomplish the same task.

The question, then, becomes *what is a sane strategy to merge the tables together so that the maximum benefit is derived?* It is in answering this question that the physical database designer earns his or her reward.

But merging tables together is only one design technique that can save I/O. Another very useful technique is that of creating an array of data. In Figure 3.28, there is data that is normalized so that each occurrence of a sequence of data resides in a different physical location. Retrieving each occurrence, $n$, $n + 1$, $n + 2$, . . . , requires a physical I/O in order to get the data. If the data were placed in a single row in an array, then a single I/O would suffice to retrieve it, as shown at the bottom of the figure.

Of course, it does not make sense to create an array of data in every case. Only when there are a stable number of occurrences, where the data is accessed in sequence, where the data is created and/or updated in a statistically well-behaved sequence, and so forth, does it make sense to create an array of data.

Interestingly, in the data warehouse these circumstances occur regularly because of the time-based orientation of the data. Data warehouse data is always relevant to some moment in time, and units of time occur with great regularity. In the

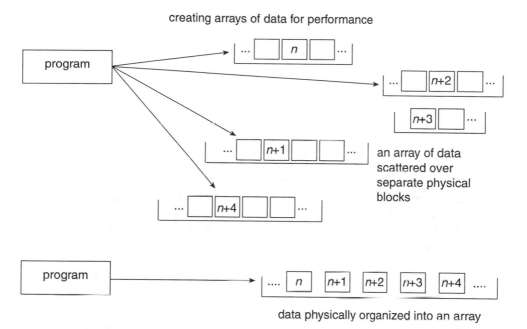

**Figure 3.28**   Under the right circumstances, creating arrays of data can save considerable resources.

data warehouse, creating an array by month, for example, is a very easy, natural thing to do.

Another important design technique that is especially relevant to the data warehouse environment is that of the deliberate introduction of redundant data. Figure 3.29 shows an example where the deliberate introduction of redundant data pays a big dividend. In the top of the figure, the field—description—is normalized and exists nonredundantly. In doing so, all processes that need to see the description of a part have to access the base parts table. The access of the data is very expensive, although the update of the data is optimal.

In the bottom of Figure 3.29, the data element—description—has been deliberately placed in the many tables where it is likely to be used. In doing so, the access of data is more efficient, and the update of data is not optimal. However, for data that is widely used (such as description), and for data that is stable (such as description), there is little reason to worry about

**selective use of redundancy**

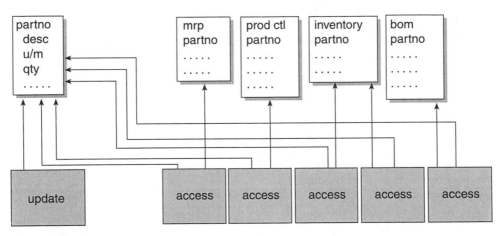

Description is nonredundant and is used frequently, but is seldom updated.

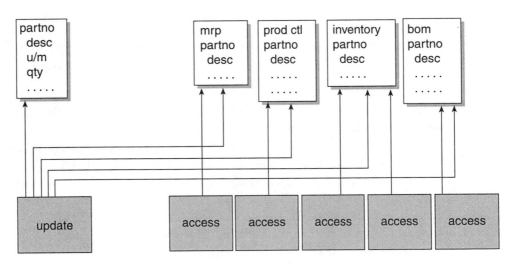

**Figure 3.29** Description is redundantly spread over the many places it is used. It must be updated in many places when it changes. But it seldom, if ever, changes.

update. In particular, in the data warehouse environment there is no concern whatsoever for update.

Another useful technique is the further separation of data when there is a wide disparity in the probability of access. Figure 3.30 shows such a case.

In Figure 3.30, concerning a bank account, the domicile of the account and the data opened for the account are normalized together with the balance of the account. Yet, the balance of the account has a very different probability of access than do the other two data elements. The balance of an account is *very* popular, while the other data are hardly ever accessed. In order to make I/O more efficient and to more compactly store the data, it makes sense to further reduce the normalized table into two separate tables, as shown.

Occasionally, the introduction of derived (i.e., calculated) data into the physical database design can reduce the amount of I/O needed. Figure 3.31 shows such a case. A program accesses payroll data regularly in order to calculate the annual pay and taxes that have been paid. If the program is run regularly and at the year's end, it makes sense to create fields of data to store the calculated data. The data has only to be calculated once. Then all future requirements can merely access the calculated field. This approach has another advantage in that once the

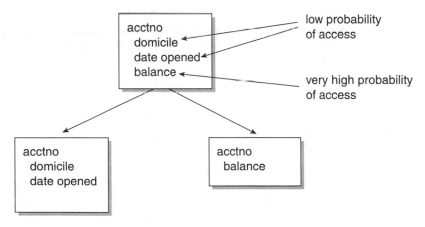

**Figure 3.30**   Further separation of data based on a wide disparity in the probability of access.

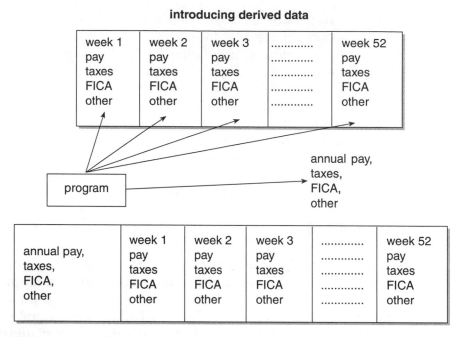

**Figure 3.31** Derived data, calculated once, then forever available.

field is calculated it will not have to be calculated again, eliminating the risk of faulty algorithms from incorrect evaluations.

One of the most innovative techniques in building a data warehouse is what can be termed a "creative" index, or a creative profile (a term coined by Les Moore). Figure 3.32 shows an example of a creative index. A creative index is created as data is passed from the operational environment to the data warehouse environment. Since each unit of data has to be handled in any case, it requires very little overhead to calculate or create an index at this point.

The creative index does a profile on items of interest to the end user, such as the largest purchases, the most inactive accounts, the latest shipments, and so on. If the requirements that might be of interest to management can be anticipated (admittedly, they cannot in every case), then at the time of passing data to the data warehouse it makes sense to build a creative index.

**creative indexes/profiles**

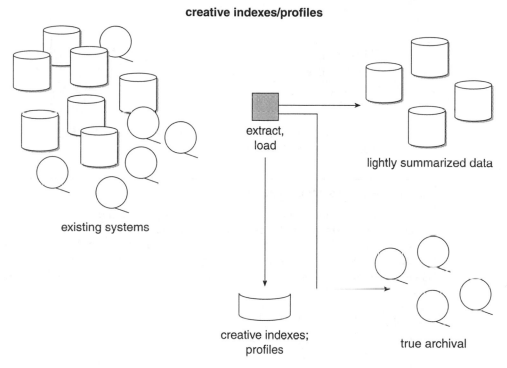

existing systems

extract,
load

lightly summarized data

creative indexes;
profiles

true archival

**Figure 3.32**   Examples of creative indexes:
- The top ten customers in volume are___
- The average transaction value for this extract was $*nnn.nn*.
- The largest transaction was $*nnn.nn*.
- The number of customers who showed activity without purchasing was *nn*.

A final design technique that the data warehouse designer needs to be aware of is the management of referential integrity in the data warehouse environment. Figure 3.33 shows that referential integrity appears as "artifacts" of relationships in the data warehouse environment.

In the operational environment, referential integrity appears as a dynamic link among tables of data. But the volume of data in a data warehouse, the fact that the data warehouse is not updated, and the fact that the data warehouse represents data over time and relationships do not stay static over time, mandate that a different approach be taken to referential integrity in the data warehouse and referential integrity

In operational systems, the relationships between databases are handled by referential integrity.

But, in the data warehouse environment:

- There is much more data than in the operational environment.
- Once in the warehouse, the data doesn't change.
- There is a need to represent more than one business rule over time.
- Data purges in the warehouse are not tightly coordinated.

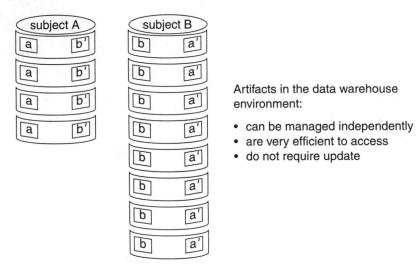

Artifacts in the data warehouse environment:

- can be managed independently
- are very efficient to access
- do not require update

**Figure 3.33** Referential integrity in the data warehouse environment.

data warehouse environment. In a word, relationships of data are represented by an artifact in the data warehouse environment. This means that some data will be duplicated, and some data will be deleted when other data is still in the warehouse. In any case, trying to replicate referential integrity in the data warehouse environment is a patently incorrect approach.

## SNAPSHOTS IN THE DATA WAREHOUSE

Data warehouses are built for a wide variety of applications and users, such as customer systems, marketing systems, sales systems, and quality control systems. Despite the very diverse applications and types of data warehouse, there is a common thread that runs through all of them. Internally, each of the data warehouses centers around a structure of data called a "snapshot."

Figure 3.34 shows what the basic components of a data warehouse snapshot look like.

Snapshots are created as a result of some event occurring. There are several kinds of events that can trigger a snapshot. One kind of event that causes the creation of a snapshot is the recording of information about a discrete activity, such as the writing of a check, the placing of a phone call, the receipt of a shipment, the completion of an order, or the purchase of a policy. In the case of a discrete activity, some business occurrence has come to pass and the business needs to make note of it. In general, discrete activities occur randomly.

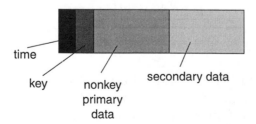

**Figure 3.34**   A data warehouse record of data is a snapshot taken one moment in time and includes a variety of types of data.

The other type of common event that triggers a snapshot is the regular passage of time. At a particular moment in time, a snapshot is triggered. Typical regular passages of time include the end of the day, the end of the week, and the end of the month. Of course, the regular passage of time is predictable and not at all random.

The snapshot that is triggered by an event has four basic components:

- a key
- a unit of time
- primary data that relates only to the key, and
- secondary data that is captured as part of the snapshot process that has no direct relationship to the primary data or key

Of these components of a data warehouse, only secondary data is optional.

The key can be unique or nonunique. The key can be a single element of data. But more often in a data warehouse, the key is a composite made up of many elements of data that serve to identify the primary data. The key identifies the record and the primary data.

The unit of time is created in terms of elements of time, such as year, month, day, hour, and quarter. The unit of time usually (but not always) refers to the moment when the event being described by the snapshot has occurred. Occasionally the unit of time refers to the moment when the capture of data takes place. (In some cases there is a distinction made between when an event occurs and when the information about the event is captured. In other cases there is no distinction made.) In the case of events triggered by the regular passage of time, the element of time may be implied rather than directly attached to the snapshot.

The primary data is the nonkey data that relates directly to the key of the record. As an example, suppose the key identifies the sale of a product. The element of time describes when the sale was finalized. The primary data describes what product was sold at what price, conditions of the sale, location of the sale, and who the representative parties of the sale were.

The secondary data—if it exists—identifies other extraneous information captured at the moment in time the snapshot record was created. An example of secondary data that relates to a sale is incidental information about the product being sold (such as how much is in stock at the moment of sale). Other secondary information about a sale might be the prevailing interest rate for a bank's preferred customers at the moment of sale. There can be any number of types of incidental information that can be added to a data warehouse record, if it appears at a later time that the incidental information can be used for DSS processing. Note that the incidental information that is added to the snapshot may or may not be a foreign key.

Once the secondary information is added to the snapshot—if it is added at all—a relationship between the primary and secondary information can be inferred, as shown in Figure 3.35. The snapshot implies that there is a relationship between secondary and primary data. Nothing other than the existence of the relationship is implied. And the relationship is implied only as of the instant of the snapshot. Nevertheless, by the juxtaposition of secondary and primary data in a snapshot record, at the instant the snapshot was taken, there is an inferred relationship of data. Sometimes this inferred relationship is called "an artifact of a relationship." The snapshot record that has been described is the most general and most widely found case of a record in a data warehouse.

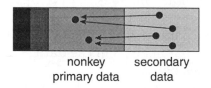

nonkey      secondary
primary data      data

**Figure 3.35** The artifacts of a relationship are captured as a result of the implied relationship that can be made by secondary data residing in the same snapshot as primary data.

## METADATA

An important aspect of the data warehouse environment is that of metadata. Metadata is data about data. Metadata has been a part of the information processing milieu for as long as there have been programs and data. But it is in the world of data warehouses that metadata takes on a new level of importance. It is with metadata that the most effective use of the data warehouse is made. Metadata allows the end user/DSS analyst to navigate through the possibilities.

Metadata sits above the warehouse and keeps track of what is where in the warehouse. Typically, the things the metadata store tracks are:

■ the structure of data as known to the programmer
■ the structure of data as known to the DSS analyst
■ the source data feeding the data warehouse
■ the transformation of data as it passes into the data warehouse
■ the data model
■ the relationship between the data model and the data warehouse
■ the history of extracts

## MANAGING REFERENCE TABLES IN A DATA WAREHOUSE

When most people think of data warehousing, thoughts turn to the normal large databases that are constantly being used by organizations to run the day-to-day business of a company, such as customer files, sales files, and so forth. Indeed, these common files form the backbone of the data warehousing effort. However, there is another type of data that belongs in the data warehouse that is often ignored: reference data.

Reference tables are often taken for granted, and that creates a special problem. In many cases reference tables are not included as part of the data warehouse. For example, suppose a company has some reference tables in 1995 and starts to create its data warehouse in 1995. Time passes and much data is loaded into the data warehouse. In the meantime the reference table is used operationally and occasionally changes. In 1999 there arises a need to go from the data warehouse to the reference table. A reference is made from 1995 data to the reference table. But the reference table has not been kept historically accurate and the reference from 1995 data warehouse data to reference entries accurate as of 1999 produces very inaccurate results. For this reason, the data warehouse needs to include reference data as well as normal data.

Reference data is peculiarly applicable to the data warehouse environment because it is through the use of reference data that the volume of data in a data warehouse can be significantly reduced. There are many design techniques for the management of reference data in the data warehouse environment. Two techniques will be discussed here, which are at opposite ends of the spectrum. (There are *many* alternatives and variations on the design options shown.)

Figure 3.36 shows the first design option, which suggests that every six months a snapshot of an entire reference table be taken. In the example a snapshot is taken on January 1, another taken on July 1, and so forth. This approach is a very good one because it is very simple. There is nothing complicated about taking a snapshot of a small table every six months. But this approach is logically incomplete. For example, suppose some activity had occurred to the reference table on March 15. Sup-

```
Jan 1                          July 1                         Jan 1
  AAA - Amber Auto               AAA - Amber Auto               AAA - Alaska Alt
  AAT - Allison's                AAR - Ark Electric             AAG - German Air
  AAZ - AutoZone                 BAE - Brit Eng                 AAR - Ark Electric
  BAE - Brit Eng                 BAG - Bill's Garage            BAE - Brit Eng
  . . . . . . . . . . . . . .    . . . . . . . . . . . . . .    . . . . . . . . . . . . . .
```

**Figure 3.36** A snapshot is taken of a reference table in its entirety every six months—one approach to the management of reference tables in the data warehouse environment.

pose a new entry—ddw—had been added, then on May 10 the entry for ddw had been deleted. Taking a snapshot every six months would not logically capture the activity that had transpired from March 15 to May 10. The first approach to the management of reference tables, then, is one that is simple but logically incomplete.

A second approach to the management of reference tables in the data warehouse environment is shown in Figure 3.37, which shows that at some starting point in time a snapshot is made of a reference table. Throughout the year, all the activities against the reference table are collected. In order to determine the status of a given entry to the reference table at a moment in time, the activity is reconstituted against the reference table. In such a manner, logical completeness of the table can be reconstructed for any moment in time. However, such a reconstruction is a nontrivial matter. Such an undertaking may represent a very large and complex task. This second approach is logically complete but very complex to execute.

The two approaches that have been outlined here are opposite in intent. The first approach is simple but logically incomplete. The second approach is very complex but logically complete. There are *many* design alternatives that lie between the two extremes that we have discussed. However they are designed and implemented, reference tables need to be managed as a regular part of the data warehouse environment.

```
Jan 1                            Jan 1  - add TWQ -     Taiwan Dairy
  AAA - Amber Auto               Jan 16 - delete AAT
  AAT - Allison's                Feb 3  - add AAG -     German Power
  AAZ - AutoZone                 Feb 27 - change GYY - German Govt
  BAE - Brit Eng                 ....................................
  ................               ....................................
  ................
```

A complete snapshot is taken on the first of the year.

Changes to the reference table are collected throughout the year and are able to be used to reconstruct the table at any moment in time.

**Figure 3.37** Another approach to the management of reference data.

## CYCLICITY OF DATA

One of the intriguing issues of data warehouse design is the cyclicity of data. Cyclicity of data refers to the length of time a change of data in the operational environment takes to be reflected in the data warehouse. Consider the data shown in Figure 3.38.

The current information is shown for Judy Jones. The data warehouse contains the historical information about Judy. Now suppose it is discovered that Judy has changed addresses. Figure 3.39 shows that as soon as that change is discovered it is reflected into the operational environment as quickly as possible.

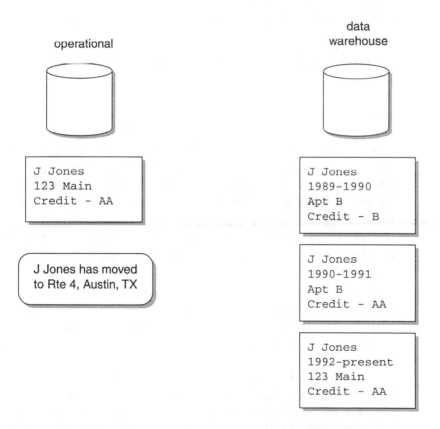

**Figure 3.38**  What happens when the corporation finds out that J Jones has moved?

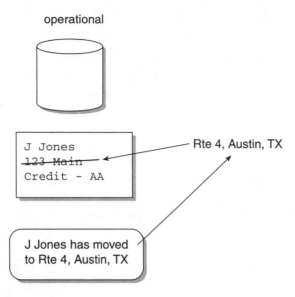

operational

J Jones
~~123 Main~~
Credit - AA

Rte 4, Austin, TX

J Jones has moved
to Rte 4, Austin, TX

**Figure 3.39**   The first step is to change the operational address of J Jones.

Once the data is reflected in the operational environment, the changes need to be moved to the data warehouse. Figure 3.40 shows that the data warehouse has a correction made to the ending date of the most current record and has a new record inserted, reflecting the change in Judy Jones's record.

The issue is, how soon should this adjustment to the data warehouse data be made? As a rule, at least 24 hours should pass from the time the change is known to the operational environment until the change is reflected into the data warehouse (Figure 3.41). There should be no rush to try to move the change into the information warehouse as quickly as possible. There are several reasons for the need to put a "wrinkle of time" in the data.

The first reason is that the tighter the operational environment is coupled to the data warehouse, the more expensive and complex the technology is. A 24-hour wrinkle of time can easily be accomplished with conventional technology.

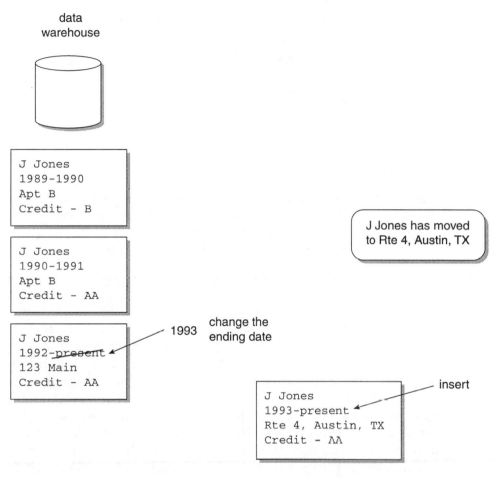

**Figure 3.40** The activities that occur in the data warehouse as a result of the change of address.

But a more powerful reason is that the wrinkle of time imposes a certain discipline on the environments. With a 24-hour wrinkle there is no temptation to do operational processing in the data warehouse and data warehouse processing in the operational environment. Another benefit of the wrinkle of time is opportunity for data to settle before it is moved to the data warehouse.

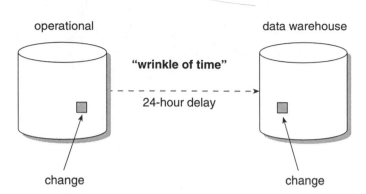

operational                                          data warehouse

**"wrinkle of time"**

24-hour delay

change                                                      change

**Figure 3.41** There needs to be at least a 24-hour lag—a "wrinkle of time"—between the time a change is known to the operational environment and the time when the change is reflected into the data warehouse.

## COMPLEXITY OF TRANSFORMATION AND INTEGRATION

At first glance, when data is moved from the legacy environment to the data warehouse environment, it appears there is nothing more going on than simple extraction of data from one place to the next. Because of the deceptive simplicity, many organizations start to build their data warehouses manually. The programmer looks at the movement of data from the old operational environment to the new data warehouse environment and declares "I can do that!" With pencil and coding pad in hand the programmer anxiously jumps into the creation of code within the first three minutes of the design and development of the data warehouse.

However, first impressions can be very deceiving. What at first appears to be nothing more than the movement of data from one place to another quickly turns into a large and complex task—far larger and more complex than the programmer bargained for.

Precisely what kind of functionality is required as data passes from the operational, legacy environment to the data warehouse environment? The following represents *some* of the functionality that is needed:

■ The extraction of data from the operational environment to the data warehouse environment requires a change in technology. This normally includes reading the operational DBMS technology, such as IMS, and writing the data out in newer, data warehouse DBMS technology, such as Informix. There is need for a technology shift as the data is being moved.

■ *The selection of data from the operational environment may be very complex.* In order to qualify a record for extraction processing, several coordinated lookups to other records in a variety of other files may have to be accomplished, requiring keyed reads, connecting logic, and so on.

■ *Operational input keys usually need to be restructured before they are written out.* Very seldom does an input key remain unaltered as it is read in the operational environment and written out to the data warehouse environment. In simple cases an element of time is added to the output key structure. In complex cases the entire input key must be rehashed or otherwise restructured.

■ *Data is reformatted.* As a simple example, input data about date is read as YY/MM/DD and is written to the output file as DD/MM/YY. (Reformatting of operational data before it is ready to go into a data warehouse often becomes much more complex than this simple example.)

■ *Data is cleansed.* In some cases, a simple algorithm is applied to input data in order to make it correct. In complex cases artificial-intelligence subroutines are invoked in order to scrub input data into an acceptable output form.

■ *Multiple input sources of data exist.* Under one set of conditions the source of a data warehouse data element is one file and under another set of conditions the source of data for the data warehouse is another file. Logic must be spelled out in order to have the appropriate source of data contribute its data under the right set of conditions.

■ *When there are multiple input files, key resolution must be done before the files can be merged together.* This means that if different key structures are used in the different input files then the merging program must have the logic embedded that allows resolution.

■ *Where there are multiple input files, the sequence of the files may not be the same or even compatible.* In this case the input files will need to be resequenced. This is not a problem unless there are many records to be resequenced, which unfortunately is almost always the case.

■ *Multiple outputs may result.* Data may be produced at different levels of summarization by the same data warehouse creation program.

■ *Default values need to be supplied.* Under some conditions an output value in the data warehouse will have no source of data. In this case, the default value that will be used must be specified.

■ *The efficiency of selection of input data for extraction often becomes a real issue.* Consider the case where at the moment of refreshment there is no way to tell operational data that needs to be extracted from operational data that does not need to be extracted. When this occurs, the entire operational file needs to be read. Reading the entire file is especially inefficient because only a fraction of the records are actually needed from the file. This type of processing causes the online environment to be active, which further squeezes other processing in the online environment.

■ *Summarization of data often needs to be done.* Multiple operational input records are combined into a single "profile" data warehouse record. In order to do summarization, the detailed input records to be summarized must be properly sequenced. In the case where different record types contribute to the single summarized data warehouse record, the arrival of the different input record types must be coordinated so that a single record is produced.

■ *Renaming of data elements as they are moved from the operational environment to the data warehouse needs to be tracked.* As a data element moves, it usually changes its name. Documentation of that change needs to be made.

■ *The input records that must be read have "exotic" or nonstandard formats.* There are a whole host of input types that must be read:
  ■ fixed-length records
  ■ variable-length records
  ■ occurs depending on
  ■ occurs clause

■ *Conversion must be made.* But the logic of conversion must be specified and the mechanics of conversion (what the "before" and "after" look like) can be quite complex. In some cases conversion logic becomes very twisted.

■ *Perhaps the worst of all: Data relationships that have been built into old legacy program logic must be understood and unraveled before those files can be used as input.* These relationships are often Byzantine, arcane, and undocumented.

■ *Data format conversion must be done.* EBCDIC to ASCII (or vice versa) must be spelled out.

■ *Massive volumes of input must be accounted for.* Where there is only a small amount of data being entered as input, many design options can be accommodated. But where there are *many* records being input, special design options (such as parallel loads and parallel reads) may have to be employed.

■ *The design of the data warehouse must conform to a corporate data model.* As such there is order and discipline to the design and structuring of the data warehouse. The input to the data warehouse conforms to design specifications of an application that was written a long time ago. The business conditions behind the application have probably changed ten times since the application was originally written. Much undocumented maintenance will have been done to the application code. In addition, the application probably will have had no integration requirements to fit with other applications. All of these mismatches must be accounted for in the design and building of the data warehouse.

■ *The data warehouse reflects historical need for information while the operational environment focuses on immediate, current need for information.*

■ *The data warehouse addresses the informational needs of the corporation while the operational environment addresses the up-to-the-second clerical needs of the corporation.*

■ *Transmission of the newly created output file that will go into the data warehouse must be accounted for.* In some cases this is very easy to do; in other cases it is not simple at all, especially when operating systems are crossed.

And there is more; this list is merely the *start* of the complexities facing the programmer when setting off to load the data warehouse.

## TRIGGERING THE DATA WAREHOUSE RECORD

The basic business interaction that causes the data warehouse to become populated with data is one that can be called an EVENT→SNAPSHOT interaction. In an EVENT→SNAPSHOT interaction, some event triggers a snapshot of data (usually in the operational environment), which in turn is moved to the data warehouse environment. Figure 3.42 symbolically depicts an EVENT→SNAPSHOT interaction.

### Events

The business event that triggers a snapshot might be the occurrence of some notable activity, such as the making of a sale, the stocking of an item, the placing of a phone call, or the delivery of a shipment. This type of business event is called an *activity-generated event*. The other type of business event that may trigger a snapshot in the data warehouse is the marking of the regular passage of time, such as the ending of the day, the ending of the week, or the ending of the month. This type of business event is called a *time-generated event*.

Events that are caused by business activities are random in nature. Events that are triggered by the passage of time are not random in nature. The time-related snapshots are created quite regularly and predictably.

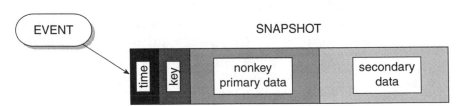

**Figure 3.42** Every snapshot in the data warehouse is triggered by some event.

## Components of the Snapshot

The snapshot that is taken and placed in the data warehouse normally contains several components. One component is the unit of time that marks the occurrence of the event. Usually (not necessarily always), the unit of time marks the moment of the taking of the snapshot. The next component of the snapshot is the key that identifies the snapshot. The third normal component of a data warehouse snapshot is the primary, nonkey data that relates to the key. And an optional component of a snapshot is secondary data that has been incidentally captured as of the moment of the taking of the snapshot and placed in the snapshot. Sometimes this secondary data is called an "artifact" of the relationship.

In the simplest case in a data warehouse, each operational activity that is of importance to the corporation will trigger a snapshot. In this case there is a one-to-one correspondence between the business activities that have occurred and the number of snapshots that are placed in the data warehouse. When there is a one-to-one correspondence between the activities in the operational environment and the snapshots in the data warehouse, the data warehouse tracks the history of all the activity relating to a subject area.

## Some Examples

An example of a simple snapshot being taken every time there is an operational, business activity might be found in a customer file. Every time a customer moves, every time a customer changes phone numbers, every time a customer changes jobs, the data warehouse is alerted and a continuous record of the history of the customer is made. One record tracks the customer from 1989 to 1991. The next record tracks the customer from 1991 to 1993. The next record tracks the customer from 1993 to the present. Each activity of the customer results in a new snapshot being placed in the data warehouse.

As another example of every business activity resulting a snapshot record being created in the data warehouse, consider the premium payments on an insurance policy. Suppose premiums are paid semiannually. Every six months a snapshot record is created in the data warehouse describing the payment of the premium—when it was paid, how much, and so on.

Where there is little volume of data, where the data is stable (i.e., the data infrequently changes), and where there is a need for meticulous historical detail, the data warehouse can be used to track each occurrence of a business event by storing the details of every activity that has ever occurred.

## PROFILE RECORDS

But there are many cases where data in the data warehouse does not meet these criteria. In some cases there will be massive volumes of data. In other cases the content of data changes very frequently. And in still other cases, there is no business need for meticulous historical detail of data. When one or more of these conditions prevails, a different kind of data warehouse record can be created. The record that can be created can be called an *aggregate* or a *profile* record. A profile record is one that groups together many different detailed occurrences of operational data into a single record. The single profile record that is created represents the many operational records in aggregation.

Profile records represent snapshots of data just like individual activity records. The difference between the two is that individual activity records in the data warehouse represent a single event while profile records in the data warehouse represent multiple events.

Like individual activity records, profile records are triggered by some event that has occurred—either a business activity or the marking of the regular passage of time. Figure 3.43 shows how an event causes the creation of a profile record.

A profile record is created from the grouping together of many detailed records. As an example, a phone company may at the end of the month take all of a customer's phone activities for the month and wrap those activities into a single customer record in the data warehouse. In doing so, a single representative record can be created for the customer that reflects all his or her monthly activity. Or a bank may take all the monthly activities of a customer and create an aggregate data warehouse

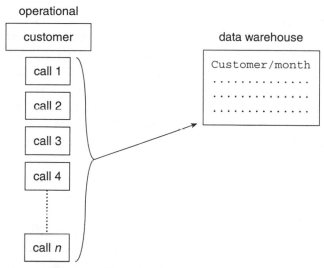

The monthly call records are aggregated in order to provide a single composite record.

**Figure 3.43**  The creation of a profile record from a series of detailed records.

record that represents all of his or her banking activities for the month.

The aggregation of operational data into a single data warehouse record may take many forms, for example:

■ Values taken from operational data can be summarized.
■ Units of operational data can be tallied, where the total number of units are captured.
■ Units of data can be processed to find the highest, lowest, average, and so forth.
■ First and last occurrences of data can be trapped.
■ Data of certain types, falling within the boundaries of several parameters, can be measured.
■ Data that is effective as of some moment in time can be trapped.
■ The oldest and the youngest data can be trapped.

There are as many ways to do representative aggregation of operational data as there are algorithms and imagination.

Another very appealing side benefit to the creation of profile records is that of organizing the data in a compact and convenient form for the end user to access and analyze. When this is done properly, the end user is very comfortable with the bringing together of many records into a single record because he or she only has to look in a single place to find out what is needed. The data architect saves the end user from having to do much laborious and tedious processing by prepackaging the data into an aggregate record in the data warehouse.

## MANAGING VOLUME

In many cases the volume of data that needs to be managed in the data warehouse is a real issue. Creating profile records is a very effective technique for the management of the volume of data. The reduction of the volume of data that is possible in moving detailed records in the operational environment into a profile record in the data warehouse is remarkable. It is possible (indeed, normal) to achieve a 2-to-3 order of magnitude reduction of data by the creation of profile records in a data warehouse. Because of this possibility, the technique of creating profile records is a very powerful one that should be in the portfolio of every data architect. Indeed, more so than any other design or data management technique, when it comes to managing the volume of data in a data warehouse, the creation of aggregate/profile records is the first and most powerful technique that the data warehouse architect should consider.

There is, however, a downside to the technique of profiling records in the data warehouse. Whenever the use of the profile technique is contemplated, it must be recognized that a certain capability or functionality of the data warehouse is lost. Of necessity, detail is lost whenever aggregation is done. But losing detail is not necessarily a bad thing. The designer of the profile record needs to insure that the detail that is lost is not important to the DSS analyst that will ultimately be using the data warehouse. The first line of defense (and easily the most effective one) the data architect has to ensure that the detail that is lost is not terribly important is to build the profile records iteratively. By doing so, the data architect has the maneuverability to make changes gracefully. The first iteration of the design of the contents of the profile record suggests the second iteration of design, and so forth. As long as the iterations of data warehouse development are small and fast, there is little danger that the end user will find many important requirements left out of the profile record. The danger comes when profile records are created and the first iteration of development is large. In this case the data architect probably will paint himself or herself into a nasty corner because important detail will have been omitted because the data warehouse is so large that its contents *cannot* be changed gracefully.

A second approach (that can be used in conjunction with the iterative approach) to ensure that important detail is not permanently lost in the creation of profile records is to create an alternative level of historical detail along with the profile record, as shown in Figure 3.44.

The alternative detail is not designed to be used frequently. The alternative detail is stored on slow, inexpensive, sequential storage and is difficult to get to and awkward to work with in any case. But the detail is there should it be needed. When management states that they *must have* a certain detail, however

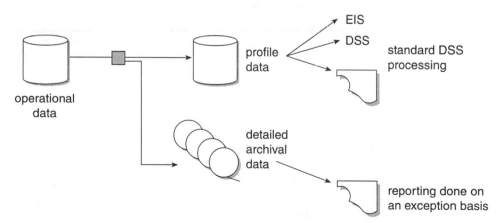

**Figure 3.44**  An alternative to the classical data warehouse architecture—all the detail that is needed is available while good performance for most DSS processing is the norm.

arcane, it can always be retrieved, albeit at a cost of time and money.

## CREATING MULTIPLE PROFILE RECORDS

Multiple profile records can be created from the same detail. In the case of a phone company, individual call records can be used for the creation of a customer profile record, for a district traffic profile record, for a line analysis profile record, and so forth.

The profile records can be used to go into the data warehouse or a datamart that is fed by the data warehouse. When the profile records go into a data warehouse, they are for general-purpose usage. When the profile records go into the datamart, they are customized for the department that uses the datamart.

The aggregation of the operational records into a profile record is almost always done on the operational server. This is because the operational server is large enough to be able to manage large volumes of data and because that is where the data resides in any case. Usually the act of creating the profile record is one of sorting data and merging it together. Once the process of creating the snapshot becomes complicated and drawn out, it is questionable whether the snapshot should be taken at all.

The metadata records that are written for profile records are very similar to the metadata records written for single activity snapshots with the exception that the process of aggregating the records becomes an important piece of metadata. (Technically speaking, the record of the process of aggregation is "meta-process" information, not "metadata" information.)

## GOING FROM THE DATA WAREHOUSE TO THE OPERATIONAL ENVIRONMENT

The operational environment and the data warehouse environment are about as different as any two environments can be. They are different in terms of content, technology, usage, communities served, and a hundred other ways. The interface between the two environments is well documented. Data under-

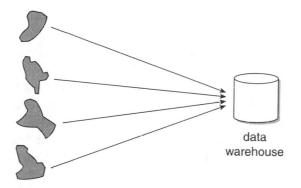

legacy applications

**Figure 3.45**   The normal flow of data in the legacy application/data warehouse architected environment.

goes a fundamental transformation as it passes from the operational environment to the data warehouse environment. The normal flow of data from the operational environment to the data warehouse environment is shown in Figure 3.45.

The question occasionally arises, *is it possible for data to pass from the data warehouse environment to the operational environment?* In other words, *is it possible for data to pass in a reverse direction from that normally experienced?* From the standpoint of technology, the answer certainly is *yes, such a passage of data is technologically possible.* However, it is not normal for the data to flow "backward."

## NORMAL PROCESSING

Under normal circumstances data does not flow from the data warehouse to the operational environment. For a variety of reasons—the sequence in which business is conducted, the high performance needs of operational processing, the aging of data, the strong application orientation of operational processing, and so forth—the flow of data from the operational environment to the data warehouse environment is natural and normal. But there are a few isolated circumstances where data does indeed flow backward.

## DIRECT ACCESS OF DATA WAREHOUSE DATA

Figure 3.46 illustrates the dynamics of the simplest of those circumstances—the direct access of data from the data warehouse by the operational environment. A request has been made within the operational environment for data that resides in the data warehouse. The request is transferred to the data warehouse environment, and the data is located and transferred to the operational environment. Apparently, from the standpoint of dynamics, the transfer could not be easier.

There are a number of serious and uncompromising limitations to the scenario of the direct access of data in the data warehouse. Some of the limitations are as follows:

- The request must be a casual one in terms of response time. It may take as long as 24 hours for it to be satisfied. This means that the operational processing that requires the data warehouse data is decidedly not of an online nature.
- The request for data needs to be for a minimal amount of data. The data being transferred is measured in terms of bytes, not megabytes or gigabytes.
- The technology managing the data warehouse needs to be compatible with the technology managing the operational environment in terms of capacity, protocol, and so on.
- The formatting of data after it is retrieved from the data warehouse in preparation for transport to the operational environment must be nonexistent (or minimal).

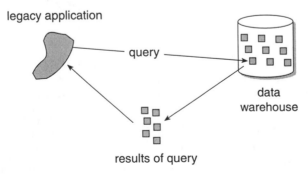

**Figure 3.46** A direct query against the data warehouse from the legacy applications environment.

These conditions preclude most data ever being directly transferred from the data warehouse to the operational environment. It is easy to see why there is a minimal amount of backward flow of data in the case of direct access of data.

## INDIRECT ACCESS OF DATA WAREHOUSE DATA

Because of the severe and uncompromising conditions of transfer, *direct* access of data warehouse data by the operational environment is a rare occurrence. However, *indirect* access of data warehouse data is another matter entirely. Indeed, one of the most effective uses of the data warehouse is the indirect access of data warehouse data by the operational environment. Some examples of indirect access of data warehouse data will suffice to illustrate this point.

### An Airline Commission Calculation System

One effective indirect use of data warehouse data occurs in the airline environment. In order for the example to make sense there needs to be some knowledge of the workings of the airline reservation and ticketing environment.

Consider the airline ticketing transaction depicted in Figure 3.47. A travel agent has contacted the airline reservation clerk

**Figure 3.47**   A typical business interchange.

on behalf of a customer. The customer has requested a ticket for a flight and the travel agent wants to know:

- Is there a seat available?
- What is the cost of the seat?
- What is the commission paid to the travel agent?

If the airline pays too much of a commission, they will get the agent's business but they will have lost money. If the airline pays too little commission, the travel agent will "shop" the ticket and the airline will lose it to an airline that pays a larger commission. It is in the airline's best interest to calculate the commission it pays very carefully, because the calculation has a direct effect on its bottom line.

The interchange between the travel agent and the airline clerk must occur in a fairly short amount of time—within two to three minutes. In this two-to-three-minute window the airline clerk must enter and complete several transactions, such as:

- Are there any seats available?
- Is seating preference available?
- What connecting flights are involved?
- Can the connections be made?
- What is the cost of the ticket?
- What is the commission?

If the response time of the airline clerk (who is running several transactions while carrying on a conversation with the travel agent) starts to be excessive, the airline will find that it is losing business merely because of the poor response time. It is in the best interest of the airline to ensure brisk response time throughout the dialogue with the travel agent.

The calculation of the optimal commission becomes a critical component of the interchange. The optimal commission is best calculated by looking at a combination of two factors—current bookings and the load history of the flight. The current bookings tell how heavily the flight is booked and the load history yields a perspective of how the flight has been booked in the past. Between current bookings and historical bookings an optimal

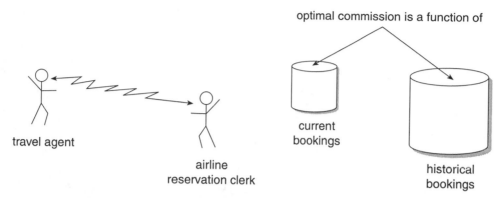

**Figure 3.48**  Optimal commission is calculated by comparing current bookings versus historical bookings.

commission can be calculated. Figure 3.48 shows the elements of the calculation.

It is a temptation to try to do the bookings and flight history calculations online. However, the amount of data that needs to be manipulated is such that response time suffers if the commission is calculated online. Instead the calculation of commission and analysis of flight history is done offline, where there are ample machine resources. Figure 3.49 shows the dynamics of offline commission calculation.

The offline calculation and analysis is done periodically and a small, easy-to-access flight status table is created. When the airline clerk has to interact with the travel agent, it is an easy matter to look at current bookings and the flight status table. The result is a very fast and smooth interaction with the travel agent and the ability to use the data stored in the data warehouse.

## A Retail Personalization System

Another example of the indirect usage of data warehouse data in the operational environment occurs in the retail personalization system. In the retail personalization system, a customer reads a catalog or other flyer issued by the retailer. The customer is inspired to make a purchase or to at least inquire about

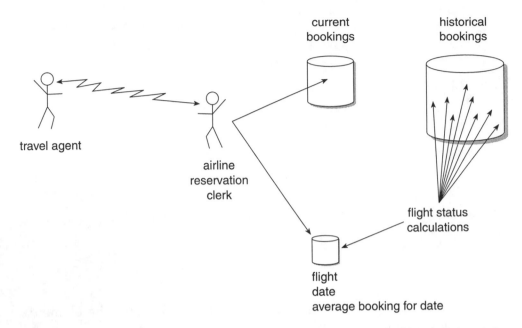

**Figure 3.49**  The flight status file is created periodically by reading the historical data. It is then a very quick matter for the airline agent to get current bookings and to compare those bookings against the historical average.

the catalog. A phone call to the retailer ensues. Figure 3.50 shows the interaction between the retailer and the customer.

The interchange is about 5 to 8 minutes in length. During this time the retail sales representative has a fair amount of processing to do—identify the customer, take down the specifics of the order, and so forth. The response time is critical, otherwise the customer will lose interest.

While the customer is placing the order or making an inquiry, the retail sales representative finds out some other information relevant to the interchange, such as:

■ the last time the customer made a purchase
■ the last type of purchase made
■ the market segment(s) in which the customer belongs

While engaging the customer in conversation, the sales representative says such things as:

**Figure 3.50** The consumer sees a catalog in the mail and wants more information.

"I see it's been since February that we last heard from you."

"How was that blue sweater you purchased?"

"Did the problems you had with the pants get resolved?"

In short, the retail sales representative is able to personalize the conversation. The personalization has the effect of making the customer more amenable to purchases.

In addition, the retail sales clerk has market segment information available, such as:

- male/female
- professional/other
- city/country
- children
  - ages
  - sex
- sports
  - fishing
  - hunting
  - beach, etc.

Because the phone call can be personalized and the direct marketing segment for a customer is available when the customer calls in, the retail sales representative is able to ask pointed questions such as:

"Did you know we have an unannounced sale on swimsuits?"

"We just got in some Italian sunglasses that I think you might like."

"The forecasters predict a cold winter for duck hunters. We have a special on waders right now."

The customer has already taken the time to make a phone call. The personalization of the phone call and the knowledge of what products the customer is interested in give the retailer a very good chance at raising revenue with no further outlay of cash or advertising. The personalization of the phone call is achieved by the indirect use of the data warehouse. Figure 3.51 shows the dynamics of how personalization is achieved.

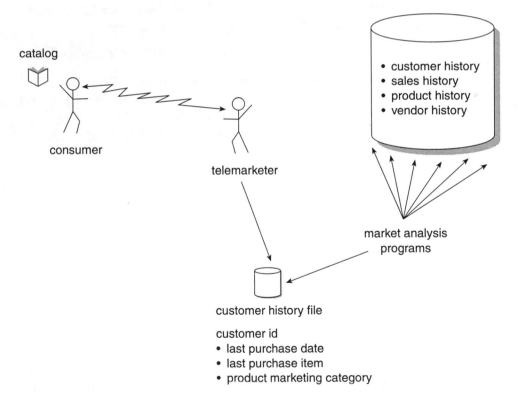

**Figure 3.51** The customer history is at the disposal of the telemarketer at a moments notice.

In the background (i.e., in the data warehouse environment), there is an analysis program that is constantly reading and analyzing customer records. The analysis program scans and analyzes historical customer data in a very sophisticated manner. Periodically, the analysis program spins off a file to the operational environment that contains such information as:

- last purchase date
- last purchase type
- market analysis/segmenting

When the customer rings in, the online prepared file is waiting for use by the retail sales representative.

### Credit Scoring

Another example of the indirect usage of a data warehouse in the operational environment is that of credit scoring in the banking/finance environment. Credit scoring is the activity of qualifying (or not qualifying) a person for a loan. Figure 3.52 shows a case of credit scoring in an interactive mode.

In Figure 3.52 a customer walks up to the teller's window and asks for a loan. The teller takes in some basic information about the customer and decides whether the loan should be approved or not. The interchange occurs in a very short amount of time—five to ten minutes.

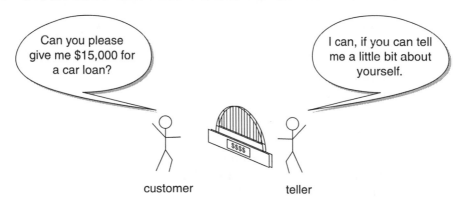

**Figure 3.52**   Online loan processing.

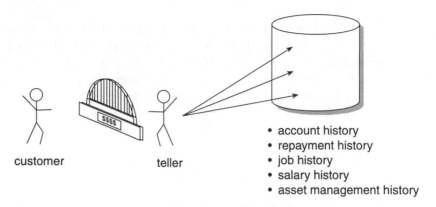

- account history
- repayment history
- job history
- salary history
- asset management history

**Figure 3.53** Checking the customer's history before approving the loan.

In order to determine whether the loan should be approved, a certain amount of processing needs to be done, as shown in Figure 3.53.

The loan request is first put through a simple screening process. If the loan is for a small enough amount and if the person has a stable financial background, then it may be approved with no further processing. However, if the loan is for a fair amount and/or the customer does not have a stable, predictable background, then a further check is required.

The background check relies on the data warehouse. In truth the check is an eclectic one, in which many aspects of the customer are investigated, such as:

- past payback history
- home/property ownership
- financial management
- net worth
- gross income
- gross expenses
- other intangibles

This extensive background check requires quite a bit of diverse historical data. Completing this part of the loan qualification process requires more than a few minutes.

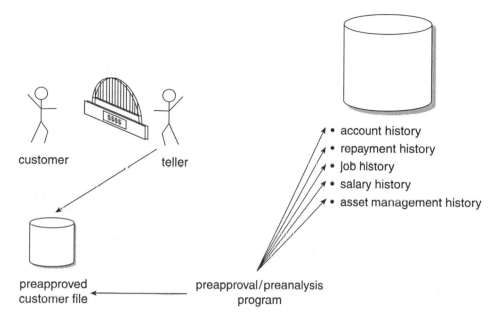

**Figure 3.54**  The preapproved customer credit file is accessible by the bank teller in an instant.

In order to satisfy the most customers in the shortest amount of time, an analysis program is written. Figure 3.54 shows how the analysis program fits in with the other components of credit scoring. The analysis program is run periodically, and produces a prequalified file for use in the operational environment. In addition to other data, the prequalified file includes:

■ customer identification
■ approved credit limit
■ special approval limit

Now when the customer wishes to apply for and get a loan, in a high-performance, online mode the teller qualifies (or does not qualify) the loan request from the customer. Only if the customer asks for a loan for an amount greater than the preapproved limit does there need to be an interaction by a loan officer.

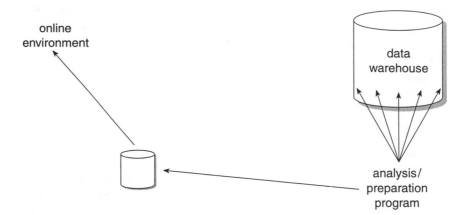

**Figure 3.55** The way that data warehouse data is made available to the online operational environment—indirectly.

## INDIRECT USAGE OF DATA WAREHOUSE DATA

There is, then, an emerging pattern to the indirect usage of data warehouse data. That pattern is shown in Figure 3.55.

The data warehouse is analyzed periodically by a program that examines relevant characteristics and criteria. The analysis then creates a small file in the online environment that contains succinct information about the business of the enterprise. The small online file is used quickly and efficiently, fitting in with the style of the other processing that occurs in the operational environment.

The following are few considerations of the elements of the indirect usage of data warehouse data:

■ The analysis program:
  ■ has many characteristics of artificial intelligence
  ■ has free rein to run on any data warehouse data that is available
  ■ is run in the background, where processing time is not an issue (or at least not a large issue)
  ■ is run in harmony with the rate at which data warehouse changes

- The periodic refreshment:
  - occurs infrequently
  - operates in a replacement mode
  - moves the data from the technology supporting the data warehouse to the technology supporting the operational environment
- The online preanalyzed data file:
  - contains only a small amount of data per unit of data
  - may contain collectively a large amount of data (because there may be many units of data)
  - contains precisely what the online clerk needs
  - is not updated, but is periodically refreshed on a whole sale basis
  - is part of the online high performance environment
  - is efficient to access
  - is geared for access of individual units of data, not massive sweeps of data

## STAR JOINS

For all of the practical use of a data model as one of the foundations of design for the data warehouse, there are some shortcomings. Consider the simple data model in Figure 3.56.

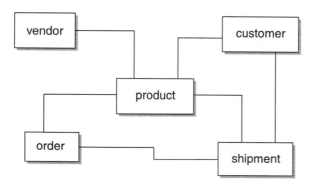

**Figure 3.56**   A simple two-dimensional data model gives the impression that all entities are equal.

The data model in the figure shows four simple entities with relationships. If all that is considered is the data model for database design, the inference can be drawn that all entities are equal. In other words, from a design standpoint the data model appears to make all entities peers with each other. Approaching database design for the data warehouse solely from the perspective of the data model produces a "flat" effect. In actuality, for a variety of reasons, entities in the world of data warehousing are anything but peers. Some entities demand their own special treatment. In order to see why the data model perspective of the data and the relationships in an organization distorted, consider a three-dimensional perspective of data in the data warehouse based on the amount of data that will populate the entities of data as they are built in the data warehouse. Figure 3.57 shows such a three-dimensional perspective. Entities representing vendor, customer, product, and shipment will be sparsely populated, while entity for orders will be heavily populated. There will be *many* more occurrences of data residing in the table or tables representing the order entity than there will be for any other entity. Because of the massive volume of data that will be populating entity order, a different design treatment is required.

The design structure that is required to manage large amounts of data residing in an entity in a data warehouse is called a "star join." As a simple example of a star join, consider the data structure shown in Figure 3.58. ORDER is at the center

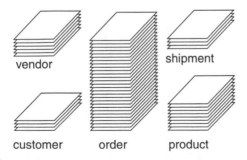

**Figure 3.57** A three-dimensional perspective of the entities shows that the entities are anything but equals. Some entities contain far more occurrences of the data than other entities.

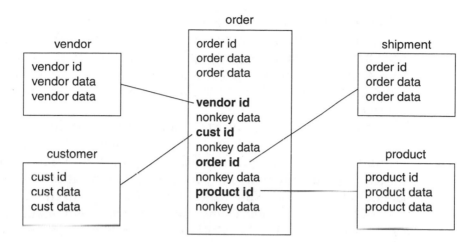

**Figure 3.58** A simple star join in which the entity "order" is populated with many occurrences and other entities are prejoined with the data.

of the star join. ORDER is the entity that will be heavily populated. Surrounding ORDER are the entities PART, DATE, SUPPLIER, and SHIPMENT. Each of the surrounding entities will have only a modest number of occurrences of data. The center of the star join—ORDER—is called the "fact table." The surrounding entities—PART, DATE, SUPPLIER, and SHIPMENT—are called "dimension tables." The fact table contains unique identifying data for ORDER, as well as data unique to the order itself. The fact table also contains prejoined foreign key references to tables outlying itself—the dimension tables. The foreign key relationships may be accompanied by nonforeign key information inside the star join if in fact the nonforeign key information is used frequently with the fact table. As an example, the description of a PART may be stored inside the fact table along with PART number if in fact description is used frequently as part of ORDER processing.

There can be any number of foreign key relationships to the dimension tables. A foreign key relationship is created when there is a need to examine the foreign key data along with data in the fact table.

One of the interesting aspects of the creation and usage of the star join is that in many cases textual data is divided from numeric data. Consider the diagram shown in Figure 3.59. Textual data often ends up in the dimension tables and numeric data ends up in the fact table. Such a division occurs in *almost* every case.

The benefit of creating star joins is to streamline data for DSS processing. By prejoining data and by creating selective redundancy, the designer greatly simplifies and streamlines data for access and analysis, which is exactly what is needed for the data warehouse. Note that if star joins were used outside of the DSS data warehouse environment, there would be many drawbacks. Outside the DSS data warehouse environment, where update occurs and where data relationships are managed up to the second, a star join most likely would be a very cumber-

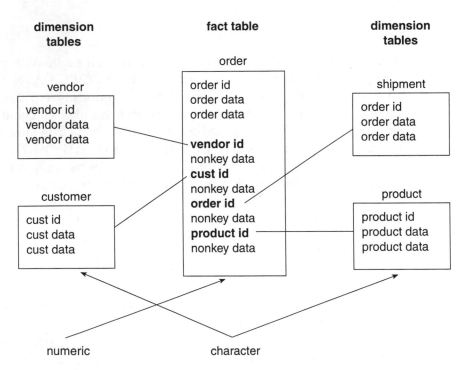

**Figure 3.59** In many cases the fact table is populated by numeric data and foreign keys, while the dimension table is populated by character data.

some structure to build and maintain. But because the data warehouse environment is a load-and-access environment, because the data warehouse contains historical data, and because massive amounts of data need to be managed, the star join data structure is ideal.

Does the advent of the star join structure imply that the data model is not the proper foundation for design for the data warehouse? The answer is: not at all. The data model is still a very useful structure for the design of much of the data warehouse environment. However, the star join has its rightful place. Figure 3.60 shows how the star join and the data model fit as foundations for data warehouse DSS design. The star joins applies as a design foundation to the very large entities that will

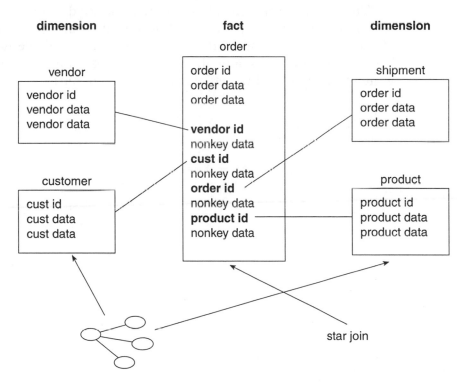

**Figure 3.60**  Classical data modeling applies to the dimension tables (i.e., the non populous entities) and star join design applies to the fact tables (i.e., the populous entities).

exist in the data warehouse. The data model applies as a design foundation to the nonvoluminous entities found in the data warehouse.

## SUMMARY

The design of the data warehouse begins with the data model. The corporate data model is used for the design of the operational environment, and a variation of the corporate data model is used for the data warehouse. The data warehouse is constructed in an iterative fashion. Requirements for the data warehouse *cannot* be known a priori. The construction of the data warehouse is under a development life cycle completely different from that of classical operational systems.

The primary concern of the data warehouse developer is that of managing volume. To that end, granularity and partitioning of data are the two most important issues of database design. There are, however, many other physical design issues, most of which center around the efficiency of access of data.

# Granularity in the Data Warehouse

The single most important design issue facing the data warehouse developer is that of determining the granularity in the data warehouse. When the granularity of a data warehouse is properly set, the remaining aspects of design and implementation flow smoothly; when it has not been set, every other aspect is awkward.

The tradeoff in choosing the right levels of granularity—as discussed earlier—centers around managing the volume of data and storing data at such a high level of granularity that detailed usage of the data cannot be made.

## RAW ESTIMATES

The starting point for determining the appropriate level of granularity is to do a raw estimate of the number of rows of data and the DASD (direct access storage device) that will be in the data warehouse. Admittedly, in the best of circumstances, only an estimate can be made. But all that is required at the inception of building the warehouse is an order of magnitude estimate in any case.

There is an algorithmic path to calculating the space occupied by a data warehouse, as shown in Figure 4.1. The first step

**Estimating rows/space for the warehouse environment**
1. For each known table:
    How big is a row (in bytes)
        −biggest estimate
        −smallest estimate
    For the 1-year horizon
        What is the maximum number of rows possible?
        What are the minimum number of rows possible?
    For the 5-year horizon
        What is the maximum number of rows possible?
        What is the minimum number of rows possible?
    For each key of the table
        What is the size of the key (in bytes)
    Total maximum 1-year space = biggest row × 1-year max rows
    Total minimum 1-year space = smallest row × 1-year min rows
        plus index space

2. Repeat (1) for all known tables.

**Figure 4.1**  Space/rows calculations.

is to identify all the tables that will be built. Next, estimate the size of the row in each table. It is likely that the exact size will not be known. A lower-bound estimate and an upper-bound estimate are sufficient.

Next, on the one-year horizon, estimate the maximum number of rows and the minimum number of rows in the table. This estimate is the one that gives the designer the greatest problem. If the table is for customers, use today's estimate of customers, factoring in business conditions and the corporate business plan. If there is no existing business today, estimate total market multiplied by expected market share. If the market share is unpredictable, use an estimate of what a competitor has achieved. In short, start with a reasonable estimate of customers gathered from one or more sources.

If the warehouse is to contain activity, go from estimated number of customers to estimated activity per unit of time. Again, the same logic is used, looking at current business profiles, a competitor's profile, economist projections, and so forth.

Once the estimate of number of units of data in the data warehouse is made (using a high and a low projection), the estimation process is repeated, but for the five-year horizon, not the one-year horizon.

After the raw data projections are made, the index data space projections are calculated. For each table—for each key in the table—identify the length of the key and whether the key will exist for each entry in the primary table.

Now the high and low numbers for the occurrences of rows in the tables are multiplied respectively by the maximum and minimum lengths of data. In addition, the number of index entries is multiplied by the length of the key and added to the total amount of data.

## INPUT TO THE PLANNING PROCESS

The estimate of rows and DASD then serves as input to the planning process, as shown by Figure 4.2.

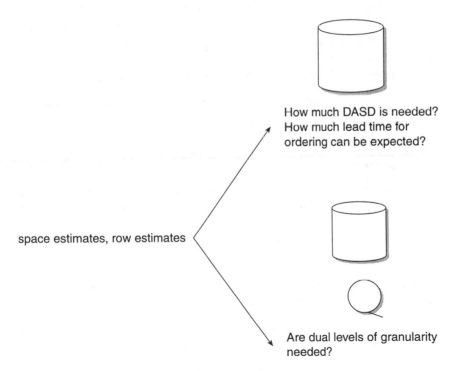

How much DASD is needed?
How much lead time for
ordering can be expected?

space estimates, row estimates

Are dual levels of granularity
needed?

**Figure 4.2**  Using the output of the space estimates.

At the point that the estimates are made, accuracy is really only important to the order of magnitude.

## DUAL OR SINGLE LEVELS OF GRANULARITY?

Once the estimates are made, the next step is to compare the total number of rows in the warehouse environment to the charts shown in Figure 4.3. Depending on how many total rows there will be in the warehouse environment, different approaches to design and development will have to be made. On the one-year horizon, if there will be less than 10,000 rows, then practically any design and implementation will work. For the one-year horizon, if there will be 100,000 total rows or less, then design must be done carefully. If there will be more than 1,000,000 rows in total in the first year, dual levels of granularity will be called for. And if the total number of rows in the data warehouse environment is to exceed 10,000,000 rows, dual levels of granularity will be mandated, and a very careful design and implementation will be required.

On the five-year horizon, the totals shift by about an order of magnitude. The theory is that after five years:

■ There will be more expertise available in managing the data warehouse volumes of data.

| 1-year horizon | | 5-year horizon | |
|---|---|---|---|
| 10,000,000 | dual level of granularity and careful design | 20,000,000 | dual level of granularity and careful design |
| 1,000,000 | dual levels of granularity | 10,000,000 | dual levels of granularity |
| 100,000 | careful design | 1,000,000 | careful design |
| 10,000 | practically any design works | 100,000 | practically any design works |

Figure 4.3  The thresholds of granularity.

■ Hardware costs will have dropped to some extent.
■ More powerful software tools will be available.
■ The end user will be more sophisticated.

All of these factors point to a different volume of data that can be managed over a long period of time.

An interesting point is that the total number of bytes used in the warehouse has little to do with the design and granularity of the data warehouse. In other words, it does not matter whether the record is 25 bytes long or 250 bytes long. The chart shown in Figure 4.3 still applies. The reason has as much to do with the indexing of data as anything else. The same number of index entries is required regardless of the size of the record being indexed. Only under exceptional circumstances does the actual size of the record being indexed play a role in determining whether the data warehouse should contain dual levels of granularity.

## WHAT THE LEVELS OF GRANULARITY WILL BE

Once the simple analysis is done (and in truth, most companies discover that they need dual levels of granularity), the next step is to determine exactly what the level of granularity is to be. The starting point is common sense and a certain amount of intuition. Creating a lightly summarized level of data that is at a very low level of detail doesn't make sense because too many resources will be required to process the data. Creating a lightly summarized level of detail that is too high means that much analysis will have to be done at the true archival level. So the first cut at the lightly summarized level of granularity is to make an educated guess.

But an educated guess is only the starting point. To refine the guess, a certain amount of iterative analysis is needed, as shown in Figure 4.4. In order to determine the proper level of granularity for the lightly summarized data, the only real way to make the determination is to put the data in front of the end user. It is only after the end user has actually seen the data that a definitive answer can be given. Figure 4.4 shows the iterative loop that must transpire.

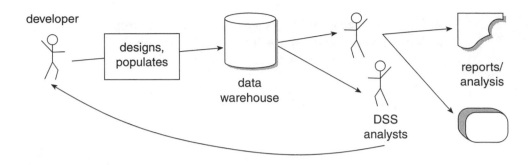

developer

designs,
populates

data
warehouse

DSS
analysts

reports/
analysis

Rule of Thumb:

If 50% of the first iteration of design is correct, the design effort has been a success.

- building very small subsets quickly and carefully listening to feedback
- prototyping
- looking at what other people have done
- working with an experienced user
- looking at what the organization has now
- JAD sessions with simulated output

**Figure 4.4** "Now that I see what can be done, I can tell you what would really be useful."—the attitude of the end user.

## SOME FEEDBACK LOOP TECHNIQUES

The following are some techniques that apply to making the feedback loop a harmonious one:

■ Build the first parts of the data warehouse in very small, very fast steps, and carefully listen to the end users' comments. Be prepared to make adjustments quickly.

■ Use prototyping if such a tool is available, and allow the feedback loop to function using observations gleaned from the prototype.

■ Look at how other people have built their levels of granularity and learn from their experience.

■ Go through the feedback process with an experienced user who is aware of the process that is occurring. Under no circumstances keep your users in the dark as to the dynamics of the feedback loop.

■ Look at whatever the organization has now that appears to be working.

■ Execute JAD sessions and simulate the output in order to achieve the desired feedback.

There are many ways that granularity of data can be raised, such as the following:

■ Summarize data from the source as it goes into the target.

■ Average or otherwise calculate data as it goes into the target.

■ Push highest/lowest set values into the target.

■ Push only data that is obviously needed into the target.

■ Use conditional logic to select only a subset of records to go into the target.

There are no limits as to how data may be lightly summarized. (The limitation is in the mind of the designer.)

There is one important point. In classical requirements systems development, it is unwise to proceed until the vast majority of the requirements are identified. But in building the data warehouse, it is unwise to not proceed if at least half of the requirements for the data warehouse are identified. In other words, if in building the data warehouse the developer waits until many requirements are identified, then the warehouse will never be built. It is vitally important that the feedback loop with the DSS analyst be initiated as soon as possible.

## LEVELS OF GRANULARITY—BANKING ENVIRONMENT

Consider the simple data structures shown in Figure 4.5 for a banking/financial environment.

To the left—at the operational level—is operational data. The details of banking transactions are found there. Sixty days' worth of activity are stored in the operational online environment.

In the lightly summarized level of processing—shown to the right of the operational data—are up to 10 years' history of activities. The activities for a given account for a given month

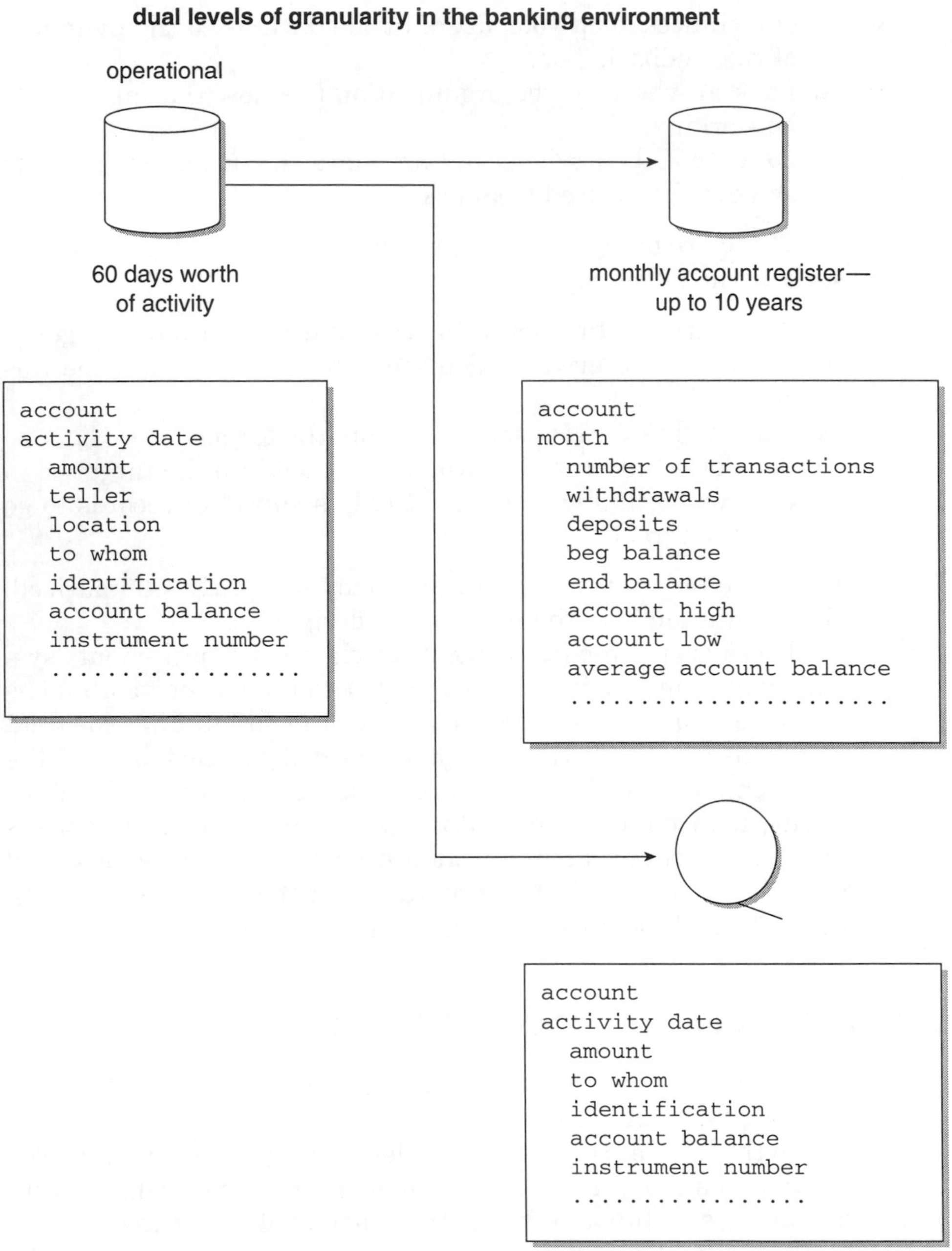

**dual levels of granularity in the banking environment**

operational

60 days worth
of activity

monthly account register—
up to 10 years

```
account
activity date
  amount
  teller
  location
  to whom
  identification
  account balance
  instrument number
  .................
```

```
account
month
  number of transactions
  withdrawals
  deposits
  beg balance
  end balance
  account high
  account low
  average account balance
  .......................
```

```
account
activity date
  amount
  to whom
  identification
  account balance
  instrument number
  ................
```

**Figure 4.5** A simple example of dual levels of granularity in the banking environment.

are stored in the lightly summarized portion of the data warehouse. While there are many records here, they are much more compact than the source records. Much less DASD and many fewer rows are found in the lightly summarized level of data.

Of course, there is the true archival level of data, in which every detailed record is stored. The true archival level of data is stored on a medium suited to bulk management of data. Note that not all fields of data are transported to the true archival level. Only those fields of data needed for legal reasons, informational reasons, and so forth, are stored. The data that has further use, even in an archival mode, is purged from the system as data is passed to the true archival level.

The true archival environment can be held in a single medium, such as magnetic tape, which is cheap for storage and expensive for access. However, it is entirely possible to store a small part of the true archival level of data online, when there is a probability that the data might be needed. For example, a bank might store the most recent 30 days of activities online. The last 30 days is true archival data, but it is still online. At the end of the 30-day period, the data is sent to magnetic tape, and space is made available for the next 30 days' worth of true archival data.

Now consider another example of data in an architected environment in the banking/financial environment, as shown by Figure 4.6.

Figure 4.6 shows customer records spread across the environment. In the operational environment is shown current value data whose content is accurate as of the moment of usage. The data that exists at the light level of summarization is the same data (in terms of definition of data) but is taken as a snapshot once a month.

Where the customer data is kept over a long span of time—for the past 10 years—a continuous file is created from the monthly files. In such a fashion the history of a customer can be tracked over a lengthy period of time.

Moving to another industry—manufacturing—the architected environment is shown in Figure 4.7.

At the operational level is the record of manufacture upon the completion of an assembly for a given lot of parts. Through-

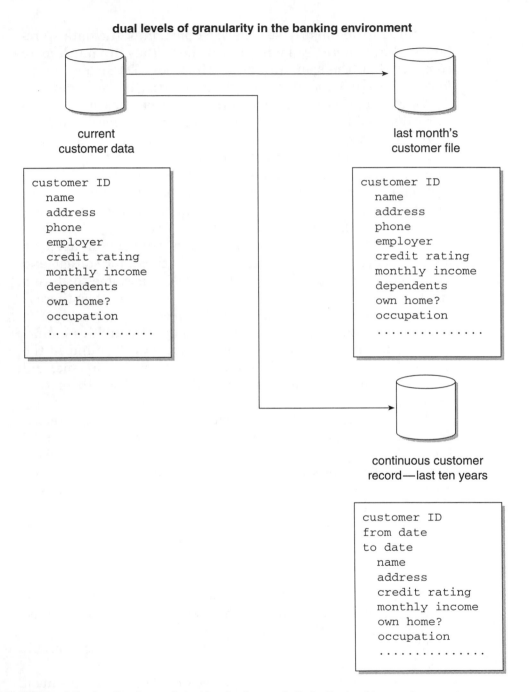

**Figure 4.6** Another form of dual levels of granularity in the banking environment.

**dual levels of granularity in the manufacturing environment**

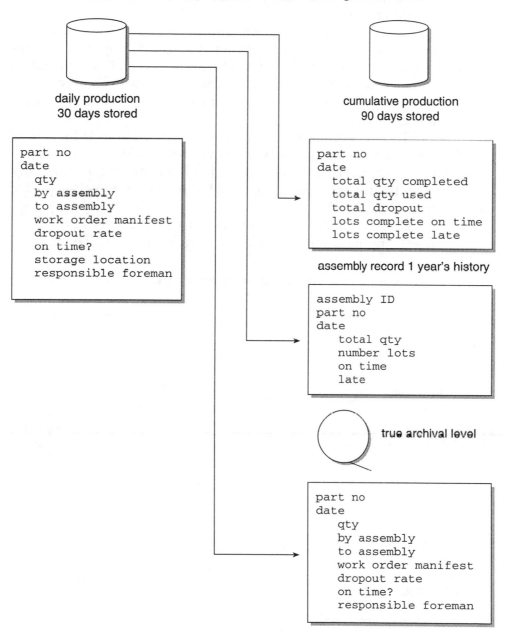

**Figure 4.7**   Some of the different levels of granularity in a manufacturing environment.

out the day there are many records that aggregate as the assembly process runs.

The light level of summarization contains two tables—one for all the activities for a part summarized by day, and another by assembly activity by part. The parts cumulative production table contains data for up to 90 days. The assembly record contains a limited amount of data on the production activity summarized by date.

The true archival environment contains a detailed record of each manufacture activity. However, as in the case of a bank, only those fields that will be needed later are stored. (Actually, those fields that have a reasonable probability of being needed later are stored.)

Another example of data warehouse granularity in the manufacturing environment is shown in Figure 4.8. There is an

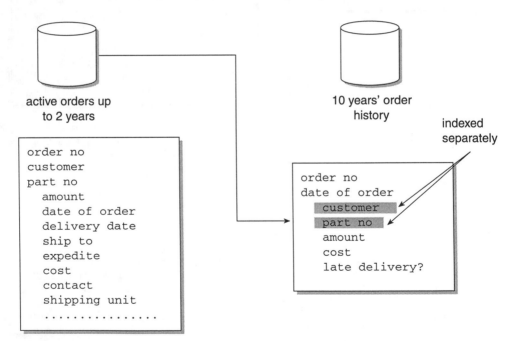

**levels of granularity in the manufacturing environment**

active orders up to 2 years

10 years' order history

indexed separately

```
order no
customer
part no
   amount
   date of order
   delivery date
   ship to
   expedite
   cost
   contact
   shipping unit
   . . . . . . . . . . . . . . .
```

```
order no
date of order
   customer
   part no
   amount
   cost
   late delivery?
```

**Figure 4.8** There are so few order records that there is no need for a dual level of granularity.

active-order file in the operational environment. All orders that need activity are stored there. In the data warehouse is stored up to 10 years' worth of order history. The order history is keyed on the primary key and several secondary keys. Only the data that will be needed for future analysis is stored in the warehouse. The volume of orders was so small that going to a true archival level was not necessary. Of course, should there start to be a plethora of orders, then it may well be necessary to go to a lower level of granularity.

Another adaptation of a shift in granularity is seen in the data in the architected environment of an insurance company, shown in Figure 4.9. Premium payment information is collected

**dual levels of granularity in the insurance environment**

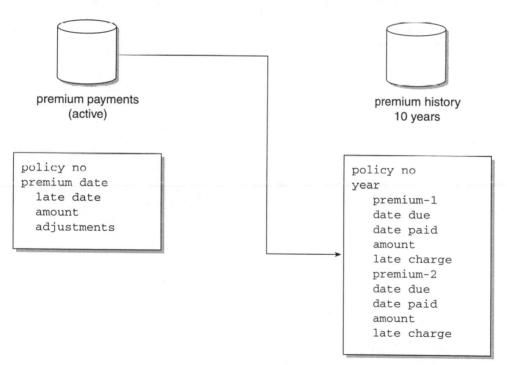

**Figure 4.9**   Because of the low volume of premiums, there is no need for dual levels of granularity, and because of the regularity of premium billing, there is the opportunity to create an array of data.

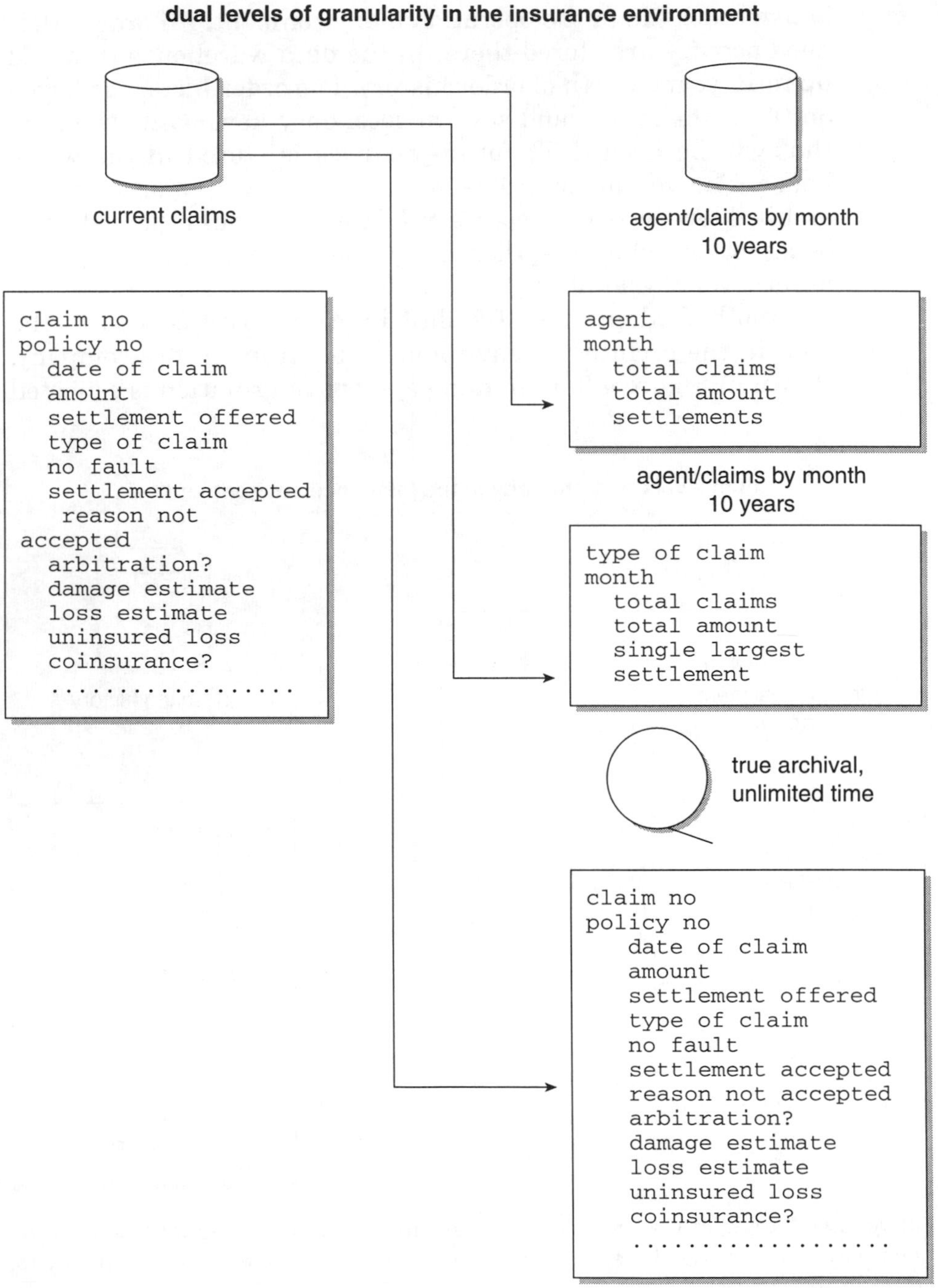

**dual levels of granularity in the insurance environment**

current claims          agent/claims by month
                             10 years

```
claim no
policy no
   date of claim
   amount
   settlement offered
   type of claim
   no fault
   settlement accepted
   reason not
accepted
   arbitration?
   damage estimate
   loss estimate
   uninsured loss
   coinsurance?
   . . . . . . . . . . . . . . . . .
```

```
agent
month
   total claims
   total amount
   settlements
```

agent/claims by month
10 years

```
type of claim
month
   total claims
   total amount
   single largest
   settlement
```

true archival,
unlimited time

```
claim no
policy no
   date of claim
   amount
   settlement offered
   type of claim
   no fault
   settlement accepted
   reason not accepted
   arbitration?
   damage estimate
   loss estimate
   uninsured loss
   coinsurance?
   . . . . . . . . . . . . . . . . .
```

**Figure 4.10** Claims information is summarized on other than the primary key in the lightly summarized part of the warehouse. Claims information must be kept indefinitely in the true archival portion of the architecture.

in an active file. Then, after a period of time, the information is passed to the data warehouse. Because there is only a relatively small amount of data, there is no need for dual levels of granularity. However, because of the regularity of premium payments, the payments are stored as part of an array in the warehouse.

As another example of architecture in the insurance environment, consider the insurance claims information shown in Figure 4.10.

In the current claims system (the operational part of the environment), much detailed information is stored about claims. When a claim is settled (or when it is determined that a claim is not going to be settled), or when enough time passes that the claim is still pending, the claim information passes over to the data warehouse. As it passes to the data warehouse, the claim information is summarized in several ways—by agent by month, by type of claim by month, and so on. At a lower level of detail, the claim is held in the true archival level for an unlimited amount of time. As in the other cases where data passes to the true archival level, only data that has a chance of being needed in the future is kept (which is most of the information found in the operational environment).

These, then, are some examples of granularity and the architected environment as they relate to different industries.

## SUMMARY

Choosing the proper levels of granularity for the architected environment is vital to success. The normal way the levels of granularity are chosen is to use common sense, create a small part of the warehouse, and let the user access the data. Then listen very carefully to the user, and take the feedback he or she gives and adjust the levels of granularity appropriately.

The worst stance that can be taken is to try to design all the levels of granularity a priori, then build the data warehouse. Even in the best of circumstances, if 50 percent of the design is done correctly, the design is a good one. The nature of the data warehouse environment is such that the DSS analyst cannot envision what is really needed until he or she actually sees the reports.

# The Data Warehouse
# and Technology

In many ways, the data warehouse requires a simpler set of technological features than its predecessors. There is no online updating with the data warehouse; there are only minimal locking needs; only a very basic teleprocessing interface is required, and so forth. Nevertheless, there is a fair number of technological requirements for the data warehouse. This chapter will outline some of those needs.

## MANAGING LARGE AMOUNTS OF DATA

The first and most important technological requirement for the data warehouse is the ability to manage large amounts of data, as shown in Figure 5.1.

There are many ways that large amounts of data need to be managed—through addressability, through indexing, through extensions of data, through the efficient management of overflow, and so forth. There really are two dimensions to the management of large amounts of data—the capability to manage large amounts at all and the ability to manage large amounts well. Any technology that purports to support the data ware-

1st technological requirement—
the ability to manage volumes of
data

2nd technological requirement—
to be able to manage multiple
media

3rd technological requirement—
to be able to freely and easily
index and monitor data

4th technological requirement—
to interface—both receiving data
from and passing data to a wide
variety of technologies

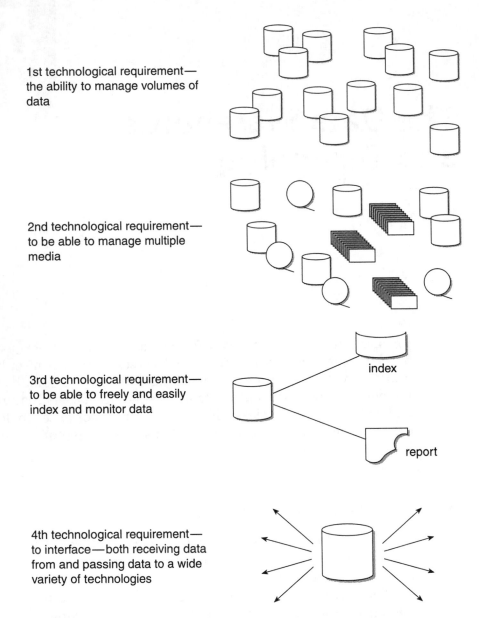

index

report

**Figure 5.1** Some basic requirements for technology supporting a data warehouse.

house must satisfy the requirements for *both* capability and efficiency.

In the ideal case, the data warehouse developer will build a data warehouse assuming that the technology can handle the volumes required. When the designer has to go to extraordinary lengths in design and implementation to map the technology to the data warehouse, then there is a problem with the underlying technology.

Not only is the basic technology and its efficiency an issue as far as the data warehouse is concerned, but the cost of storage and processing are factors as well.

## MANAGING MULTIPLE MEDIA

In conjunction with the requirement of managing large amounts of data efficiently and cost effectively, the technology underlying the data warehouse needs to be able to handle multiple storage media. It is insufficient to manage a mature data warehouse on DASD alone. There is a hierarchy of storage of data—in terms of speed of access and cost of storage. The hierarchy looks like this:

| | | |
|---|---|---|
| main memory | — very fast | —very expensive |
| expanded memory | — very fast | — expensive |
| cache | — very fast | — expensive |
| DASD | — fast | — moderate |
| optical disk | — not slow | — not expensive |
| fiche | — slow | — cheap |

The volume of data in the data warehouse and the probability of access are such that a fully populated data warehouse will reside on more than one level of storage. The technology that handles the data warehouse should be able to manage data in multiple storage media.

## INDEX/MONITOR DATA

The very essence of the data warehouse is the flexible and unpredictable access of data. This boils down to the ability to access the data quickly and easily. If data in the data warehouse cannot be easily and efficiently indexed, then the data warehouse will not be a success. Of course, there are many design practices that the designer employs to make data as flexible as possible, such as using dual levels of granularity and partitioning data. But the technology must be able to support easy indexing as well. Some of the indexing techniques that often make sense are the support of secondary indexes, the support of sparse indexes, the support of dynamic, temporary indexes, and so forth. Furthermore, the cost of creating the index and using the index cannot be significant.

In the same vein, the data in the data warehouse needs to be monitored at will. The cost of monitoring data cannot be so high and the complexity of monitoring data cannot be so bad that a monitoring program cannot be run whenever necessary.

There are many reasons for monitoring data warehouse data, including the following:

- determining if a reorganization needs to be done
- determining if an index is poorly structured
- determining if much data is in overflow
- determining the statistical composition of the data
- determining available remaining space

If the technology does not support easy and efficient monitoring of data in the warehouse, it is not appropriate.

## INTERFACES TO MANY TECHNOLOGIES

Another extremely important aspect of the data warehouse is the ability both to receive data from and pass data to a wide variety of technologies. The technology supporting the data warehouse is practically worthless if there are major constraints to the passing of data to and from the data warehouse.

The interface needs to be both efficient and easy to use and able to operate in a batch mode. Operating in an online mode is interesting but not terribly useful.

## PROGRAMMER/DESIGNER CONTROL OF DATA PLACEMENT

Because of efficiency of access and update, the programmer/ designer needs to have specific control over the placement of data at the physical block/page level, as shown in Figure 5.2.

It is all right for the technology to place the data where it thinks is appropriate, as long as the technology can be explicitly overridden when needed. It is a serious mistake for the technology to insist on the physical placement of data with no overrides from the programmer.

The programmer/designer oftentimes can arrange for the physical placement of data to coincide with its usage. In doing so, there are many economies of access to be gained.

## PARALLEL STORAGE/MANAGEMENT OF DATA

One of the most powerful features of data warehouse data management is that of parallel storage/management. When data is stored and managed in a parallel fashion, the gains in performance can be dramatic. As a rule, the performance boost is inversely proportional to the number of physical devices over which the data is scattered, assuming there is an even probability of access for the data.

The entire issue of parallel storage/management of data is too complex and important to be discussed at length here, but it should be mentioned.

### Metadata Management

For a variety of reasons, metadata becomes even more important in the data warehouse than in the classical operational environment. Metadata is vital because of the fundamental difference in the development life cycle that is associated with the data warehouse. The data warehouse operates under a heuristic, iterative development life cycle. In order to be effective, the user of the data warehouse must have access to metadata that is accurate and up to date. Without a good source of metadata to

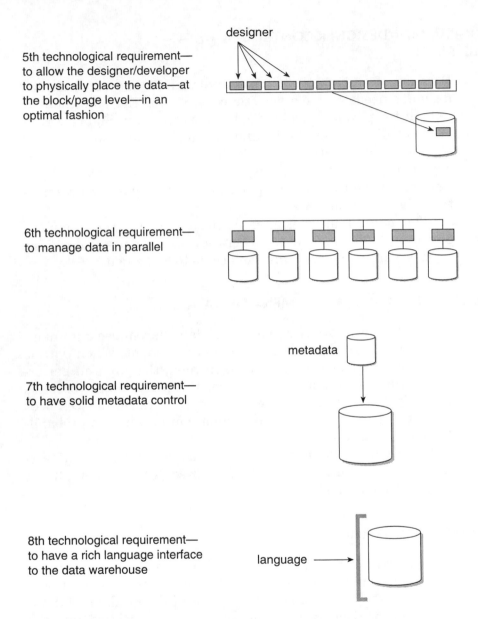

5th technological requirement—to allow the designer/developer to physically place the data—at the block/page level—in an optimal fashion

6th technological requirement—to manage data in parallel

7th technological requirement—to have solid metadata control

8th technological requirement—to have a rich language interface to the data warehouse

**Figure 5.2** More technological requirements for the data warehouse.

operate from, the job of the DSS analyst is much more difficult. Typically, metadata contains:

- data warehouse table structures
- data warehouse table attribution
- data warehouse source data (the system of record)
- mapping from the system of record to the data warehouse
- data model specification
- extract logging
- common routines for access of data

## LANGUAGE INTERFACE

The data warehouse needs to have a rich language specification. Without a robust language, interface entering and accessing data in the warehouse become difficult. In addition, the language accessing the data warehouse contents needs to be efficient.

Typically, the language interface to the data warehouse needs to:

- be able to access data a set at a time
- be able to access data a record at a time
- specifically ensure that one or more indexes will be used in the satisfaction of a call
- have an SQL interface
- be able to insert, delete, or update data

## EFFICIENT LOADING OF DATA

An important technological capability of the data warehouse is to be able to load the data warehouse efficiently, as shown in Figure 5.3.

There are several ways that data is loaded: a record at a time through a language interface or en masse with a utility. As a rule, it is much faster to load data by means of a utility. In addition, there needs to be an efficient loading of the indexes at the same time the data is loaded. In some cases, the loading of the indexes may be deferred in order to spread the workload evenly.

9th technological requirement—
to be able to load the warehouse
efficiently

10th technological requirement—
to use indexes efficiently

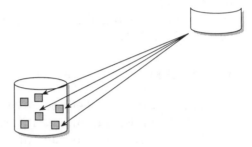

11th technological requirement—
to be able to store data in a
compact way

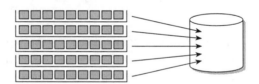

12th technological requirement—
to support compound keys

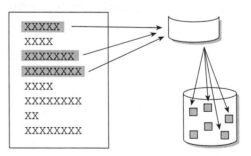

**Figure 5.3** Further technological requirements.

If loading of data warehouse data becomes an insurmountable issue, then the data warehouse becomes unusable.

## EFFICIENT INDEX UTILIZATION

Not only must the technology underlying the data warehouse be able to easily support the creation and loading of new indexes, but those indexes must be able to be accessed efficiently.

There are many ways that index access can be made efficient:

- using bit maps
- having multileveled indexes
- storing all or parts of an index in main memory
- compacting the index entries when the order of the data being indexed allows such compaction
- creating selective indexes and range indexes

In addition to the efficient storage and scanning of the index, the subsequent access of data at the primary storage level is important as well. Unfortunately, there are not nearly so many options for optimizing the access of primary data as there are for the access of index data.

## COMPACTION OF DATA

The very essence of success in the data warehouse environment is the ability to manage large amounts of data. Central to this goal is the ability to compact data. When data can be compacted it can be stored in a minimal amount of space. This is especially relevant to the data warehouse environment because data in the warehouse environment is seldom updated once inserted into the warehouse. The stability of warehouse data minimizes the problems of space management that arise when tightly compacted data is being updated.

Another advantage of compaction is that the programmer gets the absolute out of a given I/O when data is compactly stored. Of course, there is always the corresponding issue of decompaction of data upon access. While it is true that decompaction requires overhead, the overhead is measured in CPU resources, not I/O resources. As a rule, in the data warehouse environment, I/O resources are much more scarce than CPU resources, so decompaction of data is not a major issue.

## COMPOUND KEYS

A simple but important technological requirement of the data warehouse environment is the ability to support compound keys. Compound keys occur everywhere in the data warehouse environment, primarily because of the time variancy of data warehouse data.

## VARIABLE-LENGTH DATA

Another simple but very important technological requirement of the data warehouse environment is the ability to manage efficiently variable-length data, as seen in Figure 5.4.

Variable-length data can cause tremendous performance problems when it is constantly being updated and changed. But where variable-length data is stable, as in the case of a data warehouse, there is no inherent performance problem.

On the other hand, the variety of data found in the data warehouse is such that it is mandatory that variable-length structuring of data be supported.

## LOCK MANAGEMENT

A standard part of database technology is the lock manager. The lock manager is necessary to ensure that two or more people are not updating the same record at the same time. But update is not done in the data warehouse.

One of the effects of the lock manager is that it consumes a fair amount of resources, even when data is not being updated. Merely turning the lock manager on requires overhead. In order

13th technological requirement—
to manage variable-length data
efficiently

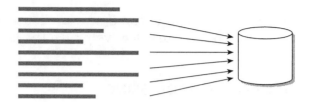

14th technological requirement—
to be able to turn on and off the
lock manager at will: to be able to
explicitly control the lock manager
at the programmer level

lock manager

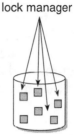

15th technological requirement—
to be able to do index-only
processing

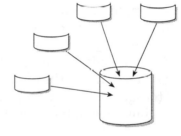

16th technological requirement—
to be able to quickly and
completely restore data from a
bulk medium

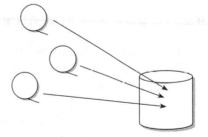

**Figure 5.4**   Still more technological requirements for the data warehouse.

to streamline the data warehouse environment, it is necessary to be able to selectively turn the lock manager off and on.

## INDEX-ONLY PROCESSING

A fairly standard database management system feature is that of being able to do index-only processing. On many occasions it is possible to service a request by simply looking in an index (or indexes). When a request can be satisfied by looking only at indexes, it is much more efficient not to have to go to the primary source of data. But not all DBMSs are intelligent enough to know that a request can be satisfied in the index.

## FAST RESTORE

A simple but important technological feature of the data warehouse environment is the ability to quickly restore a data warehouse table from non-DASD storage. When a restore can be done from secondary storage, there may be enormous savings possible. Without having the ability to quickly restore data from secondary storage, the standard practice is to double the amount of DASD and use one-half of the DASD as a recovery/restore repository.

## OTHER TECHNOLOGICAL FEATURES

The features discussed here are only the most important ones. There are many other features that should be considered, too numerous to be mentioned here.

It is noteworthy that many other features found in classical technology play only a small role (if they play a role at all). Some of those features include:

- transaction integrity
- high-speed buffering
- row/page level locking
- referential integrity
- VIEWs of data

## DBMS TYPES AND THE DATA WAREHOUSE

With the advent of data warehousing and the recognition of DSS as an integral part of the modern information systems infrastructure, a new class of DBMS has arisen. The new class of DBMS can be called a data warehouse–specific–database management system. The data warehouse–specific DBMS is optimized for data warehousing and DSS processing.

The kind of processing that occurs in a data warehouse environment can be characterized as load-and-access processing. Data is integrated, transformed, and loaded into the data warehouse from the operational legacy environment. Once in the data warehouse, the integrated data is accessed and analyzed there. Update is not normally done in the data warehouse, once the data is loaded. If corrections or adjustments need to be made to the data warehouse, they are made at off hours, when no analysis is occurring against the data warehouse data.

Another important difference between classical database environments and the data warehouse environment is that there tends to be a lot more data in the data warehouse environment, more so than has been the norm for operational systems. Data warehouses contain data that is measured in tens and hundreds of gigabytes of information, while classical databases under a general-purpose DBMSs typically manage much less data. Data warehouses end up managing lots of data because they:

- contain granular, atomic detail
- contain historical information
- contain summary as well as detailed data

In terms of basic data management capability, data warehouses are optimized around a very different set of parameters than standard operational DBMSs.

The first and most important difference between a classical general-purpose DBMS and a data warehouse–specific DBMS is that of update. A classical general-purpose DBMS must be able to accommodate record-level update as a normal part of operations. Because record-level update is a regular feature of the general-purpose DBMS, the general-purpose DBMS must offer facilities for such things as:

- locking
- COMMITs
- checkpoints
- log tape processing
- deadlock
- backout

Not only do these features become a normal part of the DBMS, they consume a tremendous amount of overhead. Interestingly, the overhead is consumed even when it isn't being used. In other words, at least some—depending on the DBMS—update and locking overhead is required by a general-purpose DBMS even when READ-ONLY processing is being executed. Depending on the general-purpose DBMS, the overhead required by update can be minimized, but it cannot be completely removed. For a data warehouse–specific DBMS, there is no need for any of the overhead of update.

A second major difference between a general-purpose DBMS and a data warehouse–specific DBMS is that of basic data management. For a general-purpose DBMS, data management at the block level includes space that is reserved for future block expansion at the moment of update or insertion. Typically this space is referred to as FREESPACE. For a general-purpose DBMS FREESPACE may be as high as 50 percent. For a data warehouse–specific DBMS, FREESPACE always equals 0 percent because there will be no need for expansion in the physical block, once loaded, since update is not done in the data warehouse environment. Indeed, given the amount of data to be managed in a data warehouse, it makes no sense to reserve vast amounts of space that may never be used.

Another relevant difference between the data warehouse and the general-purpose environment that is reflected in the different types of DBMS is that of indexing. A general-purpose DBMS environment is restricted to a finite number of indexes. This restriction exists because as updates and insertions occur, the indexes themselves require their own data management. However, in a data warehouse environment where there is no update and there is a need to optimize access of data, there is a need (and an opportunity) for many indexes. Indeed, a much more robust and sophisticated indexing structure can be employed for data warehousing than for operational, update-oriented databases.

But beyond indexing, update, and basic data management at the physical block level, there are some other very basic differences between the data management capabilities and philosophies of general-purpose DBMSs and data warehouse–specific DBMSs. Perhaps the most basic difference between the two types of DBMS is the ability to physically organize data in an optimal fashion for different kinds of access. A general-purpose DBMS typically physically organizes data for optimal transaction access and manipulation. Organizing in this fashion allows many different types of data to be physically gathered according to a common key and efficiently accessed in one or two I/Os. Data that is optimal for informational access usually has a very different physical profile. Data that is optimal for informational access is physically organized so that many different occurrences of the same type of data can be accessed efficiently in one or two physical I/Os.

Data can be physically optimized for transaction access or DSS access, but not both at the same time. A general-purpose DBMS allows data to be optimized for transaction access, and a data warehouse–specific DBMS allows data to be physically optimized for DSS access and analysis.

## CHANGING DBMS TECHNOLOGY

An interesting consideration of the information warehouse is that of changing the DBMS technology after the warehouse has already been populated. There may be several reasons why such a change is in order:

- DBMS technologies may be available today that simply were not an option when the data warehouse was first populated.
- The size of the warehouse has grown to the point that a new technological approach is mandated.
- Use of the warehouse has escalated and changed to the point that the current warehouse DBMS technology is not adequate.

In a word, it is possible to revisit the basic DBMS decision from time to time.

Should the decision be made to go to a new DBMS technology, what are the considerations? Some of the more important ones are:

■ Will the new DBMS technology meet the foreseeable requirements?
■ How will conversion from the older DBMS technology to the newer DBMS technology be done?
■ How will the transformation programs be converted?

Of all of these considerations, the last is the most vexing. Trying to change the transformation programs is a complex task in the best of circumstances.

## MULTIDIMENSIONAL DBMS AND THE DATA WAREHOUSE

One of the technologies that is often discussed in the context of the data warehouse is that of multidimensional database management systems. Multidimensional database management systems (sometimes called a "datamart") provide an information systems structure that allows an organization to have very flexible access to data, to slice and dice data any number of ways and to dynamically explore the relationship between summary and detail data. Multidimensional DBMS offers both flexibility and control to the end user and as such fits very well in a DSS environment. There is a very interesting and complementary relationship between multidimensional DBMSs and data warehouse, as shown in Figure 5.5.

The detailed data housed in a data warehouse provides a very robust and convenient source of data for the multidimensional DBMS. Data flows from the data warehouse into the multidimensional DBMS on a regular basis as the multidimensional DBMS needs to be periodically refreshed. Since legacy application data is integrated as it enters the data warehouse, the multidimensional DBMS is blessed by not having to extract and integrate the data it operates on from the operational environment. In addition, the data warehouse houses data at its lowest

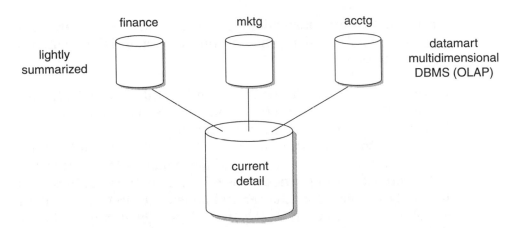

**Figure 5.5** The classical structure of the data warehouse and how current detail data and departmental data (or multidimensional DBMS, datamart) data fit together.

level, providing "bedrock" data for the lowest level of analysis that anyone using the multidimensional DBMS would ever want to go to.

There is a temptation to think that multidimensional DBMS technology should be the database technology for the data warehouse. In all but the most unusual cases this is a mistake. The properties that make multidimensional DBMS technology optimal for what it does are not the properties that are of primary importance for the data warehouse. And the properties that are the most important in the data warehouse are not those that are found in multidimensional DBMS technology.

Consider the differences between the multidimensional DBMS and the data warehouse:

■ The data warehouse holds massive amounts of data; the multidimensional DBMS holds at least an order of magnitude less data.
■ The data warehouse is geared for a limited amount of flexible access; the multidimensional DBMS is geared for very heavy and unpredictable access and analysis of data.
■ The data warehouse contains data with a very lengthy time horizon—from 5 to 10 years; the multidimensional DBMS holds a much shorter time horizon of data.

■ The data warehouse allows analysts to access its data in a constrained fashion; the multidimensional DBMS allows unfettered access.

Instead of the data warehouse being housed in a multidimensional DBMS, the multidimensional DBMS and the data warehouse enjoy a complementary relationship.

One of the interesting features of the relationship between the data warehouse and the multidimensional DBMS is that the data warehouse can provide a basis for very detailed data that is normally not found in the multidimensional DBMS. The data warehouse can contain a very fine degree of detail, which is lightly summarized as it is passed up to the multidimensional DBMS. Once in the multidimensional DBMS the data can be further summarized. In such a fashion the multidimensional DBMS can house all but the most detailed level of data. The analyst using the multidimensional DBMS can drill down in a flexible and efficient fashion over all the different levels of data found in it. Then, if needed, the analyst can actually drill down to the data warehouse. By marrying the data warehouse and the multidimensional DBMS in such a manner, the DSS analyst gets the best of both worlds. The DSS analyst enjoys the efficiency of operating most of the time in the world of the multidimensional DBMS while at the same time possessing the capability of drilling down to the lowest level of detail if necessary.

Another complementary aspect of the data warehouse coupled with the multidimensional DBMS is that summary information may be calculated and collected in the multidimensional DBMS and then stored in the data warehouse. In coupling the data this way, the summary data can be stored in the data warehouse for a much longer time than if it were stored in the multidimensional DBMS.

There is still another way that the multidimensional DBMS and data warehouse worlds are complementary. The multidimensional DBMS houses data over a modest length of time—say 12 to 15 months, depending on the application. The data warehouse houses data over a much longer time horizon—5 to 10 years. In such a manner the data warehouse becomes a source of research for multidimensional DBMS analysts. Multidimensional DBMS analysts have the luxury of knowing that huge amounts of data are available if needed, but do not have to pay the price of storing all that data in their environment when not needed.

Multidimensional DBMS come in several flavors. Some multidimensional DBMS operate on a foundation of relational technology and some multidimensional DBMS operate on a technological foundation optimal for "slicing and dicing" the data, where data can be thought of as existing in multidimensional cubes. The latter technological foundation is one that can be called a *cube foundation*.

Both foundations can support multidimensional DBMS datamarts. But there are some differences between the two types of technological foundations:

**the relational foundation for multidimensional DBMS datamarts:**

- strengths:
  - can support a lot of data
  - can support dynamic joining of data
  - has proven technology
  - is capable of supporting general purpose update processing
  - if there is no known pattern of usage of data, then the relational structure is as good as any other
- weaknesses:
  - performance is less than optimal
  - cannot be purely optimized for access processing

**the "cube" foundation for multidimensional DBMS datamarts:**

- strengths:
  - performance is optimal for DSS processing
  - can be optimized for very fast access of data
  - if pattern of access of data is known, then the structure of data can be optimized
  - can easily be "sliced and diced"
  - can be examined in many ways

- weaknesses:
  - cannot handle nearly as much data as a standard relational format
  - does not support general purpose update processing
  - may take a long time to load
  - if access is desired on a path not supported by the design of the data, then the structure is not flexible
  - support for dynamic joins of data is questionable

**Multidimensional DBMS (OLAP)** is a technology and the data warehouse is an architectural infrastructure. There is a complementary and symbiotic relationship between the two. In the normal case, the data warehouse serves as a foundation for the multidimensional DBMS—feeding selected subsets of the detailed data into the multidimensional DBMS where it is summarized and otherwise aggregated. But in some circles there is the notion that multidimensional DBMSs do not need a data warehouse for their foundation of data.

Without a data warehouse serving as the foundation for the multidimensional DBMS, the data flowing into the multidimensional DBMS comes directly from the older, legacy applications environment. Figure 5.6 shows the flow of data from the legacy environment moving directly into the multidimensional DBMS. The design is appealing because it is straightforward and easily achieved. A programmer can immediately start to work on building it. In a word, the simplicity and immediacy of the design beguiles the end user into thinking that this approach to the building of a multidimensional DBMS is proper.

**Figure 5.6** Building the multidimensional DBMS datamart from an application with no current detail.

Unfortunately, there are some major pitfalls in the architecture suggested by Figure 5.6 that are not immediately apparent. For a variety of reasons it makes sense to feed the multidimensional DBMS environment from the current level of detail of the data warehouse, rather than feeding it directly from the legacy applications operational environment.

Figure 5.7 illustrates the feeding of the multidimensional DBMS environment from the current level of detail of the data warehouse environment. Old, legacy operational data is integrated and transformed as it flows into the data warehouse. Once in the data warehouse, the integrated data is stored in the current level of detailed data. From this level of data in the data warehouse, the multidimensional DBMS is fed.

At first glance there may not appear to be substantive differences between the architectures shown in Figure 5.6 and Figure 5.7. In fact, putting data first into a data warehouse may even appear to be a wasted effort. But there is a very good reason why integrating data into the data warehouse is the first step in creating the multidimensional DBMS.

Consider the fact that under normal conditions a corporation is going to want to build multiple multidimensional DBMS. Finance will want their multidimensional DBMS. Accounting

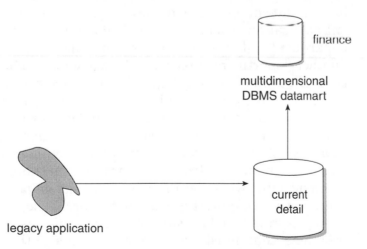

**Figure 5.7** The flow of data from the application environment to the current level detail to the multidimensional DBMS datamart.

will want theirs. Marketing, sales and others will each want their own multidimensional DBMS. Because there will be multiple multidimensional DBMSs in the corporation, the scenario shown in Figure 5.6 becomes much more complex. Figure 5.6 extended into a realistic scenario where there are multiple multidimensional DBMSs being directly and individually fed from the legacy systems environment appears as shown in Figure 5.8.

Figure 5.8 shows that multiple multidimensional DBMSs are being fed directly from the same legacy applications. What is so wrong with this architecture?

The problems are as follows:

- *The amount of development required in extraction is enormous.* Each different departmental multidimensional DBMS must have its own set of extraction programs developed for it on a customized basis. There is a tremendous overlap of extract processing. The amount of wasted development work is enormous. When the multidimensional DBMSs are fed from the data warehouse, only one set of integration and transformation programs is needed.
- *There is no integrated foundation when the multidimensional DBMSs are fed directly from the legacy systems environment.* Each departmental multidimensional DBMS has its own interpretation as to how integration from the different applications should be done. Unfortunately, the way one department integrates data is most likely not the way another department integrates the same data. The result is that there is no single integrated, definitive source of data. When the data warehouse is built, there is a single, definitive, integrated source of data that can be built upon.
- *The amount of development work required for maintenance is enormous.* A single change in an old legacy application ripples through many extraction programs. The change must be accommodated wherever there is an extraction program, and there are many. When there is a data warehouse, the effect of change is minimized because there are a minimal number of programs that must be written to manage the interface between the legacy environment and the data warehouse.

one of the primary reasons why the direct application to multidimensional dbms approach
is unworkable

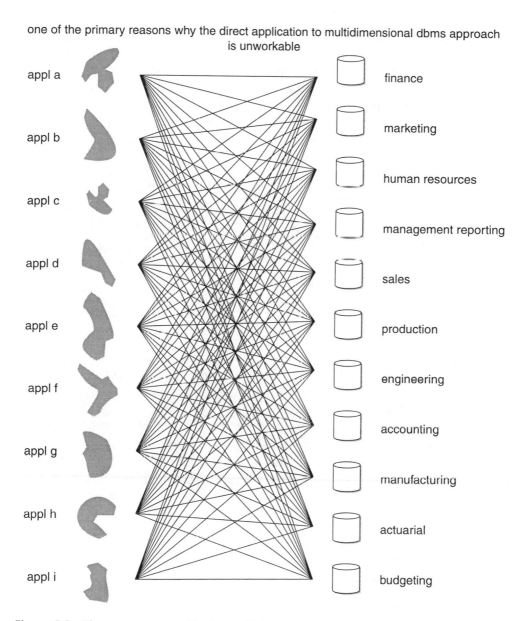

appl a          finance

appl b          marketing

appl c          human resources

appl d          management reporting

appl e          sales

appl f          production

appl g          engineering

appl h          accounting

appl i          manufacturing

                actuarial

                budgeting

**Figure 5.8**  There are many applications and there are many datamarts. An interface application is needed between each occurrence. The result of bypassing the current level of
detail is an unmanageable "spiders web."

■ *The amount of hardware resources consumed.* The same legacy data is sequentially repeatedly passed for each extraction process for each department. In the case of the data warehouse, the legacy data is passed only once for the purpose of refreshing the data in the data warehouse.

■ *The complexity of moving data directly from the legacy environment to the multidimensional DBMS environment precludes effective metadata management and control.* In the case of the data warehouse, the ability to capture and manage metadata is straightforward.

■ *The lack of reconcilability of data is an issue.* When there is a difference in opinion among various departments, each having its own multidimensional DBMS, there is no easy resolution. But with a data warehouse, resolution of conflicts is natural and easy.

## DUAL LEVELS OF GRANULARITY

One of the interesting aspects of a data warehouse is the dual environments that are often created. One environment is the DASD environment where online/interactive processing is done. The other environment is often a tape handling or mass store environment that has essentially different features. In many cases, the underlying technology that supports the DASD environment is not the same technological environment that supports the mass store environment. Mixing technologies in the data warehouse environment is normal and natural when done this way.

But there is another way that technology can be split that is not normal or natural. It is conceivable that the data warehouse environment—the DASD portion—could be split over more than one technology. Unless the split is part of a distributed data warehouse, this is not advisable.

## METADATA IN THE DATA WAREHOUSE ENVIRONMENT

The role of metadata in the data warehouse environment is very different from the role of data in the operational environment.

In the operational environment metadata is treated almost as an afterthought and is relegated to the same level of importance as documentation. However, metadata in the data warehouse environment takes on a very enhanced role. The importance of the role of metadata in the data warehouse environment is illustrated by Figure 5.9. Two different communities are served by operational data and data warehouse data. Operational data is used by the IT professional. For years, the IT professional has used metadata casually. The IT professional is computer literate and is able to find his or her way around systems because of the background and training undertaken. However, the data warehouse serves the DSS analyst community. The DSS analyst is usually a professional first and foremost. There usually is not a high degree of computer literacy in the DSS analyst community. The DSS analyst needs as much help as possible in order to use the data warehouse environment effectively, and metadata

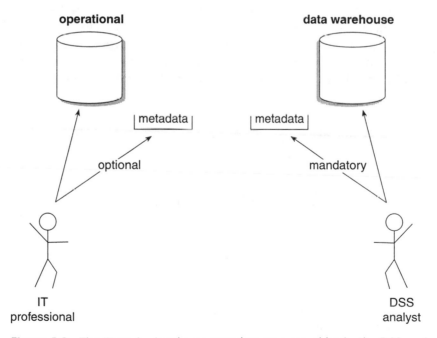

**Figure 5.9**  The IT professional uses metadata on a casual basis; the DSS analyst uses metadata regularly and as the first step of an analysis.

serves this end quite well. In addition, metadata is the first thing the DSS analyst looks at in planning how to do informational/analytical processing. Because of the difference in the communities served and because of the role that metadata plays in the day-to-day job function, metadata is much more important in the data warehouse environment than it ever was in the operational environment. But there are other reasons why data warehouse metadata is important.

Another reason for the importance of data warehouse metadata concerns managing the mapping between the operational environment and the data warehouse environment. Figure 5.10 illustrates this point.

Data undergoes a significant transformation as it passes from the operational environment to the data warehouse environment. Conversion, filtering, summarization, structural changes, and so on, all occur. There is a need to keep careful track of the transformation, and the metadata in the data warehouse is the ideal place to do it. The importance of keeping a careful record of the transformation is highlighted by the events that occur when a manager needs to trace data from the data warehouse back to its operational source (the ultimate in the drill-down process!). In this case, the record of the transformation describes exactly how to get from the data warehouse to the operational source of data.

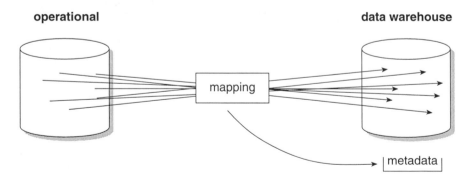

**Figure 5.10** The mapping between the operational environment and the data warehouse environment is another major reason for the need for metadata; without the mapping, controlling the interface is very difficult.

There is yet another important reason for the careful management of metadata in the data warehouse environment, as shown in Figure 5.11. Data in a data warehouse exists for a lengthy timespan—from five to ten years. Over a five-to-ten-year time span it is absolutely normal for a data warehouse to change its structure. Said another way, for a data structure to remain static over a five-to-ten-year timeframe is quite unusual. Keeping track of the changing structure of data over time, then, is a natural task for the metadata in the data warehouse.

Contrast the notion that there will be many structures of data over time in the data warehouse environment with the metadata found in the operational environment. In the operational environ-

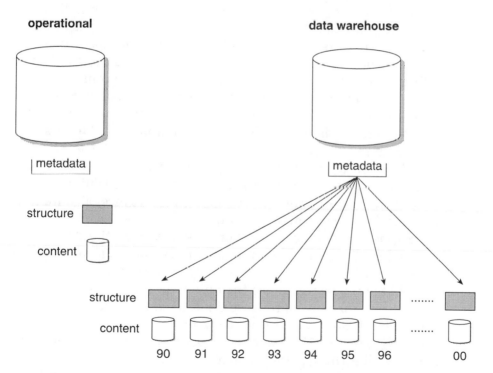

**Figure 5.11**   The data warehouse contains data over a long period of time and accordingly must manage multiple structures/definitions of data. The operational environment assumes that there is only a single correct definition of data at any one time.

ment it is assumed that at any one moment in time, there is one and only one correct definition of the structure of data.

## CONTEXT AND CONTENT

One of the intriguing aspects of data warehousing is that of the notion of the storage and management of data over a lengthy period of time. Data warehousing calls for the management of data over a five- to ten-year time frame or even longer.

In the past, classical operational information systems have focused their attention on the very current data of a corporation. In the operational world the emphasis is on how much an account balance is, right now; or how much is in inventory, right now; or what the status of a shipment is, right now. Of course every organization has a need to know about current information. But there is real value in looking at information over the spectrum of time as well. When an organization is able to look at information over a long period of time, trends become apparent that simply are not observable when looking at current information. One of the most important defining characteristics of the data warehouse is this ability to store, manage, and access data over time.

With the lengthy spectrum of time that is part of a data warehouse comes the awareness of a new dimension of data—that of *context*. In order to explain the importance of contextual information, an example is in order.

Suppose a manager asks for a report from the data warehouse for 1995. The report is generated and the manager is pleased. In fact, the manager is so pleased that a similar report for 1990 is requested. Since the data warehouse carries historical information, such a request is not hard to accommodate. The report for 1990 is generated. Now the manager holds the two reports—one for 1995 and one for 1990—in his hands and declares that the reports are a disaster!

The data warehouse architect examines the reports and sees that the financial statement for 1995 shows $50,000,000 in revenue while the report for 1990 shows a value of $10,000 for the same category. The manager declares that there is no way that any account or category could have increased in value that much in five years' time.

Before giving up, the data warehouse architect points out to the manager that there are other relevant factors that do not show up in the report. In 1990 there was a different source of data than there was in 1995. In 1990 the definition of a product was not the same as it was in 1995. In 1990 there were different marketing territories than there were in 1995. In 1990 there were different calculations, such as for depreciation, than there were in 1995. In addition, there were many different external considerations, such as a difference in inflation, taxation, economic forecasts, and so forth. Once the context of the reports is explained to the manager, the contents now appear to be quite acceptable and explainable.

In this simple but common example where the contents of data stand naked over time, the contents by themselves are quite inexplicable and unbelievable. However, when context is added to the contents of data over time, the contents and the context become quite enlightening.

In order to interpret and understand information over time, a whole new dimension of context is required. While content of information remains important, the comparison and understanding of information over time mandates that context be an equal partner to content. And in years past, context has been an undiscovered, unexplored dimension of information.

## Three Types of Contextual Information

There are three levels of contextual information that must be managed:

- simple contextual information
- complex contextual information
- external contextual information

Simple contextual information relates to the basic structure of data itself, and includes such things as:

- the structure of data
- the encoding of data

- the naming conventions used for data
- the metrics describing the data, such as:
  - how much data there is
  - how fast the data is growing
  - what sectors of the data are growing
  - how the data is being used

Simple contextual information has been managed in the past by dictionaries, directories, system monitors, and so forth. Complex contextual information describes the same data as simple contextual information, but from a different perspective. Complex contextual information addresses such aspects of data as:

- product definitions
- marketing territories
- pricing
- packaging
- organization structure
- distribution

Complex contextual information is some of the most useful and, at the same time, some of the most elusive information there is to capture. It is elusive because it is taken for granted and is in the background. It is so basic that no one thinks to define what it is or how it changes over time. And yet, in the long run, complex contextual information plays an extremely important role in understanding and interpreting of information over time.

External contextual information is information outside the corporation that nevertheless plays an important role in the understanding of information over time. Some examples of external contextual information include:

- economic forecasts:
  - inflation
  - financial
  - taxation
  - economic growth
- political information
- competitive information

- technological advancements
- consumer demographic movements

External contextual information says nothing directly about a company but says everything about the universe that the company must work and compete in. External contextual information is interesting both in terms of its immediate manifestation and in terms of changes over time. As with complex contextual information, there is very little organized attempt to capture and measure this information. It is so large and so obvious that it is taken for granted. It is quickly forgotten and difficult to reconstruct when needed.

## CAPTURING AND MANAGING CONTEXTUAL INFORMATION

One of the reasons that both complex and external contextual types of information are so hard to capture and quantify is that they are so unstructured. Compared to simple contextual information, external and complex contextual types of information are very amorphous. Another mitigating factor is that contextual information changes quickly. What is of interest and relevant one minute is irrelevant and passe the next. It is this constant flux and the amorphous state of external and complex contextual information that makes these types of information so hard to systematize.

### Looking at the Past

One can make the argument that the information systems profession has had contextual information in the past. The past attempts at dictionaries, repositories, directories, and libraries, all are movements toward the management of simple contextual information. For all the good intentions, there have been some notable limitations in these attempts that have greatly short-circuited their effectiveness. Some of the shortcomings of past attempts at the management of simple contextual information are as follows:

■ The information management attempts were aimed at the information systems developer, not the end user. As such, there was very little visibility to the end user. Consequently, the end user had very little enthusiasm or support for something that was not apparent.

■ Attempts at contextual management were passive. A developer could opt to use or not use the contextual information management facilities. Many chose to work around those facilities.

■ Attempts at contextual information management were in many cases removed from the development effort. In case after case, application development was done in 1965 and the data dictionary was done in 1985. By 1985, there were no more development dollars. Furthermore, the people that could have helped the most in organizing and defining simple contextual information were long gone to other jobs and/or companies.

■ Attempts to manage contextual information were limited to only simple contextual information. There was no attempt to try to capture or manage external or complex contextual information.

## REFRESHING THE DATA WAREHOUSE

Once the data warehouse is built, attention shifts from the building of the data warehouse to its day-to-day operations. The discovery is made that the cost of operating and maintaining a data warehouse is high. The volume of data in the warehouse grows faster than anyone had predicted. The widespread and unpredictable usage of the data warehouse by the end user DSS analyst causes contention on the server managing the warehouse. But the largest unexpected expense associated with the operation of the data warehouse is that of the periodic refreshment of legacy data into the data warehouse. What starts out as an almost incidental expense quickly turns into a very significant expense.

The first step most organizations take in the refreshment of data warehouse data is that of directly reading the old legacy databases. For some kinds of processing and under some circumstances, directly reading the older legacy files is the only way refreshment can be done. When data must be read from different legacy sources to form a single unit that is to go into the data warehouse, reading the legacy data directly is pretty much the only choice for refreshment of the data warehouse. Or when a transaction has caused the simultaneous update of multiple legacy files, a direct read of the legacy data may be the only way to do refreshment. But as a general-purpose strategy, shops discover that repeated and direct reads of the legacy data is a very costly way to go. The expense of direct legacy database reads mounts in two ways. The first expense in directly reading the legacy data is that the legacy DBMS must be online and active during the read process. The window of opportunity for lengthy sequential processing for the legacy environment is always limited. Stretching the window for the purpose of refreshing the data warehouse is never welcome. The second reason is that the same legacy data is needlessly passed many times. The refreshment scan must process 100 percent of a legacy file when only 1 percent or 2 percent of the legacy file is actually needed. This gross waste of resources occurs each time the refreshment process is done. Because of these inefficiencies, repeatedly and directly reading the legacy data for the purpose of refreshment is a strategy that has limited usefulness and applicability.

A much more appealing approach to refreshment of the data warehouse is that of trapping the data in the legacy environment as it is being updated. By trapping the data as update is occurring, there is no need to do full table scans of the legacy environment when it comes time to refresh the data warehouse. In addition, since the data can be trapped as it is being updated, there is no need to have the legacy DBMS online for the purpose of a long sequential scan. Instead, the trapped data can be processed offline.

There are two basic techniques for the trapping of data as update is occurring in the legacy operational environment. One technique is called "data replication." The other technique is called "change data capture," where the changes that have occurred are pulled out of the log or journal tapes that have been created during online update. Each approach has its pros and cons.

Replication requires that the data that is to be trapped be identified prior to the update. Then, as update occurs, the data is trapped. A "trigger" is set that causes the update activity to be captured. One of the advantages of replication is that the process of trapping can be selectively controlled. Only the data that needs to be captured is in fact captured. Another advantage of replication is that the format of the data is "clean" and well defined. The content and structure of the data that has been trapped is well documented and readily understandable to the programmer. The disadvantages of replication are that extra I/O is incurred as a result of trapping the data and that the system requires constant attention to the definition of the parameters and triggers that control trapping at the time of update due to the unstable, ever-changing nature of the data warehouse. The amount of I/O required is usually nontrivial. Furthermore, the I/O that is consumed is taken out of the middle of the high-performance day, at the time when the system can least afford it.

The second approach to the efficient refreshment of the data warehouse environment is through what is termed "changed data capture" (CDC). CDC uses the log tape as a means of capturing and identifying the changes that have occurred throughout the online day. CDC requires that the log or journal tape be read. Reading a log tape is no small matter. There are many obstacles in the way. For instance:

- The log tape contains much extraneous data.
- The log tape format is often arcane.
- The log tape contains spanned records.
- The log tape often contains addresses instead of data values.
- The log tape reflects the idiosyncracies of the DBMS and varies widely from one DBMS to another.

The main obstacle in CDC, then, is that of reading and making sense out of the log tape. But once that obstacle is passed, there are some very attractive benefits to using the log for data warehouse refreshment. The first advantage is that of efficiency.

Log tape processing requires no extra I/O, as does replication processing. The log tape is going to be written regardless of whether it will be used for data warehouse refreshment. Therefore, no incremental I/O is required for log tape CDC processing. The second advantage of CDC is that the log tape captures all update processing. There is no need to go back and redefine parameters when there is a change made either to the data warehouse or to the legacy systems environment. The log tape is as basic and stable as you can get.

The progression described here mimics the mindset of organizations as they mature in their understanding and operation of data warehouse. First the organization reads legacy databases directly in order to refresh its data warehouse. Then it tries replication. Finally, the economics and the efficiencies of operation lead them to CDC as the primary means to refresh the data warehouse. Along the way it is discovered that a few files require a direct read. Other files work best with replication. But for industrial-strength, full-bore, general-purpose data warehouse refreshment, CDC looms as the long-term final approach to data warehouse refreshment.

## SUMMARY

There are some technological features that are required for satisfactory data warehouse processing. These technological features include a robust language interface, the support of compound keys and variable-length data, and the abilities to:

- manage large amounts of data
- manage data on a diverse media
- easily index and monitor data
- interface with a wide number of technologies
- allow the programmer to place the data directly on the physical device
- store and access data in parallel
- have metadata control of the warehouse
- efficiently load the warehouse

- efficiently use indexes
- store data in a compact way
- selectively turn off the lock manager
- do index-only processing
- quickly restore from bulk storage

# The Distributed
# Data Warehouse

Most organizations build and maintain a single centralized data warehouse environment. There are many reasons why a single centralized data warehouse environment makes sense.

- The data in the warehouse is integrated across the corporation, and it is only at headquarters that an integrated view is used.
- The volume of data in the data warehouse is such that a single centralized repository of data makes sense.
- Even if data could be integrated, if it were dispersed across multiple local sites, it would be cumbersome to access.

In short, the politics, the economics, and the technology greatly favor a single centralized data warehouse. But there is a need for a distributed data warehouse in a few special cases.

## THE DISTRIBUTED DATA WAREHOUSE

To understand when a distributed data warehouse makes sense, consider some basic topologies of processing. Figure 6.1 shows a very common processing topology.

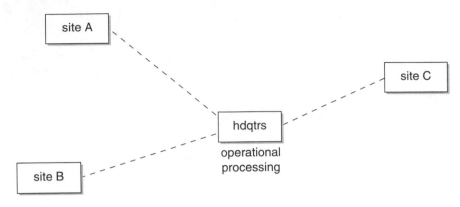

**Figure 6.1** A topology of processing representative of many enterprises.

Figure 6.1 shows that an organization has a headquarters and that all processing is done at the headquarters. If there is any processing done whatsoever at the local level, it is very basic. There might be a series of dumb terminals at the local level. But no significant processing is done locally. In this type of topology it is very unlikely that there will be a need for a distributed data warehouse.

One step up the ladder in terms of local processing sophistication is the case where basic capture activity occurs at the local level, as shown in Figure 6.2.

In Figure 6.2, there is some small amount of processing activity that occurs at the local level. Once the activity is captured, it is shipped to a central location for processing. Under this simple topology it is very unlikely that there will be a need for a distributed data warehouse.

Now, contrast the processing topology shown in Figure 6.3 with the previous two. In Figure 6.3, there is a fair amount of processing that occurs at the local level. As far as operational processing is concerned, the local sites are autonomous. Only on occasion and for certain types of processing will data and activities be sent to the central organization. It is for this type of organization that some form of distributed data warehouse makes sense.

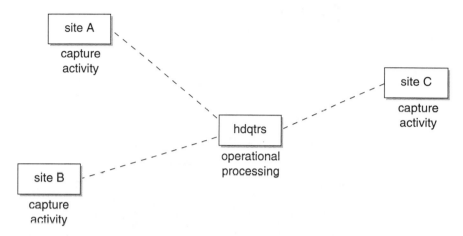

**Figure 6.2**   In some cases, very basic activity is done at the site level.

There is more than one type of distributed data warehouse, as shall be discussed. It is a mistake to think that the distributed data warehouse is a binary proposition. Instead, there are degrees of distributed data warehouse.

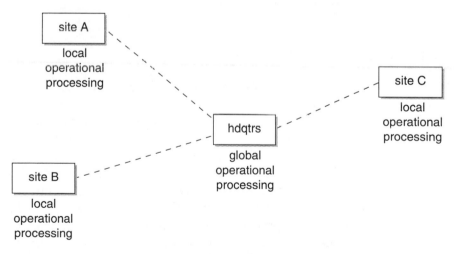

**Figure 6.3**   At the other end of the spectrum of distributed data warehouse much of the operational processing is done locally.

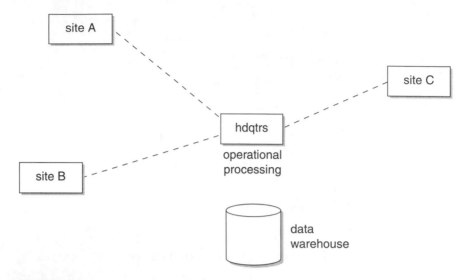

**Figure 6.4** Most organizations have a centrally controlled, centrally housed data warehouse.

Most organizations that do not have a great deal of local autonomy and processing have a central data warehouse, as shown in Figure 6.4.

## THE LOCAL DATA WAREHOUSE

There is a form of data warehouse known as a local data warehouse. The local data warehouse contains data that is of interest only to the local level. Figure 6.5 shows a simple example of a series of local data warehouses.

In Figure 6.5, there is a local data warehouse for different geographical regions or for different technical communities. The local data warehouse serves the same function that any other data warehouse serves, except the scope of the data warehouse is local. In other words, the local data warehouse contains data that is historical in nature and is integrated within the local site. There is no coordination of data or structure of data from one local data warehouse to another.

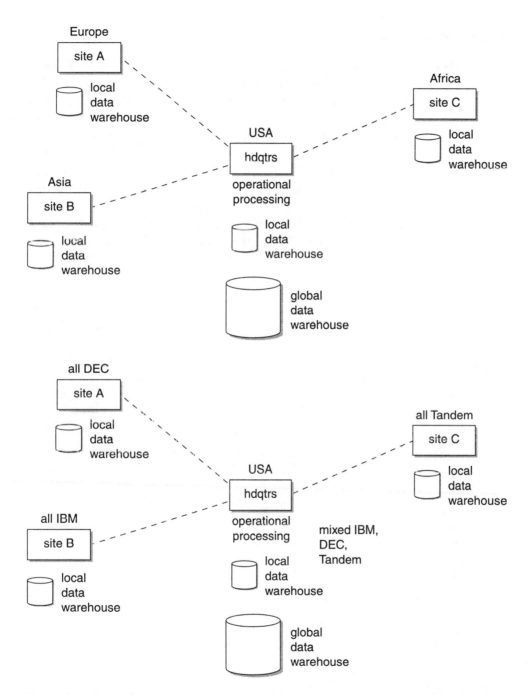

**Figure 6.5**   Some circumstances where you might want to create a two-tiered level of data warehouse.

## THE GLOBAL DATA WAREHOUSE

Of course, there can also be a global data warehouse, as shown in Figure 6.6. The global data warehouse has as its scope the corporation or the enterprise. Each of the local data warehouses within it has as its scope the local site that it serves. The scope of the global data warehouse is the corporation. The global data warehouse contains historical data as do the local data warehouses. The source of the data for the local data warehouses is shown in Figure 6.7, where we see that each local data warehouse is fed by its own operational systems.

An interesting issue is that of commonality of data among the different local data warehouses. Figure 6.8 shows that each

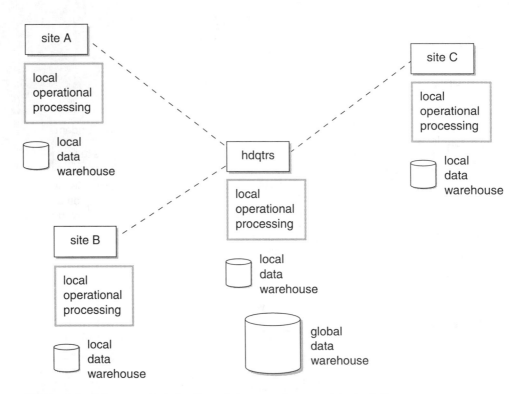

**Figure 6.6**  What a typical distributed data warehouse might look like.

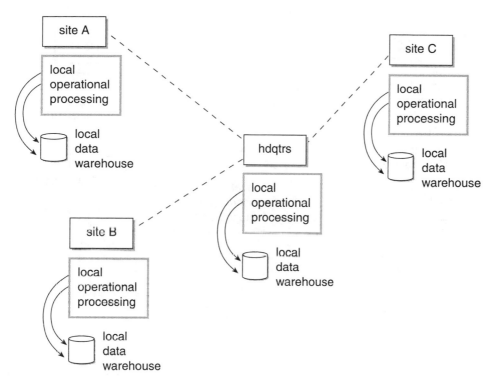

**Figure 6.7**   The flow of data from the local operational environment to the local data warehouse.

local data warehouse has its own unique structure and content of data.

Any intersection or commonality of data from one local data warehouse to another is purely coincidental. There is no coordination whatsoever of data or processing between the local data warehouses shown in Figure 6.8.

But it is reasonable to assume that a corporation will have at least some natural intersections of data from one local site to another. If there is such an intersection, it is best contained in a global data warehouse. Figure 6.9 shows that the global data warehouse is fed from existing local operational systems.

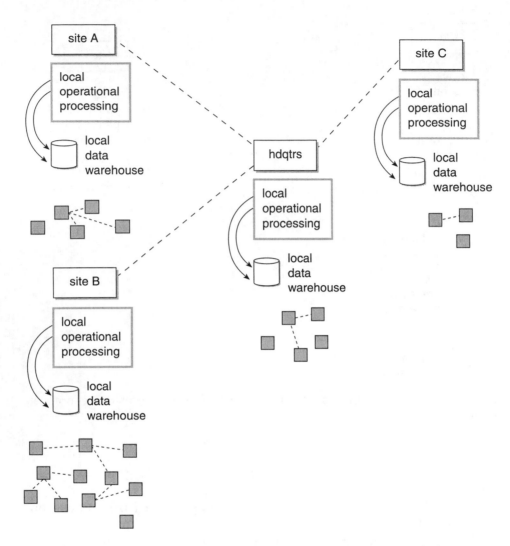

**Figure 6.8** The structure and content of the local data warehouses are very different.

## MUTUAL EXCLUSIVITY OF DATA

Not shown, but implicit in Figure 6.9, is the assumption that any data in the local data warehouse is not found in the global data warehouse, and vice versa. For this reason, it is not necessary to feed the global data warehouse from the local data warehouses.

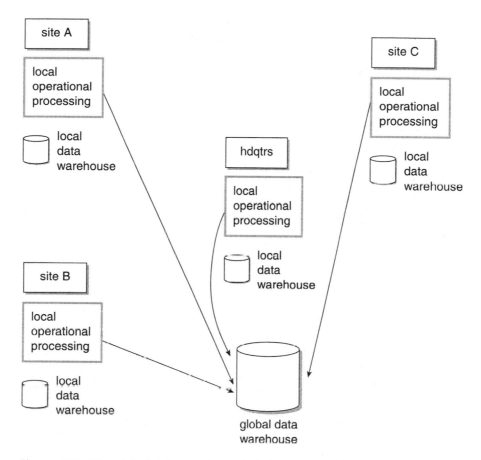

**Figure 6.9**   The global data warehouse is fed by the outlying operational systems.

The global data warehouse contains data that is common across the corporation and data that is integrated. Central to the success of the distributed data warehouse environment is the mapping of data from the local operational systems to the data structure of the global data warehouse, as seen in Figure 6.10.

Figure 6.10 shows that there is a common structure of data for the global data warehouse. The common data structure encompasses all common data across the corporation. But there is a different mapping of data from each local site into the global data warehouse. In other words, the global data warehouse is

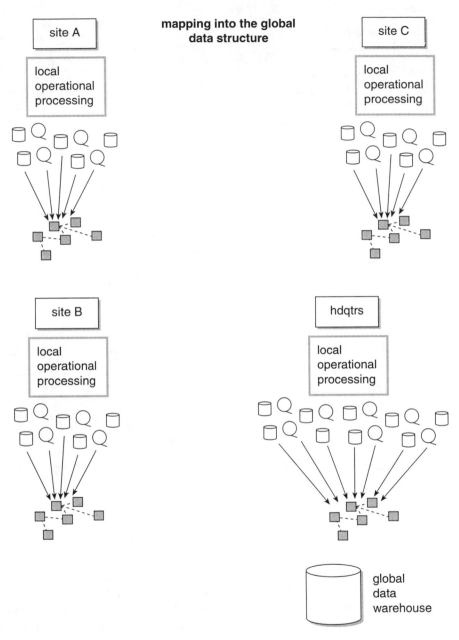

**Figure 6.10** There is a common structure for the global data warehouse. Each local site maps into the common structure differently.

designed and defined centrally, but the mapping of the data from existing local operational systems is a choice made by the local designer and developer.

It is entirely likely that the mapping from local operational systems into global data warehouse systems will not be done as precisely as possible the first time. But over time, as feedback from the user is accumulated, the mapping at the local level improves.

A variation of the data warehouse is that of allowing global data warehouse "staging" areas to be kept at the local level. Figure 6.11 shows that each local area stages global warehouse data before passing the data to the central location. In many circumstances, this approach may be technologically mandatory. There is an important issue associated with this approach— should the locally staged global data warehouse be emptied after it is transferred to the global level? If the data is not deleted locally, then there will be redundant data. However, under certain conditions, some amount of redundancy may be called for. This issue must be decided and policies and procedures put into place.

There are many subject areas that may be candidates for the first global data warehouse development effort. The area that many corporations begin with is corporate finance. Finance is a good starting point because:

- It is relatively stable.
- It enjoys high visibility.
- It is only a fraction of the business of the organization (except, of course, for organizations whose business is finance).
- It entails only a modicum of data.

When building the global data warehouse one must recognize that there are some anomalies. The global data warehouse does not fit the classical structure of a data warehouse as far as the levels of data are concerned. One of the anomalies is that the detailed data resides at the local level, while the lightly summarized data resides at the centralized global level. For example, suppose that the headquarters of a company is in New York and that there are outlying offices in Texas, California, and Illinois.

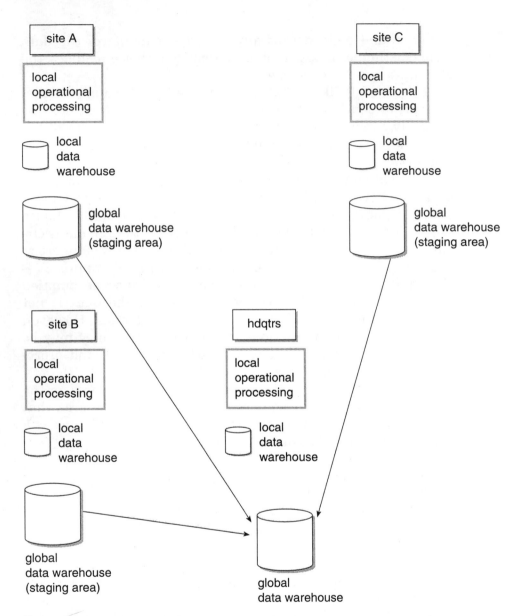

**Figure 6.11** There is the possibility of staging the global data warehouse at the local level, then passing it to the global data warehouse at the headquarters level.

The details of sales and finance are managed independently and at a detailed level in Texas, California, and Illinois. The data model is passed to the outlying regions and the needed corporate data is translated into the form that is necessary to achieve integration across the corporation. Upon having made the translation at the local level, the data is transmitted to New York. The raw, untranslated detail still resides at the local level. Only the transformed, lightly summarized data is passed to headquarters. This is a variation on the theme of the classical data warehouse structure.

## REDUNDANCY

In conjunction with the issue of redundancy of data arises the issue of redundancy between local data warehouses and global data warehouses. Figure 6.12 shows that, as a policy, there is no redundant data between the local levels and the global levels of data (and in this regard, it matters not whether global data is stored locally in a staging area or centrally). The minute there exists redundant data between the local data warehouse and the global data warehouse, it is an indication that the scope of

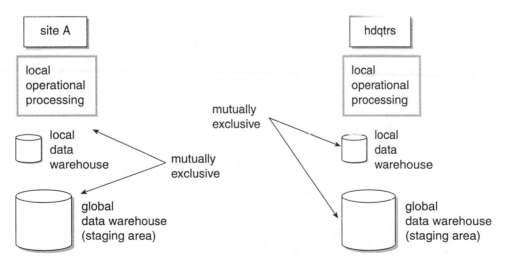

**Figure 6.12** Data can exist in either the local data warehouse or the global data warehouse, but not both.

the different warehouses has not been defined properly. And when there is a difference of opinion between the local and global scopes, it is only a matter of time before spider web systems start to appear. For this reason, it should be a matter of policy that global data and local data be mutually exclusive.

## ACCESS OF GLOBAL DATA

In line with policies required to manage the different data warehouses, there is the issue of access of data. At first, this issue seems to be almost trivial. But there are some important ramifications.

Figure 6.13 shows that some local sites are accessing global data. Depending upon what is being asked for, this may or may not be an appropriate usage of data warehouse data. If the global data is being used informationally and on a onetime-only basis, then its access at the local level is probably alright.

As a principle, local data should be used locally and global data should be used globally. The question must be raised, *why is global analysis being done locally?* As a rule, there is no good reason for it.

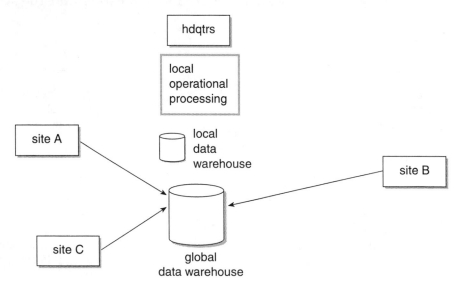

**Figure 6.13** An important issue that needs resolution is whether local sites should be accessing the global data warehouse.

Another issue is that of the routing of requests for information into the architected information environment. When there was only a single central data warehouse, there was little issue over where a request for information was routed. But when data is distributed over a complex landscape, such as a distributed data warehouse landscape, as shown in Figure 6.14, then there is some amount of work required to make sure the request is being addressed at the appropriate place.

For example, asking a local site to determine what total corporate salaries are is an incorrect thing to do. By the same token, asking the central data warehouse group what a contractor was paid last month at a particular site for a particular service is likewise an inappropriate thing to do.

A related yet separate issue not addressed in this chapter is that of global operational data. This chapter has taken the stance that every local site will have its own unique data and processing. But it is entirely possible that there will be a degree of commonality between the operational systems found at each local site.

Underlying the whole issue of distributed data warehouse is the issue of complexity. In a simple central data warehouse environment, roles and responsibilities are fairly straightforward. But in a distributed data warehouse environment, the issues of scope, coordination, metadata, responsibilities, transfer of data, local mapping, and so on, make the environment complex indeed.

## OTHER DISTRIBUTED CONSIDERATIONS

The spread of a company over multiple locations is not the only appeal of a distributed data warehouse. There are other rationales as well. One case for a distributed warehouse is that of placing a data warehouse on the technology of a vendor that is distributed. Client/server technology fits this requirement nicely.

The first question is, *can a data warehouse be placed on distributed technology?* The answer is yes. The next question is, *what are the advantages and disadvantages of using distributed technology for a data warehouse?* The first advantage of a distributed data warehouse is that the entry cost is cheap. In other words, the cost of hardware and software for a data warehouse

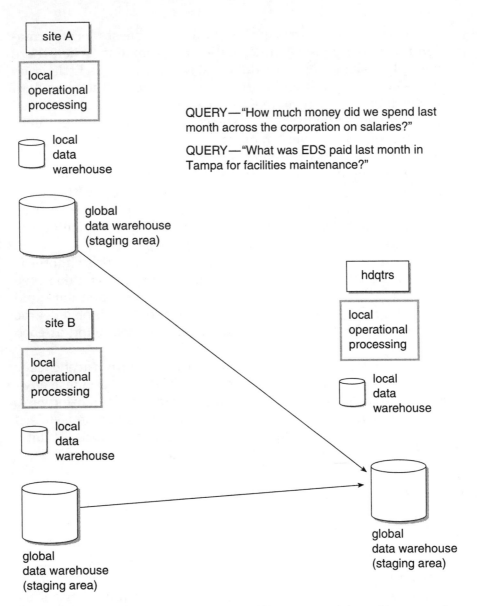

QUERY—"How much money did we spend last month across the corporation on salaries?"

QUERY—"What was EDS paid last month in Tampa for facilities maintenance?"

**Figure 6.14** Queries need to be routed to different parts of the architecture to be properly answered.

when initially loaded onto distributed technology is much less than if the data warehouse were initially loaded onto classical large, centralized hardware. The second advantage of using distributed technology for a data warehouse is that there is no theoretical limit to how much data can be placed in the data warehouse. If the volume of data inside the warehouse begins to exceed the limit of a distributed processor, then another processor can be added to the network and the progression of adding data continues in an unimpeded fashion.

The progression shown in Figure 6.15 depicts a world in which there may be an infinite amount of data in the data warehouse. This is appealing because a data warehouse will contain much data (but not an infinite amount!).

There are however, some considerations. As the data warehouse starts to expand beyond a few processors (i.e., servers), there starts to appear an excessive amount of traffic on the network. Figure 6.16 shows this effect.

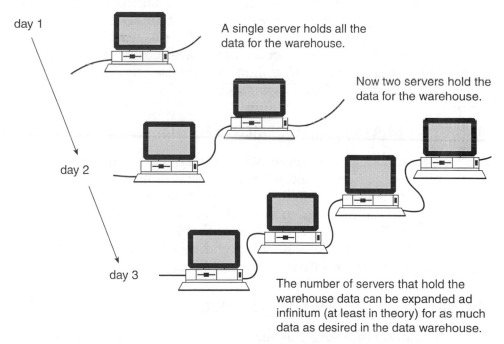

day 1

A single server holds all the data for the warehouse.

Now two servers hold the data for the warehouse.

day 2

day 3

The number of servers that hold the warehouse data can be expanded ad infinitum (at least in theory) for as much data as desired in the data warehouse.

**Figure 6.15**   The progression of adding more servers to hold the data warehouse data.

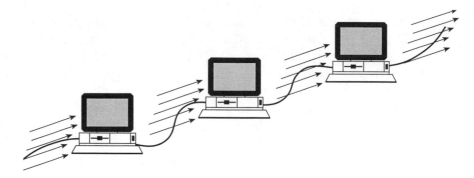

**Figure 6.16** Excessive network traffic starts to appear when the warehouse is spread over multiple servers.

In addition, when data is spread over multiple servers, there is a problem when a query needs to access a large amount of data from more than one server. Figure 6.17 depicts a query that wishes to access a large amount of data from multiple servers.

There are of course, techniques and approaches to deal with a data warehouse that is distributed over multiple servers. Ironically, the problems grow with time, as the warehouse becomes fully populated. In the early days of a distributed data warehouse, the problems discussed here are hardly obvious. In the more mature days of a data warehouse, however, the data becomes more difficult to manage.

## MANAGING MULTIPLE DEVELOPMENT EFFORTS

The first step many corporations take in data warehousing is to put up a data warehouse for a financial or marketing organization. Once success follows the initial warehouse effort, other parts of the corporation naturally desire to build upon the successful first effort. In short order the data warehouse architect has the problem of managing and coordinating multiple data warehouse efforts within the organization.

## THE NATURE OF THE DEVELOPMENT EFFORTS

The first issue facing the data architect who must manage multiple data warehouse development efforts is that of the nature of

data
warehouse

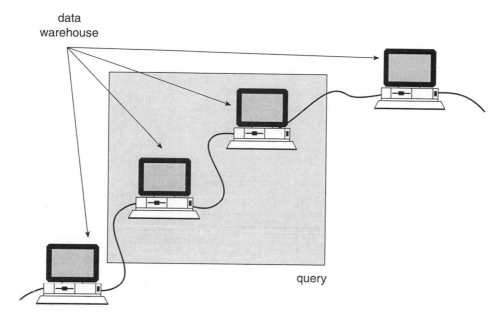

query

**Figure 6.17** A query that accesses a large amount of data from multiple data warehouse servers.

the development efforts. Unless the data architect knows what kinds of data warehouse development efforts are occurring and how they relate to the overall architecture, he or she will have a *very* difficult time managing and coordinating those efforts. Different types of data warehouse development efforts require very different approaches to management because the issues of development are very different, depending upon the approach.

There are four typical cases where multiple data warehouse development efforts occur. These cases are outlined in Figure 6.18.

In the first, rare case shown in Figure 6.18, a business has totally separate and unintegrated lines for which data warehouses are being independently built by different development groups. The diverse lines of business report to the corporation, but other than sharing a company name there is no business integration or sharing of data within the company. Such a corporate structure is not unknown, but is not common. In this rare case—where there is no business integration whatsoever—there is very little danger that one data warehouse development effort

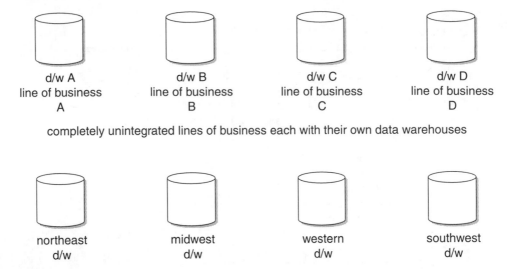

completely unintegrated lines of business each with their own data warehouses

the same data warehouse but with distributed parts

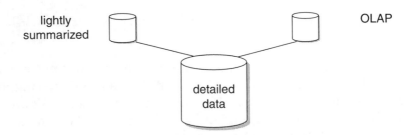

different levels of data within the same data warehouse

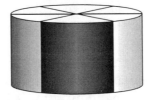

different non-distributed parts of the detailed level of the data warehouse

**Figure 6.18** Four possible meanings to—"multiple groups building the data warehouse"—each interpretation is *very* different from the other interpretations.

will conflict with another. Accordingly, there is little or no need for cross management and coordination of data warehouse development efforts.

The second case of multiple data warehouse efforts occurring simultaneously happens where a corporate distributed data warehouse is being built and various development groups are creating different parts of the same data warehouse. In this case the same level of data is being built by different groups of developers, but the level of data being built is distributed across different locations. This case is as common as the previous case is rare. This case requires close coordination among the groups and discipline in order to achieve a collectively satisfying result. The danger of not coordinating this effort is that much waste may occur through redundant storage and manipulation of massive amounts of data. If data is created redundantly, the resulting data warehouse may well be ineffective because there will be a classical "spider's web" in the DSS environment. Because this case is so common, it requires a great deal of attention.

The third case of multiple data warehouse development occurring simultaneously occurs when different groups are building different levels of data (i.e., summarized data and detailed data) in the data warehouse environment. This is also very common. For a variety of reasons this case is much easier to manage than either of the two previous cases mentioned.

The fourth case occurs when multiple groups are trying to build different parts of the current level of detail of the data warehouse environment in a nondistributed manner. This is a somewhat rare phenomenon, but when it occurs, it *mandates* special attention. There is much at stake in this last case and the data architect must be aware of what the issues are and how they relate to success.

Each of these cases will be discussed separately, along with their issues, advantages, and disadvantages.

## Completely Unrelated Warehouses

The building and operation of completely unrelated warehouses is shown in Figure 6.19. A corporation has four lines of business—golf course management, a steel mill, retail banking, and

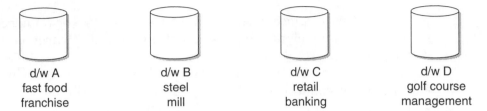

**Figure 6.19** Four totally independent enterprises where there is little or no integration of data at the business level.

a fast-food franchise. There is no integration of the businesses whatsoever. The ongoing data warehouse efforts have no reason to be coordinated. All the way from modeling to selection of base technology (i.e., platform, DBMS, access tools, development tools, etc.), each of the different businesses could operate as if it were completely autonomous.

For all the autonomy of the lines of business, there is one level at which they are, of necessity, integrated; the financial balance sheet. If the different lines of business report to a single financial entity, then there must be integration at the balance sheet level. There may well be a need to build a corporate data warehouse that reflects the corporate finances. Figure 6.20 shows a corporate financial data warehouse sitting above the different businesses.

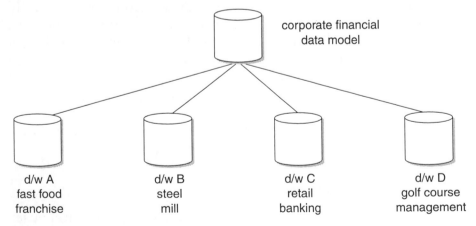

**Figure 6.20** There is common corporate financial data across even the most disparate of business enterprises.

The financial corporate data warehouse contains simple (and abstract) entities such as expenses, revenues, capital expenditures, depreciation, and the like. There is very little, if any, business data beyond that found on every balance sheet. (In other words, there is no attempt at a common corporate description of customer, product, sale, etc. in the financial data warehouse.) Of course, the data feeding the corporate financial data warehouse depicted in Figure 6.20 may come either from the "local" data warehouse or from the operational systems found at the individual operating company level.

There is a real need for metadata at the local level. There is also a need for metadata if there is a corporate financial data warehouse, at the corporate financial level. But in this case there is no real need to tie any of the metadata together.

## THE DISTRIBUTED DATA WAREHOUSE

Unlike the case of the unrelated warehouses, most businesses have some degree of integration between their disparate parts. Very few businesses are as autonomous as depicted in Figure 6.20. A much more common scenario for the development of multiple data warehouse efforts is shown in Figure 6.21.

In Figure 6.21 a corporation has different sites in different parts of the world. There is one organizational entity in the United States and Canada, another in South America, one in the Far East, and finally one in Africa. Each site has its own unique data. There is no overlap of data—particularly of detailed transaction data—from one site to the next. The company desires to create a data warehouse for each of the disparate companies as a

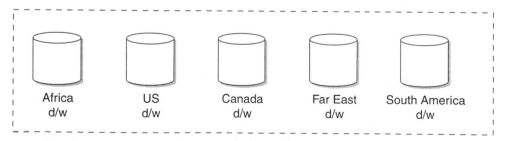

**Figure 6.21**  Logically the same data warehouse.

first effort in achieving an architected environment. There is some degree of business integration among the different organizations. At the same time it is assumed that there are different business practices carried on in each locale that are distinct and unique to that locale. Such an organization of corporate entities is common to many companies.

The first step many organizations make toward data warehousing is to create a "local" data warehouse at each geographical entity. Figure 6.22 shows the creation of a local data warehouse.

Each locale builds its own unique autonomous data warehouse according to its needs. It is noteworthy that there is *no* redundant *detailed data* among the different locales, at least as far as transaction data is concerned. In other words, a unit of data reflecting transactions that belongs in Africa would never be found in the "local" data warehouse for Europe.

There are several pros and cons to this approach to building the distributed corporate data warehouse. One advantage is that it is quick to accomplish. Each local group has control over its design and resources. There is the feel of autonomy and control that makes each local organization happy. As such the benefits of the data warehouse can be proven throughout the corporation on a real-time basis. Within six months the local data warehouses can be up and running and the organization at

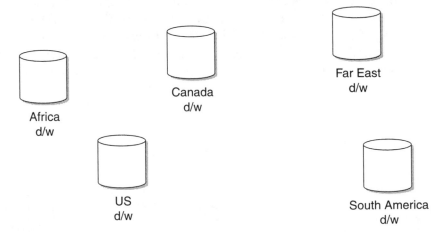

**Figure 6.22** Local data warehouses are built at each of the autonomous operating divisions.

the local level can be deriving the benefits. The disadvantage is that if there is any commonality in the structure (not the content) of data across the organization, this approach does nothing to recognize or rationalize that commonality.

## Coordinating Development Across Distributed Locations

An alternative approach is to try to coordinate the local data warehouse development efforts across the different local organizations. This sounds good in theory, but in execution it has not proved to be effective. The local development groups never collectively move at the same pace, and the local groups look on the central development group trying to coordinate the many local development efforts as a hindrance to progress. A separate data model is built to provide the foundation of the data warehouse design for each of the separate locales.

One day, after the worth of data warehousing has been proven at the local level, the corporation decides to build a corporate data warehouse (Figure 6.23). The corporate data ware-

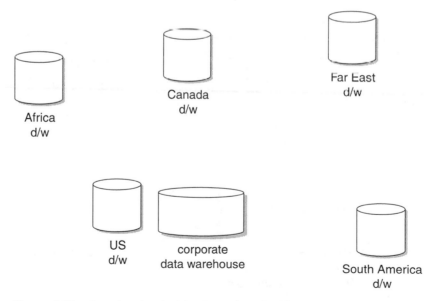

**Figure 6.23**   One day the decision is made to build a corporate data warehouse.

house will reflect the business integration across the different divisions and locales. The corporate data warehouse will be related to, but still distinct from, the local data warehouses. The first step in building the corporate data warehouse is to create a corporate data model for that portion of the business that will be reflected in the corporate data warehouse. As a general rule, the corporate data model that is built for the first iteration of the corporate data warehouse will be small and simple, and will be limited to a subset of the business. Figure 6.24 illustrates the building of the corporate data model after which the corporate data warehouse will be shaped.

### The Corporate Data Model-Distributed

The corporate data model reflects the integration of business at the corporate level. As such the corporate data model may overlap considerably with portions of the local data models. Such an overlap is healthy and normal. In other cases the corporate data

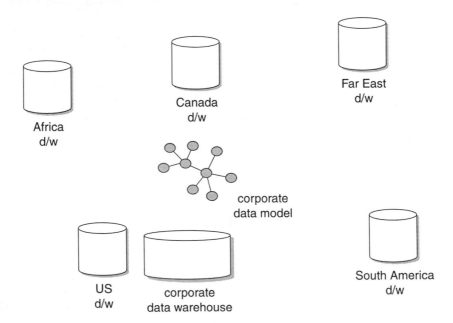

**Figure 6.24**  The corporate data model is created.

model will be different from the local data models. In any case, it is up to the local organization to determine how the fit is to be made between the corporate need for data and the local ability to provide it. The local organization knows their own data better than anyone and they are best equipped to show how local data needs to be shaped and reshaped in order to meet the specifications of the corporate design of data for the data warehouse.

While there may very well be overlap in the structural design of data from one local level to the next, there is no overlap to any great extent in the content of data. Figure 6.25 shows the building and population of the corporate data warehouse from the local levels.

The source of the data going to the corporate data warehouse

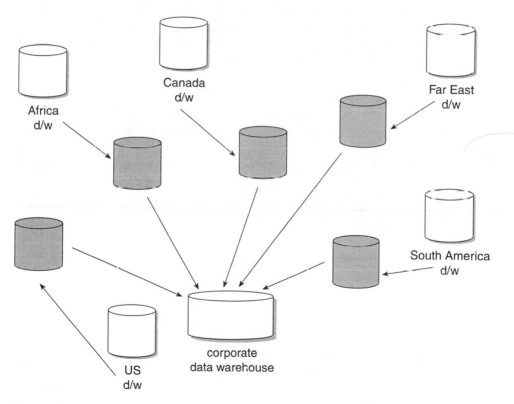

**Figure 6.25** The corporate data warehouse is loaded from the different autonomous operating companies.

can come from the local data warehouse or from the local operational systems. The determination of the system of record should be a decision that is made entirely at the local level. Most certainly several iterations of definition of the system of record will be needed.

In addition, an important design issue is how to create and transport the local system of record data from the technology found at the local level into the technology of the corporate data warehouse. In some cases the official "staged" data is kept at the local level. In other cases the staged data is passed on to the corporate environment with no access at the local level.

As a rule the data in the corporate data warehouse is simple in structure and concept. Figure 6.26 shows that data in the corporate data warehouse appears to be detailed data to the DSS analyst at the corporate level, and at the same time appears to be summary data to the DSS analyst at the local level. This apparent contradiction is reconciled by the fact that the appearance of summarization or of detail is strictly in the eyes of the beholder.

The corporate data warehouse of the distributed database can be contrasted with the corporate financial data warehouse of the completely unrelated companies. Figure 6.27 makes this comparison.

In many ways the data warehouse of the distributed corpo-

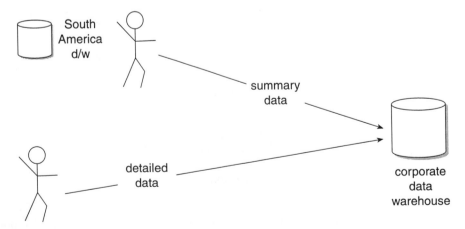

**Figure 6.26** What is summary at one level is detailed at another.

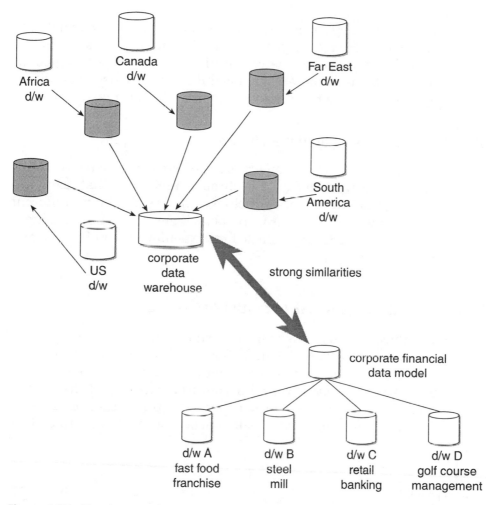

**Figure 6.27**   The data warehouse of a distributed corporation can be very similar to that of unrelated companies.

ration is very similar to the data warehouse of the unrelated companies. There are similarities in design and operation. There is one major difference, however. The corporate distributed data warehouse extends into the business itself, reflecting the integration of customer, vendor, product, and so forth. As such, the corporate distributed data warehouse represents the very fabric of the business itself. However, the corporate data warehouse for unrelated companies is for finance alone. The instant that there is a desire to use the corporate financial data warehouse for anything other than the financial relationship of the different parts of the corporation there will be disappointment with the corporate financial data warehouse. The difference between the two data warehouses, then, is one of *depth*.

### Metadata in the Distributed Warehouse

Metadata plays a very important role across the distributed corporate data warehouse. It is through metadata that coordination of structure of data is achieved across the many different locations where the data warehouse is found. Not surprisingly, metadata provides the vehicle for the achievement of uniformity and consistency.

## BUILDING THE WAREHOUSE ON MULTIPLE LEVELS

The third scenario of a company's simultaneous data warehouse development occurs when different development groups are building different levels of the data warehouse, as seen in Figure 6.28. This case is very different from the case of the distributed data warehouse development. In this case, Group A is building the high level of summarization of data, Group B is

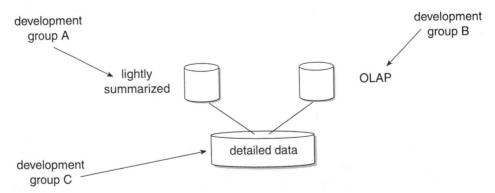

**Figure 6.28** Different development groups are developing different parts of the data warehouse environment at different levels of the architecture.

building the middle level of summarization, and Group C is building the current level of detail.

The scenario of multiple levels of data warehouse development is very common. Fortunately, it is the easiest scenario to manage, with the fewest risks. The primary concern of the data architect is that of coordinating the efforts of the different development teams, both in terms of the specification of content and structure, and in terms of timing of development. For example, if Group A is significantly ahead of Group B or C, then there is going to be a problem because when Group A is ready to populate their databases at the summary level, there may be no detailed data for them to work with.

One of the interesting aspects of different groups building different levels of summarization of the same data warehouse is that it is the group that is building the current level of detail that uses the data warehouse data model. Figure 6.29 illustrates this relationship.

The data model for the data warehouse directly reflects the design and development effort by the group doing current level detailed analysis and design. Of course, indirectly the data warehouse data model reflects the needs of *all* groups. But since other groups are summarizing off of the data found at the cur-

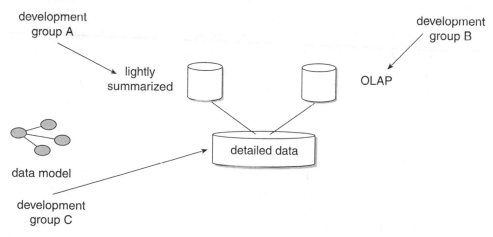

**Figure 6.29** The development organization that is developing the lowest level of detail is the organization that uses the data model.

rent level of detail, they have their own interpretation of what is needed. In most cases, the groups working on the higher levels of summarization have their own data models that reflect their own specialized needs.

One of the issues of managing multiple groups building different levels of summarization in the data warehouse is that of the technological platforms on which the data warehouse levels are built. It is normal for the different groups to choose different technological platforms. In fact, it is very unusual for the different development groups to choose the same platform. There are several reasons for this. The primary reason is that of cost. The detailed level of data requires an industrial-strength platform because of the large volume of data that will have to be handled. The different levels of summarization will require much less data, especially at the higher levels of summarization. It is overkill (and expensive) to place the higher levels of summarized data on the same platform as the detailed data (although it can be done).

Another reason why various levels of summarization within the data warehouse are often placed on other technological platforms than the platform the detailed data is on is that the alternative platforms offer a wide variety of specialized software, much of which is not to be found on the monolithic platforms that house detailed data. In any case, whether the different levels of data are on a single platform or on multiple platforms, it is mandatory that metadata be carefully stored and managed, so that continuity from one level of detail to the next can be maintained.

Because different platforms are commonly used for the different levels of data in a data warehouse that are being developed by different groups, the issue of interconnectivity arises. Figure 6.30 shows the need for interconnectivity from one level to the next.

There are several aspects to interconnectivity that need to be addressed. One issue is that of compatibility of access at the *call* level. In other words, is there compatible syntax between the two technologies that make up the detailed and the summary data between any two levels of the warehouse? If there is not at least some degree of compatibility of call level syntax, then there is a

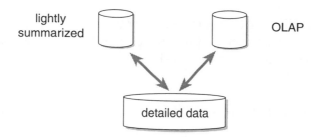

**Figure 6.30**  Interconnectivity between the different levels of the data warehouse is an important issue.

problem with usability of the interface. Another aspect of the interconnectivity issue is the effective bandwidth of the interface. If there is very heavy traffic being created by processing that occurs on either level of the data warehouse, then the interface between the two environments can become a bottleneck.

However the groups that work on the data warehouse are coordinated, there needs to be an assurance that the group that manages the lower level detail will form a proper foundation of data for those groups that will be summarizing the data and creating a new level. This need is depicted in Figure 6.31.

The coordination between the groups can be as simple as an agreement on a data model that satisfies the needs of all parties. Or the agreement can be much more elaborate, if circumstances warrant.

The coordination of the development efforts is another matter. There needs to be a time-sequenced arrangement between

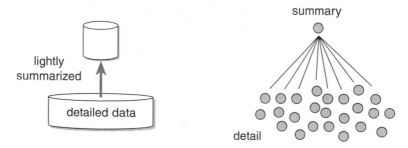

**Figure 6.31**  The detailed level forms the foundation for the summary level of data.

the different development groups so that no one development group will arrive at a point of needing data that has not yet been gathered at a lower level.

## MULTIPLE GROUPS BUILDING THE CURRENT LEVEL OF DETAIL

An infrequent set of circumstances occurs when multiple development groups attempt to build the current level of detail in a data warehouse in a nondistributed manner. Figure 6.32 illustrates this phenomenon.

As long as the groups that are developing the current level of detail are developing mutually exclusive sets of data, there is little difficulty. In this case, as long as the development groups are working from a common data model and there is technological compatibility among the different groups' platforms, then there is little risk. Unfortunately, it is seldom the case that multiple groups are developing mutually exclusive sets of detailed data warehouse data. It is much more common for the multiple

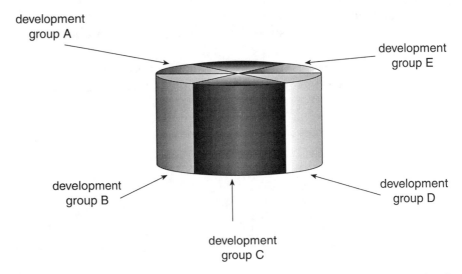

**Figure 6.32** Different development groups that are developing the current level of detail for the data warehouse.

development groups to be designing and populating some or all of the same data, as seen in Figure 6.33.

There are a series of problems that arise when the groups overlap. The first problem is that of cost—in particular the cost of storage and of processing. The volumes of data that are found at the current detailed level are such that *any* amount of redundancy must be questioned, much less wholesale redundancy. The cost of processing the detail is likewise a major issue.

The second, more insidious issue is that of the introduction of the spider's web into the DSS environment. With massive amounts of redundant detailed data, it is almost axiomatic that misinterpretation of data caused by redundancy will occur, where there is no effective reconcilability. So creating large amounts of redundant detailed data is a very undesirable condition for the detailed level of data in the data warehouse, defeating its purpose. *If multiple development groups are going to be doing concurrent design and population in the current level of detail, great care must be taken to ensure that no redundant detailed data will be created.*

In order to ensure that no redundant data is being developed

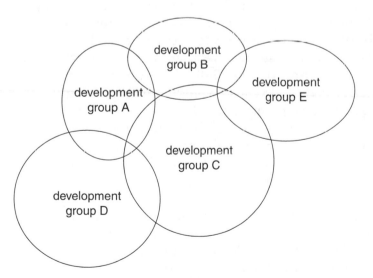

**Figure 6.33**   Overlap between the different development groups insofar as the data that is being developed by the group.

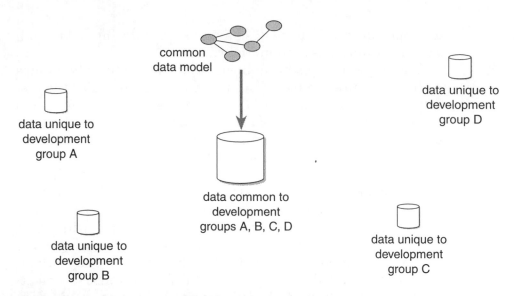

**Figure 6.34** A data model identifies data that is common to all the development groups.

at the detailed level of the data warehouse, it is necessary to create a data model that reflects the common detailed data. Figure 6.34 shows that multiple development groups have combined their interests to create a common data model. In addition to the currently active development groups, other groups that will have future requirements but who are not currently in a development mode may also contribute their requirements. Of course, if a group knows it will have future requirements but is unable to articulate them, then those requirements cannot be factored into the common detailed data model.

The common detailed data model reflects the collective need among the different groups for detailed data in the data warehouse.

The data model forms the basis of the design for the data warehouse. Figure 6.35 shows that the data model will be broken up into many tables as design progresses, each of which physically becomes part of the warehouse.

Because the data model is broken into multiple physical tables at the moment of implementation, the development

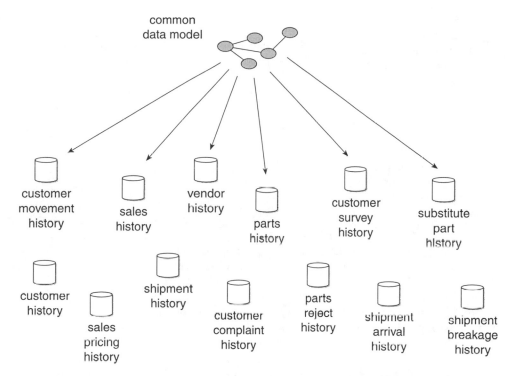

**Figure 6.35** The data warehouse is physically manifested over multiple physical tables and databases.

process for the data warehouse can proceed in an iterative manner. There is no need to build all of the tables at once. In fact, there is good reason to build only a few tables at a time, so that the end user feedback can be factored into the modification of the table if necessary with a minimum of fuss. In addition, because the common data model is broken into multiple tables, adding new tables at a later point in time to reflect requirements that are now unknown is not a problem.

## Different Requirements at Different Levels

It is normal that the different groups have requirements that are unique to them (Figure 6.36). These unique requirements result in what can be termed "local" current level detail. The

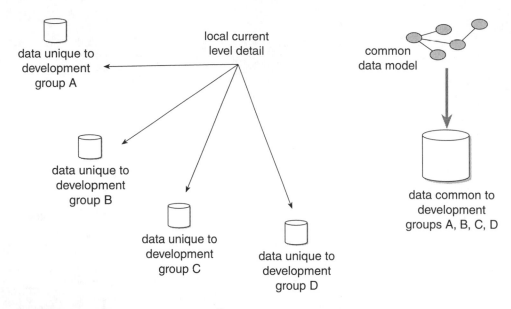

**Figure 6.36** Just because data is not common to all development groups does not mean that it does not belong in the current level detail of the data warehouse.

local data is certainly part of the data warehouse. It is, however, distinctively different from the "common" part. The local data has its own data model, usually much smaller and simpler than the common detailed data model.

There is, of necessity, nonredundancy of data across *all* of the detailed data. Figure 6.37 makes this point clear.

Of course, the nonredundancy of the data is restricted to nonkey data. There *is* redundancy of data at the key level because a form of foreign key relationships is used to relate the different types of data together. Figure 6.38 shows the use of foreign keys that relate the different tables of data together.

The foreign keys that are found in the tables shown in Figure 6.38 are quite different from the classical foreign key relationships that are governed by referential integrity. Because the data in the data warehouse is gathered by and stored in terms of snapshots of data, the foreign key relationships that are found are organized in terms of "artifacts" of relationships. For an in-depth explanation of artifacts of relationships, refer to the Prism Solutions Tech Topic on the subject found in the References.

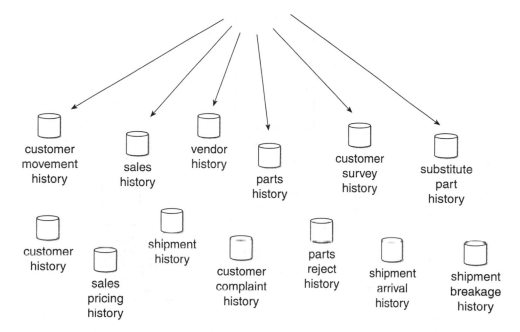

**Figure 6.37**   Nonredundancy of nonkey data throughout the many tables that make up the detailed level of the data warehouse.

An issue that arises is whether to place all of the detailed tables—common and local—under the same technology. Figure 6.39 shows the case where all tables are placed under the same technology. There are many good arguments for placing *all* the detailed data under a single technological platform. One argument is that the cost of a single platform versus multiple platforms is much less. Another argument for a single platform is that the cost of support and training will be less. About the only argument for multiple platforms for detailed data is that with multiple platforms, there may not be the need for a single massively large platform, and as a consequence, the cost of the multiple smaller platforms may be less than a single larger platform. In any case, many organizations adopt the strategy of a single platform for all their detailed data warehouse data and the strategy works well.

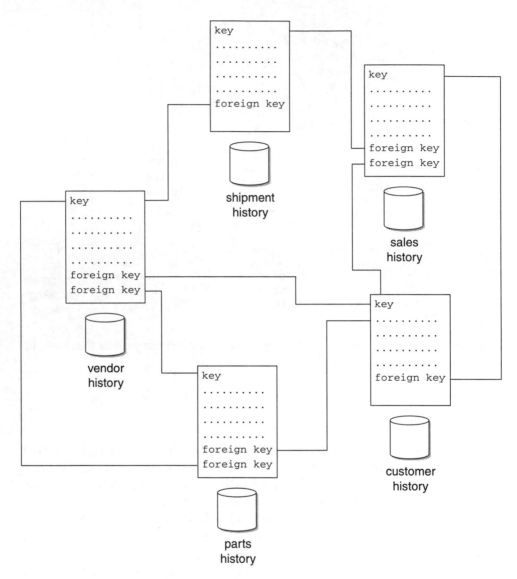

**Figure 6.38** Foreign keys in the data warehouse environment.

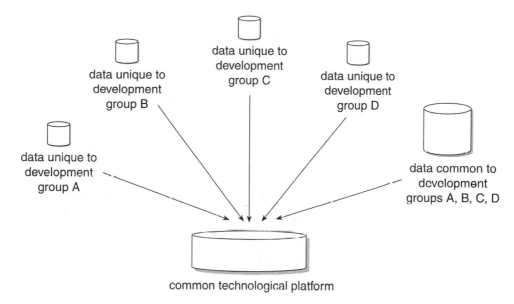

data unique to development group C

data unique to development group B

data unique to development group D

data unique to development group A

data common to development groups A, B, C, D

common technological platform

**Figure 6.39** The different types of data in the detailed level of the data warehouse all on a common platform.

## Other Types of Detailed Data

Another strategy is to use different platforms for the different types of data found at the detailed level. Figure 6.40 shows one example of this option. Some of the local data is on one platform, the common data is on another platform, and yet other local data is on another technological platform. This option is certainly one that is valid, and good for satisfying the different political needs of the organization. With this option each group doing development can feel like it has some degree of control of at least its own peculiar needs. Unfortunately, this option has several major drawbacks. One drawback is that multiple technologies must be purchased and supported. Another is that the end user needs to be trained in different technologies. And finally, the boundaries between the technologies may not be able to be easily crossed. Figure 6.41 illustrates this dilemma.

If there are to be multiple technologies supporting the different levels of detail in the data warehouse, it will be necessary to

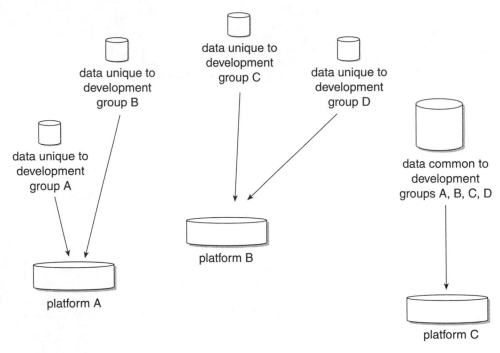

**Figure 6.40** In this case the different parts of the detailed level of the data warehouse are scattered across different technological platforms.

cross the boundaries between the technologies frequently. To that end technology such as IBI's EDA/SQL fits very nicely. Unfortunately, even with an elegant piece of software such as EDA/SQL there are still architectural problems. Some of the problems that remain are shown in Figure 6.42.

One problem is in the passage of data. If the EDA/SQL interface is used for the passage of small amounts of data, then there is no problem with performance. But if EDA/SQL is used for the purpose of passing large amounts of data, then EDA/SQL can become a performance bottleneck. Unfortunately, in a DSS environment it is almost impossible to know how much data will be accessed by any one request. Some requests access very little data; other requests access large amounts of data. This problem

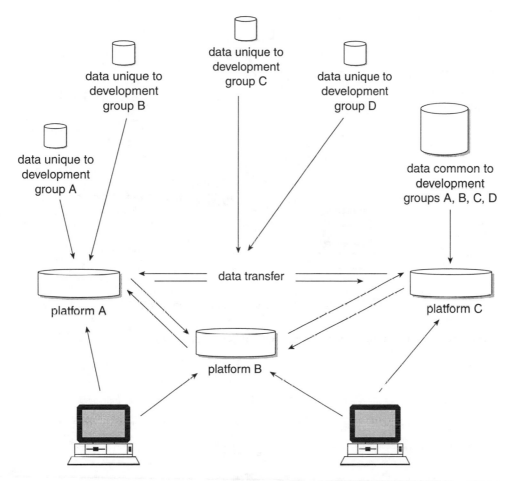

**Figure 6.41**   Data transfer and multiple table queries present special technological problems.

of resource utilization and management manifests itself when detailed data resides on multiple platforms.

Another related problem is that of "leaving" detailed data on one side of the data warehouse after it has been transported from the other side. This casual redeployment of detailed data has the effect of creating redundancy of data at the detailed level, something that is not acceptable.

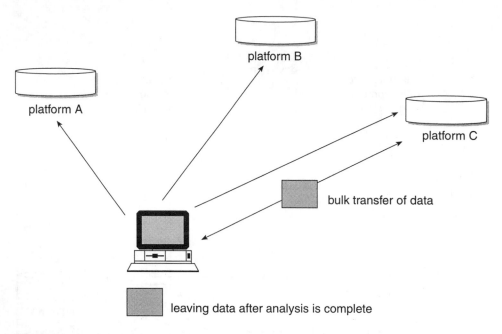

platform B

platform A

platform C

bulk transfer of data

leaving data after analysis is complete

**Figure 6.42** Some problems with interfacing different platforms.

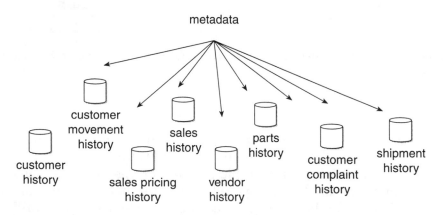

metadata

customer
movement
history

sales
history

parts
history

customer
history

sales pricing
history

vendor
history

customer
complaint
history

shipment
history

**Figure 6.43** Metadata sits on top of the actual data contents of the data warehouse.

## Metadata

In any case, however detailed data is managed, whether on a single technology or on multiple technologies, the role of metadata is not diminished. Figure 6.43 shows that metadata is needed to sit on top of the detailed data warehouse data.

## MULTIPLE PLATFORMS FOR COMMON DETAIL DATA

There is one other possibility that is worth mentioning, and that is the possibility of using multiple platforms for common detail of data. Figure 6.44 outlines this possibility.

But while such a possibility is certainly an option, it is almost never a good choice. It is difficult enough to manage common current detailed data. The volumes of data that are found at that level present their own unique problems for management. Adding the complicating factor of having to cross multiple technological platforms merely makes life more difficult. Unless there are very unusual mitigating circumstances, this option is not recommended.

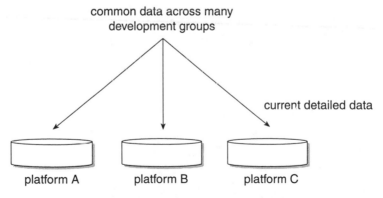

**Figure 6.44** Common detailed data across multiple platforms—a real red flag in *all* cases.

## SUMMARY

Most environments operate from a single centralized data warehouse. But in some circumstances there can be a distributed data warehouse. There may be local data warehouses that house data unique to and of interest to the local operating site. There may also be a globally distributed data warehouse. The structure and content of the distributed global data warehouse are decided centrally. The mapping of data into the global data warehouse is decided locally.

The coordination and administration of the distributed data warehouse environment is much more complex than that of the single-site data warehouse.

# Executive Information Systems and the Data Warehouse

EIS—executive information systems—is one of the most potent forms of computing. Through EIS the executive analyst can pinpoint problems and detect trends that are of vital importance to management. In a sense, EIS represents one of the most sophisticated usages of the computer.

EIS processing is tailored to help the executive make decisions. EIS becomes the executive's window into the corporation. EIS processing looks across broad vistas and picks out the aspects that are relevant to the running of the business. Some of the typical uses of EIS are:

- trend analysis and detection
- key ratio indicator measurement and tracking
- drill-down analysis
- problem monitoring
- competitive analysis

## A SIMPLE EXAMPLE

As an example of how EIS analysis might appear to an executive, consider Figure 7.1, which shows information on policies

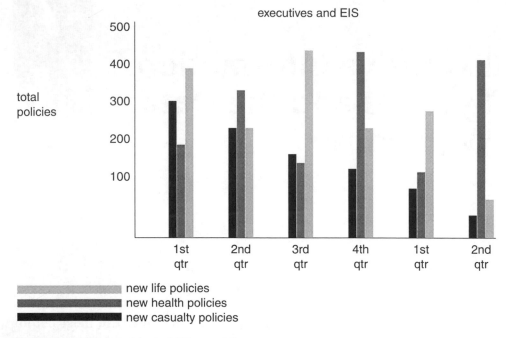

**Figure 7.1** A chart typical of EIS processing.

offered by an insurance company. Quarter by quarter, the new life, health, and casualty policy sales are tracked. The simple graph shown in Figure 7.1 is a good starting point for an executive's probing into the state of the business. Once the executive has seen the overall information, he or she can probe more deeply, as shown by the trend analysis in Figure 7.2.

In Figure 7.2, the executive has isolated new casualty sales from new life sales and new health sales. Looking just at new casualty sales, the executive identifies a trend. Each quarter new casualty sales are dropping off. Having identified the trend, the executive can further investigate why sales are dropping.

The EIS analysis alerts the executive as to what the trends are. It is then up to him or her to discover the underlying reasons for the trends.

The executive is interested in both negative and positive trends. If business is getting worse, why, and at what rate?

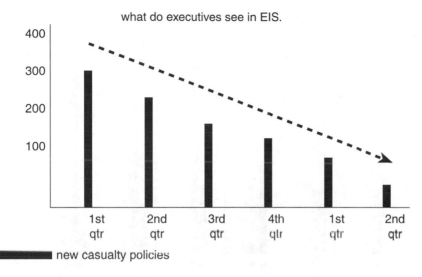

**Figure 7.2** Trends—new casualty policy sales are slacking off.

What can be done to remedy the situation? Or, if business is picking up, are responsible for the upturn? What can be done to accelerate the success factors? Can the success factors be applied in other parts of the business?

But trends are not the only type of analysis that is accommodated by EIS. Another type of useful analysis is that of comparisons. Figure 7.3 shows a comparison that might be found in an EIS analysis.

Looking at fourth-quarter data, first-quarter data, and second-quarter data in Figure 7.3, the question can be asked, *Why is there such a difference in sales of new health policies for the past three quarters?* The EIS processing alerts the manager to these differences. It is then the job of the EIS analyst to determine the underlying reasons.

For the manager of a large, diverse enterprise, EIS allows a look at the activities of the enterprise in many ways. Trying to keep track of a large number of activities is much more difficult than trying to keep track of just a few activities. In that sense, EIS can be used to expand the scope of control of a manager.

But trend analysis and comparisons are not the only means the manager has to use EIS effectively. Another approach is "slice-and-dice." Here the analyst takes basic information and

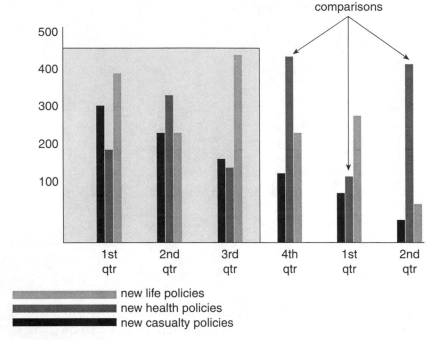

**Figure 7.3** Why is there an extreme difference in sales of new health policies for the past three quarters?

groups it one way and analyzes it, then groups it another way and reanalyzes it. Slicing and dicing allows the manager to have many different perspectives of the activities that are occurring.

## DRILL-DOWN ANALYSIS

In order to do slicing and dicing, it is necessary to be able to "drill down" data. Drilling down data refers to the ability to start at a summary number and to break that summary into a successively finer set of summarizations. By being able to get at the detail beneath a summary number, the manager can get a feel for what is happening, especially where the summary number is surprising. Figure 7.4 shows a simple example of drill-down analysis.

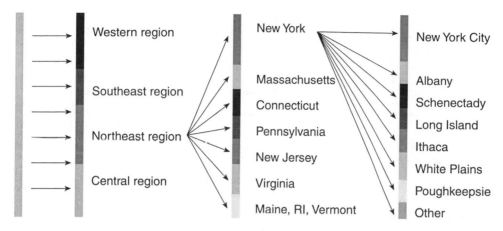

**Figure 7.4**  In order to make sense of the numbers shown by EIS, the numbers need to support a drill-down process.

In Figure 7.4, the manager has seen second-quarter summary results and wants to explore them further. The manager then looks at the regions that have contributed to the summary analysis. The regions' figures that are analyzed are the Western region, the Southeast region, the Northeast region, and the Central region. In looking at the numbers of each region, the manager decides to look more closely at the Northeast region's numbers.

The Northeast's numbers are made up of totals from New York, Massachusetts, Connecticut, Pennsylvania, New Jersey, Virginia, Maine, Rhode Island, and Vermont. Of these states, the manager then decides to look more closely at the numbers for New York state. The different cities in New York state that have outlets are then queried.

In each case, the manager has selected a path of going from summary to detail, then to a successively lower level. In such a fashion, he or she can determine where the troublesome results are. Once having identified the anomalies, the manager then knows where to look for a closer explanation.

There is plenty of very sophisticated software that can be used in EIS to present the results to a manager. The difficult part of EIS is not in the graphical presentation but in discovering and preparing the numbers that go into the graphics, as seen in Figure 7.5.

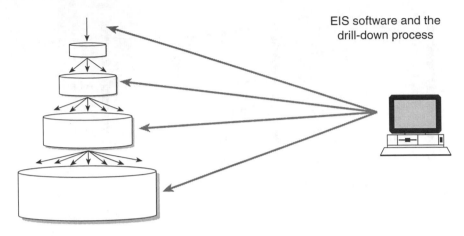

EIS software and the
drill-down process

**Figure 7.5** EIS software supports the drill-down process as long as the data that is needed is available and is structured properly.

EIS is perfectly capable of supporting the drill-down process from the graphical perspective as long as the data exists in the first place. But if the data to analyze does not exist, the drill-down process becomes very tedious and awkward, certainly not something the executive wants to do.

## SUPPORTING THE DRILL-DOWN PROCESS

Creating the basis of data on which to do drill-down analysis, then, is the major obstacle to successfully implementing the drill-down process, as seen in Figure 7.6.

Indeed, some studies indicate that $9 is spent on drill-down data preparation for every $1 spent on EIS software and hardware.

Exaggerating the problem is the fact that the executive is constantly changing his or her mind about what is of interest. Figure 7.7 shows the constantly changing nature of what interests the executive.

On day one, the executive is interested in the corporation's financial activities. The EIS analyst spends a large effort in developing the underlying data to support EIS interest. Then on

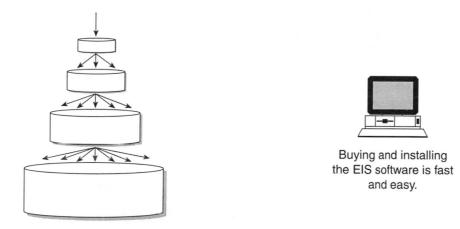

Buying and installing
the EIS software is fast
and easy.

**Figure 7.6** Creating the base of data on which to do EIS processing is the hard part.

day two, there is an unexpected production problem and management's attention is turned there. The EIS analyst scurries around and tries to gather the data needed by the executive. On day three, the EIS analyst is directed to the problems that have developed in shipping.

Management's focus shifts with every new problem or opportunity that arises. There simply is no predictable pattern to what management will be interested in tomorrow. In turn, the EIS analyst is at the end of a whip—the wrong end! The EIS analyst is forever in a *reactive* state. Furthermore, given the work that is required of the EIS analyst in order to build the base of data needed for EIS analysis, the EIS analyst is constantly swamped.

## THE DATA WAREHOUSE AS A BASIS FOR EIS

It is in the EIS environment that the data warehouse operates. The data warehouse is tailor-made for the needs of the EIS analyst. Once the data warehouse has been built, the job of the EIS is infinitely easier than when there is no foundation of data on which to operate. Figure 7.8 shows how the data warehouse supports the need for EIS data.

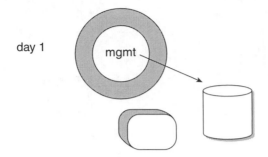

day 1

Management is interested in financial activities.

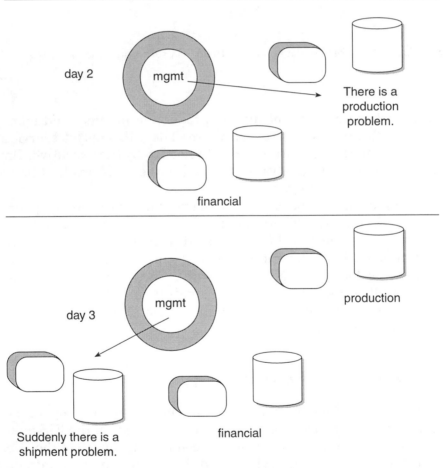

day 2

There is a
production
problem.

financial

day 3

production

Suddenly there is a
shipment problem.

financial

**Figure 7.7** • Management's attention is constantly shifting.
• The shift is in a random pattern.
• Management always wants the information *now*!
• At the end of the data, management wants the data integrated as well.

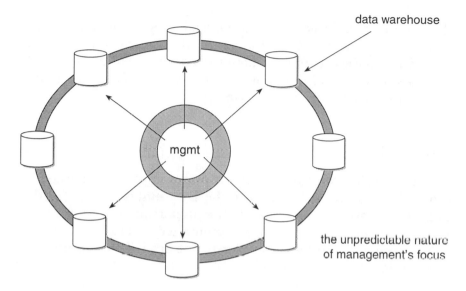

data warehouse

mgmt

the unpredictable nature
of management's focus

**Figure 7.8**   The data warehouse:
- is in place when needed
- is integrated
- has detailed and summary data
- covers all the wide topics needed by management
- has the lengthy time basis of data needed for trending

With a data warehouse, the EIS analyst:

- does not have to search for the definitive source of data
- does not have to create special extract programs from existing systems
- does not have to worry about unintegrated data
- does not have to worry about detailed and summary data and the linkage between the two
- does not have to worry about finding an appropriate time basis of data
- does not have to worry about management constantly or changing its mind about what needs to be looked at next
- has available a rich supply of summary data

In short, the data warehouse provides the basis of data that the EIS analyst needs to effectively support EIS processing.

With a fully populated data warehouse in place, the analyst can be in a *proactive* stance—not an eternally reactive stance—with regard to answering management's needs. The EIS analyst's job changes from that of data engineer to that of doing true analysis, thanks to the data warehouse.

## WHERE TO TURN

The EIS analyst can turn to various places in the architecture in order to get data. In Figure 7.9, the EIS analyst can go to the individual level of processing, the departmental (datamart) level of processing, the lightly summarized level of processing, or the true archival level in order to get data. The EIS analyst can get data from anywhere.

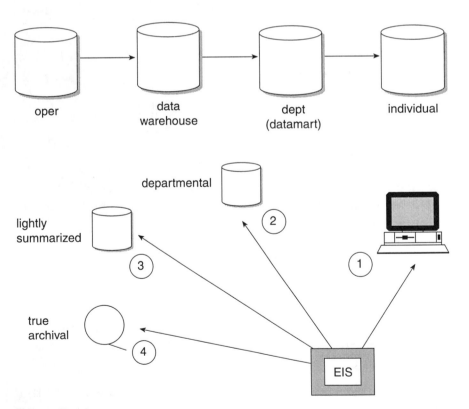

**Figure 7.9** Where EIS goes to get data.

In addition, there is a normal sequence or hierarchy in which the EIS analyst goes after data to serve management's needs (Figure 7.9).

There is a very good reason for the order shown, as indicated in Figure 7.10. By going from the individual level of processing to the true archival level of processing, the analyst does de facto drill-down analysis. The most summarized data found in the architected environment is found at the individual level. The supporting level of summary for the individual level is the departmental level. Supporting the summaries found at the departmental level is data found at the data warehouse lightly summarized level. And finally, the light summarization found at the data warehouse level is supported by true archival data. The sequence of summaries just described is precisely what is required to support drill-down EIS analysis.

Almost by default, the data warehouse lays a path for drill-down analysis. At the different levels of the data warehouse, and throughout the summarization process, data is related by means of a key structure. The key structure itself, or the deriva-

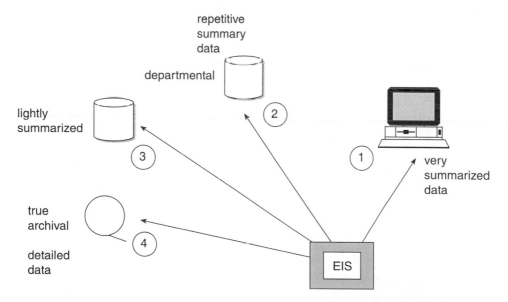

**Figure 7.10** In going from individual levels of processing to true archival data, the drill-down process is accommodated.

tions of the key structure, allow the data to be related so that drill-down analysis is an easy thing to do.

The ways that EIS is supported by the data warehouse are illustrated in Figure 7.11.

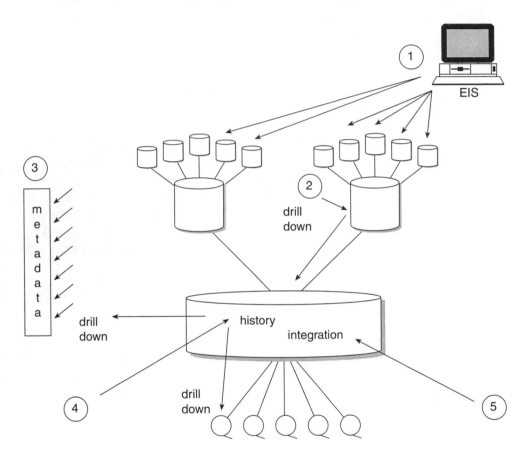

**Figure 7.11** The ways in which the data warehouse supports EIS:

1. There is a rich and available supply of summary data.
2. The structure of the data in the warehouse supports the drill-down process.
3. Metadata allows the DSS analyst to plan the development of new initiatives.
4. The history of data found in the warehouse supports management's desire for trend analysis in the EIS.
5. The integration of data before entering the warehouse is what management needs in order to look across the enterprise.

The EIS function:

- uses the data warehouse for a readily available supply of summary data
- uses the structure of the data warehouse to support the drill-down process
- uses data warehouse metadata for the DSS analyst to plan how the EIS system will be built
- uses the historical content of the data warehouse to support the trend analysis that management wishes to see
- uses the integrated data found throughout the data warehouse to look at data across the corporation

## EVENT MAPPING

A useful technique in using the data warehouse for EIS processing is that of event mapping. The simplest way to depict event mapping is to start with a simple trend line.

Figure 7.12 shows that corporate revenues have varied by month, as expected. The trend has been calculated from data found in the data warehouse. The trend of revenues in and of itself is interesting but gives only a superficial view of what is going on with the corporation. To enhance the view, events are mapped onto the trend line.

In Figure 7.13, three notable events have been mapped to

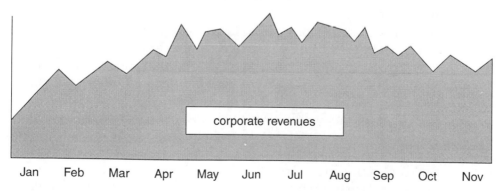

**Figure 7.12**  Simple trends.

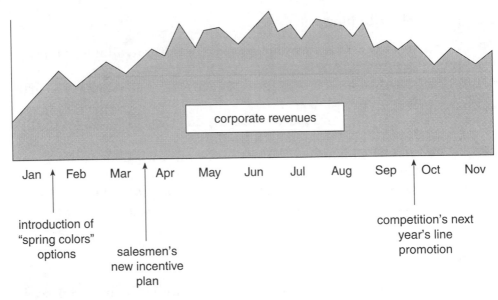

Jan   Feb   Mar   Apr   May   Jun   Jul   Aug   Sep   Oct   Nov

introduction of
"spring colors"
options

salesmen's
new incentive
plan

competition's next
year's line
promotion

corporate revenues

**Figure 7.13** Mapping events against a trend line.

the corporate revenue trend line—the introduction of a "spring colors" line of products, the advent of a salesmen's incentive program, and the introduction of competition. Now the relationship between corporate revenue and significant events begins to take on a different perspective. Looking at the diagram in Figure 7.13, the conclusion can be drawn that the introduction of a new line of products and a new incentive plan have boosted revenue and that competition is starting to have an effect in the latter part of the year.

For some sorts of events, event mapping is the only way to measure the results. Some events and activities cannot be measured directly and have to be measured in a correlative fashion. Cost justification and actual cost benefit cannot be measured any other way for some types of events.

However, misleading conclusions can be drawn by looking at correlative information. It often helps to look at more than one set of trends that relate to the events at hand. As an example of looking at multiple trends, Figure 7.14 shows that corporate revenues are matched against consumer confidence index to produce a diagram packed with even more perspective.

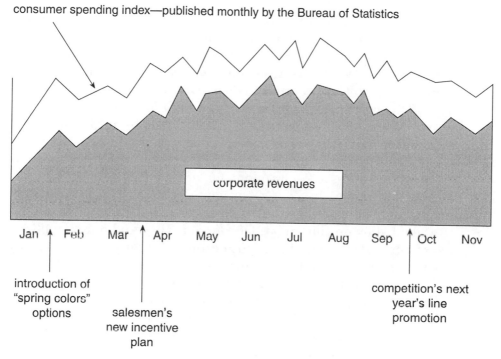

consumer spending index—published monthly by the Bureau of Statistics

corporate revenues

| Jan | Feb | Mar | Apr | May | Jun | Jul | Aug | Sep | Oct | Nov |

introduction of
"spring colors"
options

salesmen's
new incentive
plan

competition's next
year's line
promotion

**Figure 7.14**   Superimposing another trend analysis over the existing one to gain another perspective.

Looking at Figure 7.14, the executive can make up his or her own mind whether events that have been mapped have shaped sales or not.

The data warehouse can store both the internally generated revenue numbers and the externally generated consumer confidence numbers.

## DETAILED DATA AND EIS

Just how much detailed data do you need to run your EIS/DSS environment? There is one school of thought that says that you need as much detail as possible. By storing as much data as possible, you have the ability to do any kind of analysis that might happen along. Since the nature of DSS is delving into the unknown, who knows what detail you will need? To be on the safe side, you'd better keep all the detailed data you can get your hands on. Furthermore, the more historical detailed data you can get, the better, because you never can tell how far back you need to go in time in order to do a given DSS analysis.

The logic at the heart of the argument for the storage of massive amounts of detail for DSS processing is hard to argue with. Intellectually it must be correct to say that you need as much detail as possible for DSS and EIS processing. But in some important ways the argument for detailed data in EIS is like Zeno's paradox. In Zeno's paradox, logic inescapably "proves" that a rabbit can never outrun a turtle as long as the turtle has a head start on the rabbit. Of course reality and our own observations tell us something quite different, warning us that any conclusion based purely on logic is circumspect.

What, then, is so wrong with keeping all the detail in the world around when you are building a DSS/EIS environment? There are several things wrong with keeping massive amounts of detailed data around. The first is that the amount of money required for both storage and processing costs can go sky-high. The sheer cost of storing and processing huge amounts of detailed data prohibits the establishment of an effective EIS/DSS environment. The second reason why storing massive amounts of detail for DSS processing is not a good practice is that massive amounts of data form an obstacle to the effective use of analysis techniques. Given very large amounts of data to be processed, important trends and patterns can hide behind the mask of endless records of detailed data. And a third reason why massive amounts of detail are not a good idea is that with the detail, reuse of previous analysis is not fostered. As long as there is a massive amount of detail around, DSS analysts are encouraged to create new analyses from scratch. Such a practice is wasteful and potentially harmful, when new analysis is not done in quite the same way as older analysis, very similar analysis and conflicting results are obtained.

There is, then, a very real case for storing summary data as well as detailed data. DSS and EIS processing ought to make as much use of summary data as they do of detailed data. Summary data is much less voluminous and much easier to manage than detailed data. From an access and presentation perspective, summary data is ideal for management. Summary data represents a foundation on which future analysis can build and for which existing analysis does not have to be repeated. For these reasons alone, summary data is an integral part of the DSS/EIS environment.

## Keeping Only Summary Data in the EIS

But there are some very real problems with keeping just summary data. The first problem is that summary data implies a process—the summary is *always* created as a result of the process of calculation. The calculation may be very simple or the calculation may be complex. In any case, there is no such thing as summary data that stands alone—summary data of necessity stands with its process. In order to effectively use summary data, the DSS analyst *must* have access to and an understanding of the process that has been used to shape it. As long as DSS and EIS understand this relationship between process and summary data and as long as EIS and DSS can profitably use the summary data that has resulted from the process of calculation, then summary data constitutes an ideal foundation for EIS and DSS. But if the analysts that are doing EIS/DSS analysis do not understand that process is intimately related to summary data, the results of the analysis can be very misleading.

The second problem with summary data is that it may or may not be at the appropriate level of granularity for the analytical purpose at hand. There needs to be a balance struck between the level of detail and the level of summarization for EIS and DSS processing.

## SUMMARY

There is a very strong affinity between the needs of the EIS analyst and the data warehouse. The data warehouse explicitly supports *all* of the EIS analyst's needs. With a data warehouse in place, the EIS analyst can be in a proactive position rather than a reactive position.

The data warehouse enables the EIS analyst to deal with:

- management's need for very quick information
- need to change their mind
- management's need to look at integrated data
- management's need to look at data over a spectrum of time
- management's need to be able to drill down

# External/Unstructured Data and the Data Warehouse

Most organizations build their first data warehouse efforts on the data whose source is existing systems (i.e., on data internal to the corporation). In almost every case, the data that comes from existing systems can be termed *internal, structured data*. The data comes from the internals of the corporation and has been already shaped into a regularly occurring format.

But there is a whole host of other data that is of legitimate use to a corporation that is not generated from the corporation's own systems. This class of data is called *external data* and usually enters the corporation in an *unstructured*, unpredictable format. Figure 8.1 shows external and unstructured data entering the data warehouse.

The data warehouse is the ideal place to store external and unstructured data. If external and unstructured data is not stored in a centrally located place, several problems are sure to arise. Figure 8.2 shows that when external and unstructured data enters the corporation in an undisciplined fashion, the identity of the source of the data is lost, and there is no coordination whatsoever in the orderly use of the data.

Typically, when external data is not entered into the data warehouse, it comes into the corporation by means of the PC.

**261**

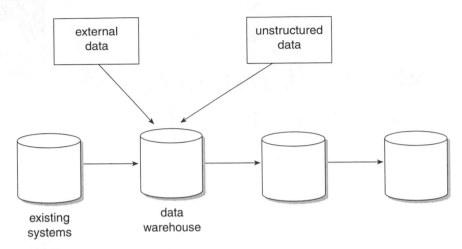

**Figure 8.1** External and unstructured data both belong in the data warehouse.

There is nothing wrong with entering data at the PC level, per se. But almost always, when data is entered at the PC level it is entered manually through a spreadsheet, and there is absolutely no attempt to capture information about the source of data in addition to the data. For example, in Figure 8.2 an analyst sees a report in the *Wall Street Journal*. The next day, the analyst uses the data from the *Wall Street Journal* as part of a report, but the original source of the data is lost as it is entered into the corporate mainstream of data.

Another difficulty with the laissez-faire approach to external data is that at a later point in time it is hard to recall the data. It is entered into the corporation's systems, used once, and then disappears. Even a few weeks later, it is hard to reaccess the data for further use, and this is unfortunate, because much of the data coming from external sources is quite useful over the spectrum of time.

The types of data that come from external sources are many and diverse. Some typical sources of interesting data include the following:

- the *Wall Street Journal*
- *Business Week*
- *Forbes*

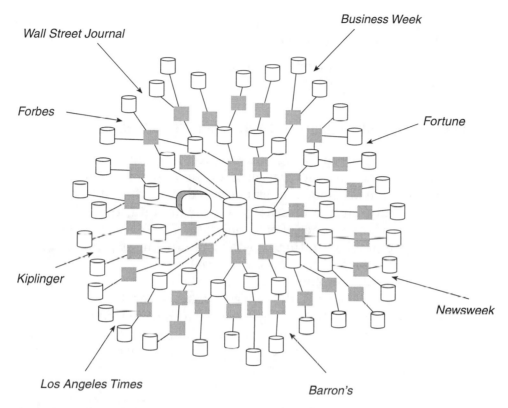

**Figure 8.2** The problem with external and unstructured data:
- Its source is stripped upon entering the corporation.
- One analyst is not aware that another analyst has brought in similar information.

- *Fortune*
- industry newsletters
- technology reports
- Dun and Bradstreet
- reports generated by consultants specifically for the corporation
- Equifax reports
- competitive analysis reports
- marketing comparison and analysis reports
- sales analysis and comparison reports
- new product announcements

In addition, there are reports internal to the corporation that are of interest as well:

- the auditor's quarterly report
- the annual report

## EXTERNAL/UNSTRUCTURED DATA IN THE DATA WAREHOUSE

There are several issues that relate to the use and storage of external and unstructured data in the data warehouse. In Figure 8.3, one problem of unstructured data is that of frequency of availability. Unlike internally appearing data, there is no real pattern of appearance of external data. The frequency of appearance is a problem in that constant monitoring must be set up to ensure that the right data is captured.

The second problem with external data is that of the form of the data. The form of the external data is totally undisciplined. In order to be useful, and in order for it to be placed in the warehouse, a certain amount of reformatting of external data must be accomplished to transform it into an internally acceptable and usable form.

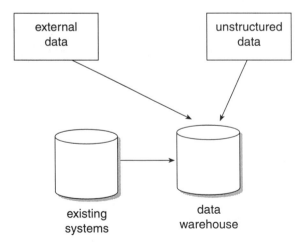

**Figure 8.3** Issues relating to external data:
- • the frequency of entry
- • the form of data
- • the unpredictability

The third factor that makes external data hard to capture is its unpredictability. External data may come from practically any source at almost any time. The unpredictable nature of the availability of external data makes it very difficult for it to be consistently and completely captured.

In addition to external data that might come out of a magazine article or a consultant's report, there is another whole class of data that is just now able to be automated—unstructured data, shown in Figure 8.4.

The two most common types of unstructured data are in the forms of images and voice. Image data is data stored as pictures. Voice data is data stored digitally and able to be translated back into a voice format. The issues of image data and voice data stem primarily from technology. The technology to capture and manipulate image and voice data is not nearly as mature as more conventional technology. In addition, even when image and voice data can be captured, their storage requires huge amounts of DASD, and their recall and display or playback can be awkward and slow.

Nevertheless, there are many possibilities in the capturing of unstructured information and its storage in a data warehouse.

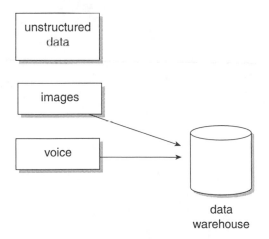

**Figure 8.4**   Some forms of unstructured data that can be stored in the data warehouse.

## METADATA AND EXTERNAL DATA

Metadata is an important component of the data warehouse in any scenario. But metadata takes on an entirely different dimension in the face of storing and managing external and unstructured data. Figure 8.5 shows the role of metadata.

Metadata is important because it is through metadata that external data is registered, accessed, and controlled in the data warehouse environment. The best explanation of the importance of metadata is witnessed by the typical contents of metadata in the data warehouse for external data, such as the following:

- document ID
- date of entry into the warehouse
- description of the document
- source of the document
- date of source of the document
- classification of the document
- index words

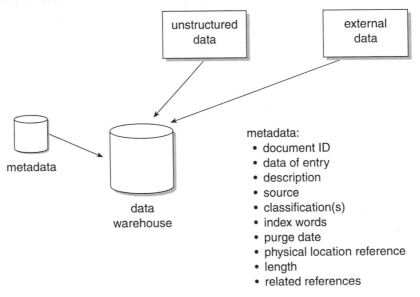

**Figure 8.5** Metadata takes on a new role in the face of external and unstructured data.

- purge date
- physical location reference
- length of the document
- related references

It is through the metadata that a manager determines much information about the external data. In many instances, the manager will look at the metadata without ever looking at the source document. Scanning metadata eliminates much work for the manager in ruling out documents that are not relevant or are out of date.

Properly built and maintained metadata, then, is absolutely essential to the operation of the data warehouse as far as external data is concerned.

In association with metadata is another type of data—notification data. Figure 8.6 shows notification data, which is merely a file created for users of the system that indicates classifications of data interesting to the users. When data is entered into

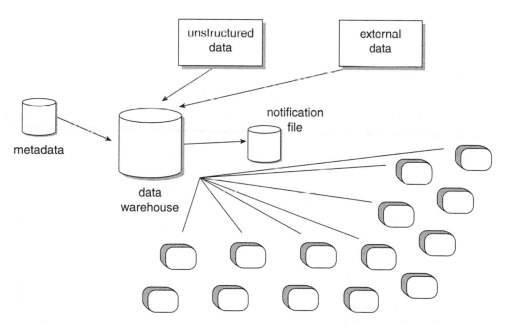

**Figure 8.6** Another nice feature of external data and metadata is the ability to create a tailored notification file.

the data warehouse and into the metadata, a check is made to see who is interested in it. Upon discovering that someone is interested in the data that has just been captured, a notification is made so that he or she will know that external data of interest has been captured.

## STORING EXTERNAL/UNSTRUCTURED DATA

External data and unstructured data can actually be stored in the data warehouse if it is convenient and cost effective to do so. But in many cases it will not be possible or economical to store all external data in the data warehouse. Instead, an entry is made in the metadata of the warehouse describing where the actual body of external data can be found, and the external data is stored elsewhere, where it is convenient, as shown in Figure 8.7. External data may be stored in a filing cabinet, on fiche, on magnetic tape, and so on. Of course, external data can be stored in the data warehouse if desired.

## DIFFERENT COMPONENTS OF EXTERNAL/ UNSTRUCTURED DATA

One of the important design aspects of external/unstructured data is that it often contains many different components, some of which are of more use than others. As an example, suppose the complete manufacturing history of a product is purchased. Certain aspects of production are very important, such as the length of time from first to final assembly. Another important production measurement is total cost of unassembled raw goods. But there are many other unimportant pieces of information that accompany the manufacturing information as well, such as actual date of production, shipment specification, and temperature at production.

In order to manage the data, an experienced DSS analyst or industrial engineer needs to determine what the most important units of data are. Then the most important units of data are stored in an online, easy-to-get-to location. There is efficiency of

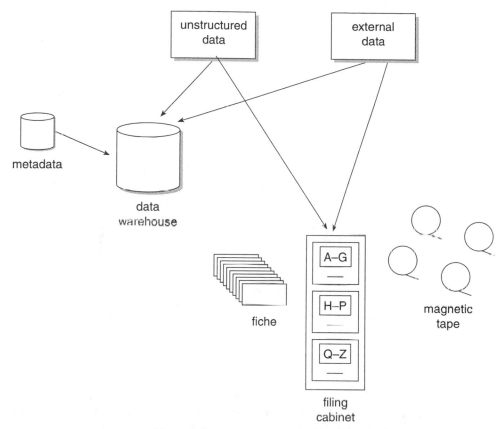

**Figure 8.7**   In every case, external data/unstructured data is registered with the metadata, but the actual data may or may not be stored in the data warehouse based on the size of the data and the probability of access.

storage and efficiency of access. The remaining less important detail is not discarded but is placed in a bulk storage location. In such a manner large amounts of unstructured data can be efficiently stored and managed.

## MODELING AND EXTERNAL/UNSTRUCTURED DATA

What is the role of the data model and external data? Figure 8.8 reflects the dilemma. The normal role of the data model is the shaping of the environment, usually in terms of design. But external data and unstructured data are not malleable to any

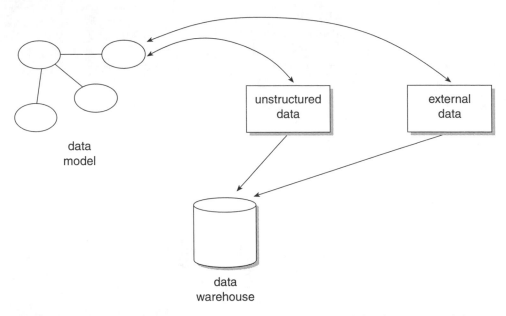

**Figure 8.8** There usually is only a faint resemblance of external data/unstructured data to the data model. Furthermore, nothing can be done about reshaping external data and unstructured data.

extent at all. Therefore it appears that there is very little relationship between the data model and external data. About the best that can be done is to note the differences between the data model and external data insofar as the interpretation of key phrases and words are concerned. Attempting to use the data model for any serious reshaping of the data is a mistake.

## SECONDARY REPORTS

Not only can primary data be put in the data warehouse, but when data is repetitive in nature, secondary reports can be created from the detailed data over time. For example, take the month-end Dow Jones average report shown in Figure 8.9.

In Figure 8.9, Dow Jones information comes into the data warehouse environment daily. The daily information is useful, but of even more interest are the long-term trends that are formed. At the end of the month, the Dow Jones average is shuf-

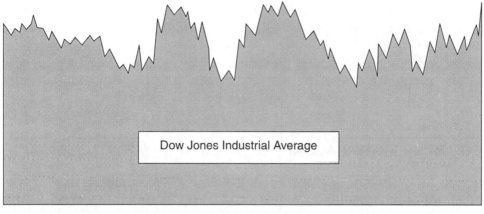

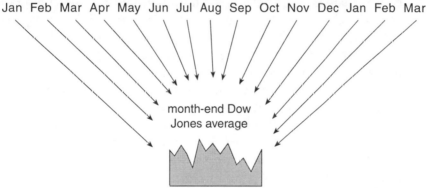

**Figure 8.9** Creating a summary report from daily or monthly recurring information.

fled off into a "secondary" report. The secondary report then becomes part of the store of external data contained in the data warehouse.

## ARCHIVING EXTERNAL DATA

Every piece of information—external or otherwise—has a useful lifetime. Once past that lifetime, it is not economical to keep the information. An essential part of managing external data is in deciding what the useful lifetime of the data is. Even after this is determined, there still remains an issue as to whether the data should be discarded or put into archives. As a rule, external data may be removed from the data warehouse and placed on less expensive storage. The metadata reference to the external data is updated to reflect the new storage place and is left in the metadata store. The cost of an entry into the metadata store is so low that once put there, it is best left there.

## COMPARING INTERNAL DATA TO EXTERNAL DATA

One of the most useful things that can be done with external data is to compare it to internal data over a period of time. The comparison is one that allows management to "see the forest for the trees." Being able to contrast very immediate and personal activities and trends against very global activities and trends allows an executive to have insights that simply are not possible elsewhere. Figure 8.10 shows such a comparison.

When the comparison between external and internal data is made, the assumption is that the comparison is made on a common key. Any other assumption, and the comparison between external and internal data loses much of its usefulness. Unfortunately, actually achieving a common key basis between external and internal data is not easy.

In order to understand the difficulty consider two cases. In one case the commodity being sold is a large, expensive item, such as a car or a television set. In order to do a meaningful comparison, sale by actual outlet needs to be measured. The actual sales by dealer is the basis for comparison. Unfortu-

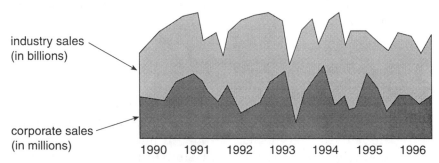

industry sales
(in billions)

corporate sales
(in millions)

1990　1991　1992　1993　1994　1995　1996

**Figure 8.10**　External data compared to internal data can be very elucidating.

nately, the key structure used for dealers by the external source of data is not the same key structure used by internal systems. Either the external source must be converted to the key structure of the internal source, or vice versa. Such a conversion is a nontrivial task.

Now consider the measurement of sales of a high-volume, low-cost item such as colas. The internal sales figures of the company reflect the sale of colas. But the external sales data has mixed the sales of colas with the sales of other beverages such as beer. Making a comparison between the two types of sales data will lead to some very misleading conclusions. In order to have a meaningful comparison, there needs to be a "cleansing" of the external sales data to include only colas. In fact, if at all possible, colas only of the variety produced and sold by the bottler should be included. Not only should beer be removed from the external sales data, but noncompeting cola types should be removed as well.

## SUMMARY

The data warehouse is capable of holding much more than internal, structured data. There is much information relevant to the running of the company that comes from sources outside the company.

External data is captured, and information about the metadata is stored in the data warehouse metadata. The metadata serves as an executive index to information. In addition, a "notification" service is often provided whenever a new entry is made into the data warehouse.

External and unstructured data may or may not actually be stored in the data warehouse.

# Migration to the Architected Environment

Any architecture that must be implemented all at once, in a big bang, is doomed to failure in today's world. There simply is too much risk, too long a period to wait until there is a payback, and the unreality of trying to freeze changes to consider any path that is evolutionary, rather than revolutionary.

It is very good news indeed that migrating to the architected data warehouse environment is a step-by-step activity that is accomplished one finite deliverable at a time. The most successful implementations of the architected environment have been those where the data warehouse has been built one iteration at a time. In doing so, the data warehouse can be built for a minimum of manpower resources and can be built with absolutely minimal disruption to the existing applications environment. Both the size and the speed of iterative development are important. Results must be delivered quickly.

In this chapter, a generic migration plan and a methodology for development are discussed. The methodology is described in detail in the appendix. The migration plan has been successfully followed by a wide number of companies. It is anything but a fanciful flight. The methodology has been gleaned from the experiences of a number of companies. Of course, each company will have its own diversions and permutations. But the migration plan and methodology have met with enough success in enough diverse companies to merit the confidence of the general-purpose developer.

## A MIGRATION PLAN

The beginning point for the migration plan is a data model. The data model represents the information needs of the corporation. It represents what the corporation needs, not necessarily what the corporation currently has. It is built with no consideration of technology.

The data model may be built internally or may have been generated from a generic data model. The data model needs to identify (at a minimum!) the following:

- the major subjects of the corporation
- the relationships between the major subjects
- the groupings of keys and attributes that more fully represent the major subjects, including
  - the attributes of the major subjects
  - the keys of the major subjects
  - the repeating groups of keys and attributes
  - connectors between major subject areas
  - subtyping relationships

In theory, it is possible to build the architected environment without a data model. However, in practice it is never done. Trying to build an architected environment without a data model is like trying to navigate without a map. It can be done, but it is very prone to trial and error. It is like a person who has never been outside of Texas landing at New York's La Guardia airport and driving to midtown Manhattan with no map and no instructions. It can be done (perhaps!), but all sensibilities suggest that a map is a superior way to go.

Figure 9.1 shows that building or otherwise acquiring a data model is the starting point for the migration process.

After the data model is in place, the next activity is the definition of the system of record. The system of record is defined in

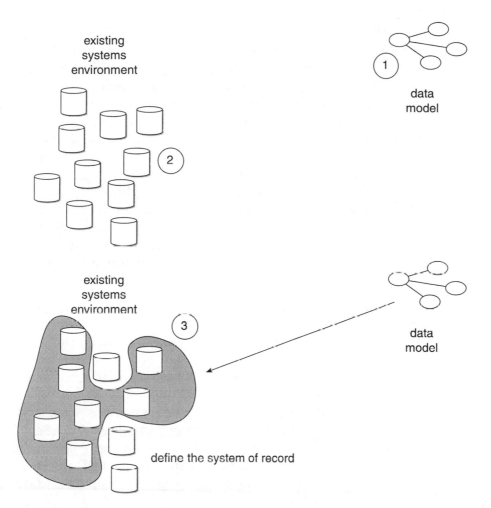

"Best" data to represent the data model:

- most timely
- most accurate
- most complete
- nearest to the external source
- most structurally compatible

**Figure 9.1**  Migration to the architected environment.

terms of the existing systems the corporation already has. Usually these systems are affectionately known as the "mess."

The system of record is nothing more than the identification of the "best" data the corporation has. The data model is used as a benchmark for determining what the best data is. In other words, the data architect starts with the data model and asks what data is in hand that best fulfills the data requirements identified in the data model. It is understood that the fit will be less than a perfect one. In some cases there will be no data in the existing systems environment that exemplifies the data in the data model. In other cases there will be many sources of data in the existing systems environment that contribute data to the systems of record, each under different circumstances.

The "best" source of existing data is determined by the following criteria:

- What data in the existing systems environment is the most complete?
- What data in the existing systems environment is the most timely?
- What data in the existing systems environment is the most accurate?
- What data in the existing systems environment is the closest to the source of entry into the existing systems environment?
- What data in the existing systems environment conforms the most closely to the structure of the data model? in terms of keys? in terms of attributes? in terms of grouping of data attributes together?

Using the data model and the criteria described above, the analyst defines the system of record.

After the system of record is defined, the next step is to design the data warehouse, as shown in Figure 9.2.

If the data modeling activity has been done properly, the design of the data warehouse is simple. Only a few aspects of the data model need to be changed to turn the data model into a data warehouse design. Principally, the following needs to be done:

- An element of time needs to be added to the key structure if one is not already present.

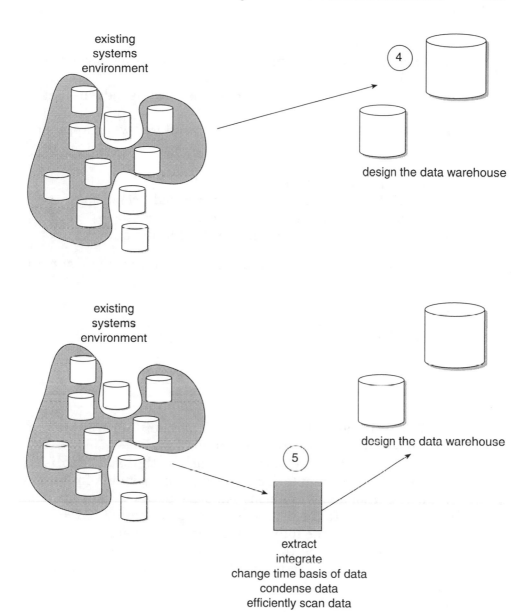

existing
systems
environment

4

design the data warehouse

existing
systems
environment

5

design the data warehouse

extract
integrate
change time basis of data
condense data
efficiently scan data

**Figure 9.2** Migration to the architected environment.

- All purely operational data needs to be eliminated.
- Referential integrity relationships need to be turned into artifacts.
- Derived data that is frequently needed is added to the design.
- The structure of the data needs to be altered when appropriate for:
  - adding arrays of data
  - adding data redundantly
  - further separating data under the right conditions
  - merging tables when appropriate
- Stability analysis of the data needs to be done.

The data warehouse, once designed, is organized by subject area. Typical subject areas are:

- customer
- product
- sale
- account
- activity
- shipment

Within the subject area there will be many separate tables, each of which is connected by a common key.

After the data warehouse is designed, the next step is to design and build the interfaces between the system of record—in the operational environment—and the data warehouses. The interfaces populate the data warehouse on a regular basis.

At first glance, the interfaces appear to be merely an extract process, and it is true that extract processing does occur. But there are many more activities that occur at the point of interface as well:

- integration of data from the operational, application-oriented environment
- the alteration of the time basis of data
- the condensation of data
- the efficient scanning of the existing systems environment

Most of these issues have been discussed elsewhere in this book.

It is of interest that the vast majority of development resources required to build a data warehouse are consumed at this point. It is not unusual for 80 percent of the effort required to build a data warehouse to be spent here. In laying out the development activities for the building of a data warehouse, most developers overestimate the time required for other activities and underestimate the time required for designing and building the operational to data warehouse interface.

Once the interface programs are designed and built, the next activity is to start the population of the first subject area, as shown in Figure 9.3.

There are many good reasons to populate only a fraction of the data needed in a data warehouse at this point. It is very likely that changes to the data will need to be made. Populating only a small amount of data means that those changes that need to be made can be made easily and quickly. Populating a large amount of data greatly diminishes the flexibility of the data warehouse. Once the end user has had a chance to look at the data and give feedback to the data architect, then it is safe to populate large volumes of data.

The population and feedback process continues for a long period (indefinitely). In addition, the data in the warehouse continues to be changed.

There must be a word of caution at this point: *If you wait for existing systems to be cleaned up, you will never build a data warehouse.* The issues and activities of the existing systems operational environment must be independent of the issues and activities of the data warehouse environment.

One observation that is worthwhile at this point is the frequency of refreshment of data warehouse data. As a rule, data warehouse data should be refreshed no more frequently than every 24 hours. By making sure that there is at least a 24-hour time delay in the loading of data, the data warehouse developer minimizes the temptation to try to turn the data warehouse into an operational environment. The data warehouse serves the DSS needs of the company, not the operational needs. Most

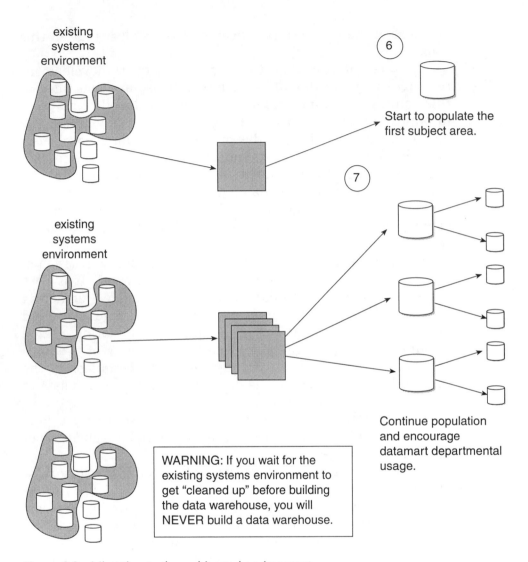

existing
systems
environment

⑥

Start to populate the
first subject area.

⑦

existing
systems
environment

Continue population
and encourage
datamart departmental
usage.

WARNING: If you wait for the
existing systems environment to
get "cleaned up" before building
the data warehouse, you will
NEVER build a data warehouse.

**Figure 9.3** Migration to the architected environment.

operational processing depends on data being accurate as of the moment of access (i.e., current value data). By insuring that there is a 24-hour delay (at the least), the data warehouse developer adds an important ingredient that maximizes the chances for success.

## THE FEEDBACK LOOP

At the heart of success in the development of the data warehouse is the feedback loop between the data architect and the DSS analyst, shown in Figure 9.4.

Figure 9.4 shows that the data warehouse is populated from existing systems. The DSS analyst uses the data warehouse as a basis for analysis. Upon finding new opportunities, the DSS

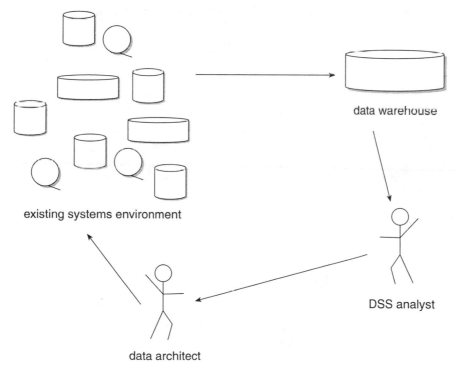

data warehouse

existing systems environment

DSS analyst

data architect

**Figure 9.4**   The crucial feedback loop between DSS analyst and data architect.

analyst conveys those requirements back to the data architect, who makes the appropriate adjustments.

There are a few observations about this feedback loop that are of vital importance to the success of the data warehouse environment:

■ The DSS analyst operates—quite legitimately—in a "give me what I want, then I can tell you what I really want" mode.
■ The shorter the cycle of the feedback loop, the more successful the warehouse effort.
■ The larger the volume of data that has to be changed, the longer the feedback loop takes.

## STRATEGIC CONSIDERATIONS

Figure 9.5 shows that the path of activities that have been described addresses the DSS needs of the organization.

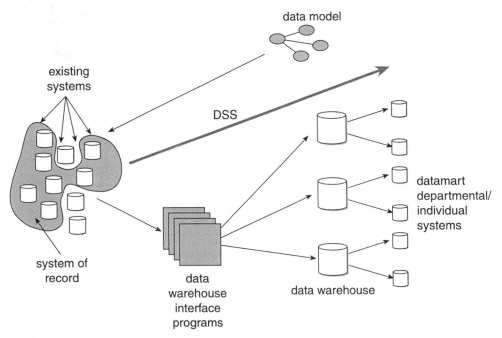

**Figure 9.5**   The first major path to be followed is the one of DSS.

The data warehouse environment is designed and built for the purpose of supporting the DSS needs of the organization, but there are needs other than DSS needs. Figure 9.6 shows that there are operational needs of the corporation as well.

In Figure 9.6, the operational world is shown as being in a state of chaos. There is much unintegrated data in the operational world. The operational world contains data and systems so old and so patched that they cannot be maintained. The requirements that originally shaped the operational applications have changed into an almost unrecognizable form, and so forth.

The migration plan that has been discussed is solely for the DSS component. But isn't there an opportunity to rectify some or much of the operational "mess" at the same time that the data warehouse is being built? The answer is that to some extent there is an opportunity to rebuild less than aesthetically pleasing aspects of the operational environment.

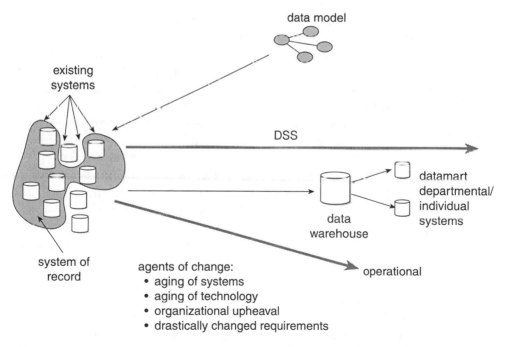

**Figure 9.6** In order to be successful, the data architect should wait for agents of change to become compelling and ally the efforts toward the architected environment with the appropriate agents.

One approach—which is on an independent track of the migration to the data warehouse environment—is to use the data model as a guideline and make a case to management that major changes need to be made to the operational environment. The industry track record of this approach is dismal. The amount of effort, the amount of resources, and the disruption to the end user in undertaking a massive rewrite and restructuring of operational data and systems is such that management seldom supports such an effort with the needed level of commitment and resources.

A better ploy is to coordinate the effort to rebuild operational systems with what is termed the "agents of change":

■ the aging of systems
■ the radical changing of technology
■ organizational upheaval
■ massive business changes

When management faces the effects of the agents of change, there is no question that changes will have to be made—the only question is how soon and at what expense. The data architect allies the agents of change with the notion of an architecture and presents management with an irresistible argument for the purpose of restructuring operational processing.

The steps the data architect takes to restructure the operational environment—which is an independent activity of the building of the data warehouse—are shown in Figure 9.7.

First a "delta" list is created. The delta list is an assessment of the differences between the operational environment and the environment depicted by the data model. The delta list is a simple listing, with very little elaboration.

The next step is the impact analysis. At this point an assessment is made of the impact of each item on the delta list. Some items may have a serious impact; other items have a negligible impact on the running of the company.

Next the resource estimate is created. This estimate is for the determination of how many resources will be required to "fix" the delta list item.

Finally, all the above are packaged into a report that goes to information systems management. Management then makes a

existing
systems

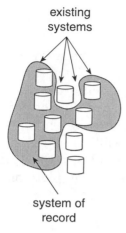

system of
record

data model

1. delta list:
   how the data model differs from
   existing systems

2. impact analysis:
   how each delta item makes
   a difference

3. resource estimate:
   how much will it cost to "fix"
   the delta item

4. report to management:
   • what needs to be fixed
   • the estimate of resources required
   • the order of work
   • the disruption analysis

**Figure 9.7**   The first steps in creating the operational "clean up" plan.

decision as to what work should proceed, at what pace, and so
forth.

## METHODOLOGY AND MIGRATION

In the appendix of this book, a methodology for building a data
warehouse is described. The methodology is actually a much
larger one in scope in that it not only contains information as to
how to build a data warehouse but it also describes how to use
the data warehouse. In addition, the classical activities of oper-

ational development are included to form what can be termed a "data-driven" methodology.

The methodology described differs from the migration path in several ways. The migration path describes general activities dynamically. The methodology describes specific activities, deliverables from those activities and the order of the activities. But the iterative dynamics of creating a warehouse are not described. In other words, the migration plan describes a sketchy plan in three dimensions, while the methodology describes a detailed plan in one dimension. Together they form a complete picture of what is required to build the data warehouse.

## A DATA-DRIVEN DEVELOPMENT METHODOLOGY

There is a universal appeal to development methodologies. Appealing to the intellect, a methodology directs the developer down a rational path, pointing out what needs to be done, in what order, and how long the activity should take. As attractive as the notion of a methodology is, the industry track record has not been good. Across the board, the enthusiasm for methodologies (data warehouse or any other) has met with disappointment upon implementation. The track record for methodologies put into implementation has generally been a rocky road.

Why have methodologies been a disappointment? There are a plethora of reasons.

- Methodologies generally show a flat, linear flow of activities. In fact, almost any methodology requires execution in terms of iterations. In other words, it is absolutely normal to execute two or three steps, stop, and repeat all or part of those steps again. Methodologies usually don't show or concern themselves with the need to revisit one or more activities. In the case of the data warehouse, this lack of support for iteration makes a methodology a very questionable subject.
- Methodologies usually show activities as occurring once and only once. Indeed, some activities need to be done (successfully) only once. However, other activities are done repeatedly

for different cases (which is a different case than reiteration for refinement).

- Methodologies usually describe a prescribed set of activities to be done. Oftentimes, some of the activities don't need to be done at all, and other activities need to be done that are not shown as part of the methodology, and so forth.
- Methodologies often tell how to do something, not what needs to be done. In describing how to do something, the effectiveness of the methodology becomes mired in detail and in special cases.
- Methodologies often do not distinguish between the sizes of the systems being developed under the methodology. Some systems are so small that a rigorous methodology makes no sense. Some systems are just the right size for a methodology. Other systems are so large that their sheer size and complexity will overwhelm the methodology.
- Methodologies often mix project management concerns with design/development activities to be done. Usually, project management activities should be kept separate from methodological concerns.
- Methodologies often do not make the distinction between operational and DSS processing. The system development life cycles for operational and DSS processing are diametrically opposed in many ways. A methodology must distinguish between operational and DSS processing and development in order to be successful.
- Methodologies often do not include checkpoints and stopping places in the case of failure. *What is the next step if the previous step has not been done properly?* is usually not a standard part of a methodology.
- Methodologies are often sold as solutions, not tools. When a methodology is sold as a solution, inevitably it is asked to replace good judgment and common sense, and this is always a mistake.
- Methodologies often generate a lot of paper and very little design. Design and development activities are not legitimately replaced by paper.
- Methodologies can be very complex, anticipating every possibility that may ever happen, or potentially happen.

Despite these drawbacks, there still is general appeal for methodologies. A general-purpose methodology—applicable to the data-driven environment—will be described in the Appendix, with full recognition of the pitfalls and track record of methodologies. The data-driven methodology that is outlined owes much to its early predecessors. As such, for a much fuller explanation of the intricacies and techniques described in the methodology, refer to the books listed in the references in the back of this book.

One of the salient aspects of a data-driven methodology is that it builds upon previous efforts—building on both code and processes that have been already developed. The only way that development on previous efforts can be achieved is through the recognition of commonality. Before the developer strikes the first line of code or designs the first database, he or she needs to know what already exists and how it affects the development process. A conscious effort must be made to use what is already in place and not reinvent the wheel. That is one of the essences of data-driven development.

## DATA-DRIVEN METHODOLOGY

What makes a methodology data driven? How is a data-driven methodology any different from any other methodology? There are at least two distinguishing characteristics of a data driven methodology.

■ A data-driven methodology does not take an application-by-application approach to the development of systems. Instead, code and data that have been built previously are built upon, rather than built around. In order to build on previous efforts, the commonality of data and processing must be recognized. Once recognized, data is built upon if it already exists, or if no data exists, data is constructed so that future development may built on it. The key to the recognition of commonality is the data model.

■ There is an emphasis on the central store of data—the data warehouse—as the basis for DSS processing, recognizing that DSS processing has a very different development life cycle than operational systems.

## SYSTEM DEVELOPMENT LIFE CYCLES

Fundamentally, shaping the data-driven development methodology is the profound difference in the system development life cycles of operational and DSS systems. Operational development is shaped around a development life cycle that begins with requirements and ends with code. DSS processing begins with data and ends with requirements.

## A PHILOSOPHICAL OBSERVATION

In some regards, the best example of methodology is the Boy Scout and Girl Scout merit badge system. The merit badge system is used to determine when a scout is ready to pass on to the next rank. It applies to both country- and city-dwelling boys and girls, the athletically inclined and the intellectually inclined, and to all geographical areas. In short, the merit badge system is a uniform methodology for the measurement of accomplishment that has stood the test of time.

Is there is any secret to the merit badge methodology? If so, it is this: The merit badge methodology does not prescribe *how* any activity is to be accomplished; instead, it merely describes what is to be done with parameters for the measurement of the achievement. The "how to do" that is required is left up to the Boy Scout or Girl Scout.

Philosophically, the approach to methodology described in the Appendix of this book takes the same perspective as the merit badge system. The results of what must be accomplished and, generally speaking, the order that things must be done in is described. How the results required are to be achieved is left entirely up to the developer.

## OPERATIONAL DEVELOPMENT/DSS DEVELOPMENT

The data-driven methodology will be presented in three parts: METH 1, METH 2, and METH 3. The first part of the methodology—METH 1—is for operational systems and processing. This part of the methodology will probably be most familiar to those used to looking at classically structured operational methodologies. METH 2 is for DSS systems and processing—the data warehouse. The essence of this component of the methodology centers around a data model as the vehicle that allows the commonality of data to be recognized. It is in this section of the appendix that the development of the data warehouse is described. The third part of the methodology—METH 3—describes what occurs in the heuristic component of the development process. It is in METH 3 that the usage of the warehouse is described.

These three sections comprise the data-driven methodology.

## SUMMARY

In this chapter, a migration plan and a methodology (found in the appendix) have been described. The migration plan addresses the issues of transforming data out of the existing systems environment into the data warehouse environment. In addition, the dynamics of how the operational environment might be organized was discussed.

A general-purpose data-driven methodology was discussed as well. The general-purpose methodology has three phases—an operational phase, a data warehouse construction phase, and a data warehouse iterative usage phase.

# A Data Warehouse Design Review Checklist

One of the most effective techniques for ensuring quality in the operational environment is that of design review. Through design review, errors can be detected and resolved prior to coding. The cost benefit of identifying errors early in the development life cycle is enormous.

In the operational environment, design review is usually done upon completion of the physical design of an application. The types of issues around which an operational design review centers are:

- transaction performance
- batch window adequacy
- system availability
- capacity
- project readiness
- user requirements satisfaction

Done properly in the operational environment, design review can save significant resources and greatly increase user satisfaction. Most importantly, when design review has been properly executed, major pieces of code do not have to be torn up and rewritten after the system has gone into production.

Design review is as applicable to the data warehouse environment as it is to the operational environment, with a few provisos.

One proviso is that systems are developed in the data warehouse environment in an iterative manner, where the requirements are discovered as a part of the development process. The classical operational environment is built under the well-defined SDLC—system development life cycle. Systems in the data warehouse environment are not built under the SDLC. Other differences between the development process in the operational environment and the data warehouse environment are the following:

- Development in the operational environment is done one application at a time. Systems for the data warehouse environment are built a subject area at a time.
- In the operational environment there is a firm set of requirements that form the basis of operational design and development. In the data warehouse environment, there is seldom a firm understanding of processing requirements at the outset of DSS development.
- In the operational environment, transaction response time is a major and burning issue. In the data warehouse environment, transaction response time had better not be an issue.
- In the operational environment, the input from systems usually comes from sources external to the organization, most often from interaction with outside agencies. In the data warehouse environment, it usually comes from systems inside the organization where data is integrated from a wide variety of existing sources.
- In the operational environment, data is nearly all current valued (i.e., data is accurate as of the moment of usage). In the data warehouse environment, data is time variant (i.e., data is relevant to some one moment in time).

There are, then, some substantial differences between the operational and data warehouse environments, and these differences show up in the way design review is conducted.

## WHEN TO DO DESIGN REVIEW

Design review in the data warehouse environment is done as soon as a major subject area has been designed and is ready to be added to the data warehouse environment. It does not need to be done for every new database that goes up. Instead, as whole new major subject areas are added to the database, design review becomes an appropriate activity.

### Who Should Be in the Design Review?

The attendees at the design review include anyone who has a stake in the development, operation, or usage of the DSS subject area being reviewed.

Normally, this includes:

- the Data Administration (DA)
- the Database Administration (DBA)
- programmers
- the DSS analysts
- end users other than the DSS analysts
- operations
- systems support
- management

Of this group, by far the most important attendees are the end users and the DSS analysts.

One important benefit from having all the parties in the same room together at the same time is the opportunity to short-circuit miscommunications. In an everyday environment where the end user talks to the liaison person who talks to the designer who talks to the programmer, there is ample opportunity for miscommunication and misinterpretation. When all the parties are gathered, there can be direct conversations that are beneficial to the health of the project being reviewed.

### What Should the Agenda Be?

The subject for review for the data warehouse environment is any aspect of design, development, project management, or usage that might prevent success. In short, any obstacle to success is relevant to the design review process. As a rule, the more controversial the subject, the more important that it be addressed during the review.

The questions that form the basis of the review process are addressed in the latter part of this chapter.

## The Results

There are three results of a data warehouse design review:

- an appraisal to management of the issues, and recommendations as to further action
- a documentation of where the system is in the design, as of the moment of review
- an "action item" list that states specific objectives and activities that are a result of the review process

## Administering the Review

The review is led by two people—a facilitator and a recorder. The facilitator is never the manager or the developer of the project being reviewed. If by some chance the facilitator is the project leader, the purpose of the review—from many perspectives—will have been defeated.

To conduct a successful review, it is mandatory that the facilitator be someone removed from the project for the following reasons:

- As an outsider, the facilitator provides an external perspective—a fresh look—at the system. This fresh look often reveals important insights that someone close to the design and development of the system is not capable of providing.
- As an outsider, a facilitator can offer criticism constructively. The criticism that comes from someone close to the development effort is usually taken personally and causes the design review to be reduced to a very base level.

## A Typical Data Warehouse Design Review

1.  Who is missing in the review? Is any group missing that ought to be in attendance? Are the following groups represented?

    ■ DA
    ■ DBA
    ■ programming
    ■ DSS analysts
    ■ end users
    ■ operations
    ■ systems programming
    ■ auditing
    ■ management

    Who is the official representative of each group?

    *ISSUE:* The proper attendance of the design review by the proper people is vital to the success of the review regardless of any other factors. Easily the most important attendee is the DSS analyst or the end user. Management may or may not attend at their discretion.

2.  Have the end user requirements been anticipated at all? If so, to what extent have they been anticipated? Does the end user representative to the design review agree with the representation of requirements that has been done?

    *ISSUE:* In theory, the DSS environment can be built without interaction with the end user—with no anticipation of end user requirements. However, if there is going to be a need to change the granularity of data in the data warehouse environment, or if EIS/artificial intelligence processing is to be built on top of the data warehouse, then some anticipation of requirements is a healthy exercise to go through. As a rule, even when the DSS requirements are anticipated, the level of participation of the end users is very low, and the end result is very sketchy. Furthermore, a large amount of time should not be allocated to the anticipation of end user requirements.

3. How much of the data warehouse has already been built in the data warehouse environment?

   ■ Which subjects?
   ■ What detail? what summarization?
   ■ How much data—in bytes? in rows? in tracks/cylinders?
   ■ How much processing?
   ■ What growth pattern is there, independent of the project being reviewed?

   *ISSUE:* The current status of the data warehouse environment has a great influence on the development project being reviewed. The very first development effort should be undertaken in a limited scope, trial-and-error basis. There should be little critical processing or data in this phase. In addition, a certain amount of quick feedback and reiteration of development should be anticipated.

   Later efforts of data warehouse development will have smaller margins for error.

4. How many major subjects have been identified from the data model? How many are currently implemented? How many are fully implemented? How many are being implemented by the development project being reviewed? How many will be implemented in the foreseeable future?

   *ISSUE:* As a rule, the data warehouse environment is implemented one subject at a time. The first few subjects should be considered almost as experiments. Later subject implementation should reflect the lessons learned from earlier development efforts.

5. Does any major DSS processing (i.e., data warehouse) exist outside the data warehouse environment? If so, what is the chance of conflict or overlap? What migration plan is there for DSS data and processing outside the data warehouse environment? Does the end user understand the migration that will have to occur? In what time frame will the migration be done?

*ISSUE:* Under normal circumstances, it is a major mistake to have only part of the data warehouse in the data warehouse environment and other parts out of the data warehouse environment. Only under the most exceptional circumstances should a "split" scenario be allowed. (One of those circumstances is a distributed DSS environment.)

If part of the data warehouse environment in fact does exist outside the data warehouse environment, there should be a plan to bring that part of the DSS world back into the data warehouse environment.

6. Have the major subjects that have been identified been broken down into lower levels of detail?

   ■ Have the keys been identified?
   ■ Have the attributes been identified?
   ■ Have the keys and attributes been grouped together?
   ■ Have the relationships between groupings of data been identified?
   ■ Have the time variances of each group been identified?

*ISSUE:* There needs to be a data model that serves as the intellectual heart of the data warehouse environment. The data model normally has three levels—a high-level model where entities and relationships are identified; a midlevel where keys, attributes, and relationships are identified; and a low level, where database design can be done. While not all of the data needs to be modeled down to the lowest level of detail in order for the DSS environment to begin to be built, at least the high-level model must be complete.

7. Is the design discussed in question 6 periodically reviewed? (How often? Informally? Formally?) What changes occur as a result of the review? How is end user feedback channeled to the developer?

*ISSUE:* From time to time, the data model needs to be updated to reflect changing business needs of the organization. As a rule, these changes are incremental in nature. It is very unusual to have a revolutionary change. There needs to be an assessment of the impact of these changes on both existing data warehouse data and planned data warehouse data.

8. Has the operational system of record been identified?

■ Has the source for every attribute been identified?
■ Have the conditions under which one attribute or another will be the source been identified?
■ If there is no source for an attribute, have default values been identified?
■ Has a common measure of attribute values been identified for those data attributes in the data warehouse environment?
■ Has a common encoding structure been identified for those attributes in the data warehouse environment?
■ Has a common key structure in the data warehouse environment been identified? Where the system of record key does not meet the conditions for the DSS key structure, has a conversion path been identified?

*ISSUE:* After the data model has been built, the system of record is identified. The system of record normally resides in the operational environment. The system of record represents the best source of existing data in support of the data model. The issues of integration are very much a factor in defining the system of record.

9. Has the frequency of extract processing—from the operational system of record to the data warehouse environment—been identified? How will the extract processing identify changes to the operational data from the last time an extract process was run?

■ by looking at time stamped data?
■ by changing operational application code?
■ by looking at a log file? an audit file?
■ by looking at a delta file?
■ by rubbing "before" and "after" images together?

*ISSUE:* The frequency of extract processing is an issue because of the resources required in refreshment, the complexity of refreshment processing, and the need to refresh data on a timely basis. The usefulness of data warehouse data is often related to how often the data warehouse data is refreshed.

One of the most complex issues—from a technical perspective—is in determining what data is to be scanned for extract processing. In some cases, the operational data that needs to pass from one environment to the next is straightforward. In other cases, it is not clear at all just what data should be examined as a candidate for populating the data warehouse environment.

10. What volume of data will normally be contained in the DSS environment? If the volume of data is large,

- Will multiple levels of granularity be specified?
- Will data be compacted?
- Will data be purged periodically?

*ISSUE:* In addition to the volumes of data processed by extraction, the designer needs to concern himself or herself with the volume of data actually in the data warehouse environment. The analysis of the volume of data in the data warehouse environment leads directly to the subject of the granularity of data in the data warehouse environment and the possibility of multiple levels of granularity.

11. What data will be filtered out of the operational environment as extract processing is done to create the data warehouse environment?

*ISSUE:* It is very unusual for all operational data to be passed to the DSS environment. Almost every operational environment contains data that is relevant only to the operational environment. This data should not be passed to the data warehouse environment.

12. What software will be used to feed the data warehouse environment?

- Has the software been thoroughly shaken out?
- What bottlenecks are there or might there be?

- Is the interface one-way or two-way?
- What technical support will be required?
- What volume of data will pass through the software?
- What monitoring of the software will be required?
- What alterations to the software will be periodically required?
- What outage will the alterations entail?
- How long will it take to install the software?
- Who will be responsible for the software?
- When will the software be ready for full-blown usage?

*ISSUE:* The data warehouse environment is capable of handling a large number of different types of software interfaces. However, the amount of break-in time and "infrastructure" time should not be underestimated. The DSS architect must not assume that the linking of the data warehouse environment to other environments will necessarily be straightforward and easy.

13. What software/interface will be required for the feeding of DSS departmental and individual processing out of the data warehouse environment?

- Has the interface been thoroughly tested?
- What bottlenecks might exist?
- Is the interface one-way or two-way?
- What technical support will be required?
- What traffic of data across the interface is anticipated?
- What monitoring of the interface will be required?
- What alterations to the interface will there be?
- What outage is anticipated as a result of alterations to the interface?
- How long will it take to install the interface?
- Who will be responsible for the interface?
- When will the interface be ready for full-scale utilization?

14. What physical organization of data will be used in the data warehouse environment? Can the data be directly accessed? Can it be sequentially accessed? Can indexes be easily and cheaply created?

*ISSUE:* The designer needs to review the physical configuration of the data warehouse environment to ensure that adequate capacity will be available and that the data, once in the environment, will be able to be manipulated in a responsive manner.

15. How easy will it be to add more storage to the data warehouse environment at a later point in time? How easy will it be to reorganize data within the data warehouse environment at a later point in time?

    *ISSUE:* No data warehouse is static and no data warehouse is fully specified at the initial moment of design. It is absolutely normal to make corrections in design throughout the life of the data warehouse environment. To construct a data warehouse environment either where midcourse corrections cannot be made or are awkward to make is to have a faulty design.

16. What is the likelihood that data in the data warehouse environment will need to be restructured frequently (i.e., columns added, dropped, or enlarged, keys modified, etc.)? What effect will these activities of restructuring have on ongoing processing in the data warehouse?

    *ISSUE:* Given the volume of data found in the data warehouse environment, restructuring it is not a trivial issue. In addition, with archival data, restructuring after a certain moment in time often becomes a logical impossibility.

17. What are the expected levels of performance in the data warehouse environment? Has a DSS service level agreement been drawn up either formally or informally?

    *ISSUE:* Unless a DSS service-level agreement has been formally drawn up, it is impossible to measure whether performance objectives are being met. The DSS service-level agreement should cover both DSS performance levels and downtime. Typical DSS service-level agreements state such things as

    - average performance during peak hours per units of data
    - average performance during off-peak hours per units of data

- worst performance levels during peak hours per units of data
- worst performance during off-peak hours per units of data
- system availability standards

One of the difficulties of the DSS environment is measuring performance. Unlike the operational environment where performance can be measured in absolute terms, DSS processing needs to be measured in relation to:

- how much processing the individual request is for
- how much processing is going on concurrently
- how many users are on the system at the moment of execution

18. What are the expected levels of availability? Has an availability agreement been drawn up for the data warehouse environment either formally or informally?

*ISSUE:* (See issue for question 17.)

19. How will the data in the data warehouse environment be indexed or accessed?

- Will any table have more than four indexes?
- Will any table be hashed?
- Will any table have only the primary key indexed?
- What overhead will be required to maintain the index?
- What overhead will be required to load the index initially?
- How often will the index be used?
- Can/should the index be altered to serve a wider usage?

*ISSUE:* Data in the data warehouse environment needs to be able to be accessed efficiently and in a flexible manner. Unfortunately, the heuristic nature of data warehouse processing is such that the need for indexes is unpredictable. The result is that the accessing of data in the data warehouse environment must not be taken for granted. As a rule, a multitiered approach to managing the access of data warehouse data is optimal:

- The hashed/primary key should satisfy most accesses.
- Secondary indexes should satisfy other popular access patterns.
- Temporary indexes should satisfy the occasional access.
- Extraction and subsequent indexing of a subset of data warehouse data should satisfy infrequent or once-in-a-lifetime accesses of data.

In any case, data in the data warehouse environment should not be stored in partitions so large that they cannot be indexed freely.

**20.** What volumes of processing in the data warehouse environment are to be expected? What about peak periods? What will the profile of the average day look like? the peak rate?

*ISSUE:* Not only should the volume of data in the data warehouse environment be anticipated, but the volume of processing should be anticipated as well.

**21.** What level of granularity of data in the data warehouse environment will there be?

- A high level?
- A low level?
- Multiple levels?
- Will rolling summarization be done?
- Will there be a level of true archival data?
- Will there be a living sample level of data?

*ISSUE:* Clearly, the most important design issue in the data warehouse environment is that of granularity of data and the possibility of multiple levels of granularity. In a word, if the granularity of the data warehouse environment is done properly, then all other issues become straightforward; if the granularity of data in the data warehouse environment is not designed properly, then all other design issues become complex and burdensome.

**22.** What purge criteria for data in the data warehouse environment will there be? Will data be truly purged or will it be compacted and archived elsewhere? What legal requirements are there? What audit requirements are there?

*ISSUE:* Even though data in the DSS environment is archival and of necessity has a low probability of access, it nevertheless has some probability of access (otherwise it should not be stored). When the probability of access reaches zero (or approaches zero), the data needs to be purged. Given that volume of data is one of the most burning issues in the data warehouse environment, purging data that is no longer useful is one of the more important aspects of the data warehouse environment.

23. What total processing capacity requirements are there:

   ■ for initial implementation?
   ■ for the data warehouse environment at maturity?

*ISSUE:* Granted that capacity requirements cannot be planned down to the last bit, it is worthwhile to at least estimate how much capacity will be required, just in case there is a mismatch between needs and what will be available.

24. What relationships between major subject areas will be recognized in the data warehouse environment? Will their implementation:

   ■ cause foreign keys to be kept up-to-date?
   ■ make use of artifacts?

What overhead is required in the building and maintenance of the relationship in the data warehouse environment?

*ISSUE:* One of the most important design decisions the data warehouse designer makes is that of how to implement relationships between data in the data warehouse environment. Data relationships are almost *never* implemented the same way in the data warehouse as they are in the operational environment.

25. Do the data structures internal to the data warehouse environment make use of:

   ■ arrays of data?
   ■ selective redundancy of data?
   ■ merging of tables of data?
   ■ creation of commonly used units of derived data?

*ISSUE:* Even though operational performance is not an issue in the data warehouse environment, performance is nevertheless an issue. The designer needs to consider the design techniques listed previously when they can reduce the total amount of I/O consumed. The techniques listed previously are classical physical denormalization techniques. Because data is not updated in the data warehouse environment, there are very few restrictions on what can and can't be done.

The factors that determine when one or the other design technique can be used include:

■ the predictability of occurrences of data
■ the predictability of the pattern of access of data
■ the need to gather artifacts of data

26. How long will a recovery take? Is operations prepared to execute a full data warehouse database recovery? a partial recovery? Will operations periodically practice recovery so that they will be prepared in the event of a need for recovery? What level of preparedness is exhibited by:

■ systems support?
■ applications programming?
■ the DBA?
■ the DA?

For each type of problem that can arise, is it clear whose responsibility the problem is?

*ISSUE:* As in operational systems, the designer must be prepared for the outages that occur during recovery. The frequency of recovery, the length of time required to bring the system back up, and the domino effect that can occur during an outage must all be considered.

Have instructions been prepared, tested, and written up? Have these instructions been kept up-to-date?

27. What level of preparation is there for reorganization/restructuring of:

■ operations?
■ systems support?

- applications programming?
- the DBA?
- the DA?

Have written instructions and procedures been set and tested? Are they up-to-date? Will they be kept up-to-date?

*ISSUE:* (See issues for question 26.)

**28.** What level of preparation is there for the loading of a database table by:

- operations?
- systems support?
- applications programming?
- the DBA?
- the DA?

Have written instructions and procedures been made and tested? Are they up-to-date? Will they be kept up-to-date?

*ISSUE:* The time and resources for loading can be considerable. This estimation needs to be done carefully and early in the development life cycle.

**29.** What level of preparation is there for the loading of a database index by:

- operations?
- systems support?
- applications programming?
- the DBA?
- the DA?

*ISSUE:* (See issue for question 28.)

**30.** If there is ever a controversy as to the accuracy of a piece of data in the data warehouse environment, how will the conflict be resolved? Has ownership (or at least source identification) been done for each unit of data in the data warehouse environment? Will ownership be able to be established if the need arises? Who will address the issues of ownership? Who will be the final authority as to the issues of ownership?

*ISSUE:* Ownership or stewardship of data is an essential component of success in the data warehouse environment. It is inevitable that at some moment in time the contents of a database will come into question. The designer needs to plan in advance for this eventuality.

31. How will corrections to data be made once data is placed in the data warehouse environment? How frequently will corrections be made? Will corrections be monitored? If there is a pattern of regularly occurring changes, how will corrections at the source (i.e., operational) level be made?

   *ISSUE:* On an infrequent, nonscheduled basis, there may need to be changes made to the data warehouse environment. If there appears to be a pattern to these changes, then the DSS analyst needs to investigate what is wrong in the operational system.

32. Will public summary data be stored separately from normal primitive DSS data? How much public summary data will there be? Will the algorithm required to create public summary data be stored?

   *ISSUE:* Even though the data warehouse environment contains primitive data, it is normal for there to be public summary data in the data warehouse environment as well. The designer needs to have prepared a logical place for this data to reside.

33. What security requirements will there be for the databases in the data warehouse environment? How will security be enforced?

   *ISSUE:* The access of data becomes an issue, especially as the detailed data becomes summarized or aggregated, where trends become apparent. The designer needs to anticipate the security requirements and prepare the data warehouse environment for them.

34. What audit requirements are there? How will audit requirements be met?

*ISSUE:* As a rule, system audit can be done at the data warehouse level, but this is almost always a mistake. Instead, detailed record audits are best done at the system of record level.

**35.** Will compaction of data be used? Has the overhead of compacting/decompacting data been considered? What is the overhead? What are the savings in terms of DASD for compacting/decompacting data?

*ISSUE:* On the one hand, compaction or encoding of data can save significant amounts of space. On the other hand, both compacting and encoding data require CPU cycles as data is decompacted or decoded upon access. The designer needs to make a thorough investigation of these issues and a deliberate tradeoff in the design.

**36.** Will encoding of data be done? Has the overhead of encoding/decoding been considered? What, in fact, is the overhead?

*ISSUE:* (See issue for question 35.)

**37.** Will metadata be stored for the data warehouse environment?

*ISSUE:* Metadata needs to be stored with any archival data as a matter of policy. There is nothing more frustrating than an analyst trying to solve a problem using archival data when he or she does not know the meaning of the contents of a field being analyzed. This frustration can be alleviated by storing the semantics of data with the data as it is archived. Over time, it is absolutely normal for the contents and structure of data in the data warehouse environment to change. Keeping track of the changing definition of data is something the designer should make sure is done.

**38.** Will reference tables be stored in the data warehouse environment?

*ISSUE:* (See issue for question 37.)

**39.** What catalog/dictionary will be maintained for the data warehouse environment? Who will maintain it? How will it be kept up-to-date? To whom will it be made available?

*ISSUE:* Not only is keeping track of the definition of data over time an issue, but keeping track of data currently in the data warehouse is important as well.

**40.** Will update (as opposed to loading and access of data) be allowed in the data warehouse environment? (Why? How much? Under what circumstances? On an exception-only basis?)

*ISSUE:* If any updating is allowed on a regular basis in the data warehouse environment, the designer should ask why. The only update that should occur should be on an exception basis and for only small amounts of data. Any exception to this severely compromises the efficacy of the data warehouse environment.

   When updates are done (if, in fact, they are done at all), they should be run in a private window when no other processing is done and when there is slack time on the processor.

**41.** What time lag will there be in getting data from the operational to the data warehouse environment? Will the time lag ever be less than 24 hours? If so, why and under what conditions? Will the passage of data from the operational to the data warehouse environment be a "push" or a "pull" process?

*ISSUE:* As a matter of policy, any time lag less than 24 hours should be questioned. As a rule, if a time lag of less than 24 hours is required, it is a sign that the developer is building operational requirements into the data warehouse. The flow of data through the data warehouse environment should always be a pull process, where data is pulled into the warehouse environment when it is needed, rather than being pushed into the warehouse environment when it is available.

**42.** What logging of data warehouse activity will be done? Who will have access to the logs?

*ISSUE: Most* DSS processing does not require logging. If an extensive amount of logging is required, it is usually a sign of lack of understanding of what type of processing is occurring in the data warehouse environment.

43. Will any data other than public summary data flow to the data warehouse environment from the departmental or individual level? If so, describe it.

*ISSUE:* Only on rare occasions should public summary data come from sources other than departmental or individual levels of processing. If much public summary data is coming from other sources, the analyst should ask why.

44. What external data (i.e., data other than that generated by a company's internal sources and systems) will enter the data warehouse environment? Will it be specially marked? Will its source be stored with the data? How frequently will the external data enter the system? How much of it will enter? Will an unstructured format be required? What happens if the external data is found to be inaccurate?

*ISSUE:* Even though there are legitimate sources of data other than a company's operational systems, if much data is entering externally, the analyst should ask why. Inevitably, there is much less flexibility with the content and regularity of availability of external data, although external data represents an important resource that should not be ignored.

45. What facilities will exist that will help the departmental and the individual user to locate data in the data warehouse environment?

*ISSUE:* One of the primary features of the data warehouse is ease of accessibility of data. And the first step in the accessibility of data is the initial location of the data.

46. Will there be an attempt to mix operational and DSS processing on the same machine at the same time? (Why? How much processing? How much data?)

*ISSUE:* For a multitude of reasons, it makes little sense to mix both operational and DSS processing on the same machine at the same time. Only where there are small amounts of data and small amounts of processing should there be a mixture. But these are not the conditions under which the data warehouse environment is most cost effective. (See the book *Data Architecture—The Information Paradigm*, Wiley, 1992 for an in-depth discussion of this issue.)

47. How much data will flow back to the operational level from the data warehouse level? at what rate? at what volume? under what response time constraints? Will the flowback be summarized data or individual units of data?

    *ISSUE:* As a rule, data flows from the operational to the warehouse level to the departmental to the individual levels of processing. There are some notable exceptions. As long as not too much data "backflows," and as long as the backflow is done in a disciplined fashion, there usually is no problem. However, if there is a lot of data engaged in backflow, then a red flag should be raised.

48. How much repetitive processing will occur against the data warehouse environment? Will precalculation and storage of derived data save processing time?

    *ISSUE:* It is absolutely normal for the data warehouse environment to have some amount of repetitive processing done against it. If only repetitive processing is done, however, or if no repetitive processing is planned, the designer should question why.

49. How will major subjects be partitioned? (By year? by geography? by functional unit? by product line?) Just how finely does the partitioning of the data break the data up?

    *ISSUE:* Given the volume of data that is inherent to the data warehouse environment and the unpredictable usage of the data, it is mandatory that data warehouse data be partitioned into physically small units that can be managed independently. The design issue is not whether partitioning is to be done. Instead, the design issue is how partitioning is to be accomplished. In general, partitioning is done at the application level rather than the system level.

The partitioning strategy should be reviewed with the following in mind:

- current volume of data
- future volume of data
- current usage of data
- future usage of data
- partitioning of other data in the warehouse
- usage of other data
- volatility of the structure of data

**50.** Will sparse indexes be created? Would they be useful?

*ISSUE:* Sparse indexes created in the right place can save huge amounts of processing. By the same token, sparse indexes require a fair amount of overhead in their creation and maintenance. The designer of the data warehouse environment should consider their use.

**51.** What temporary indexes will be created? How long will they be kept? How large will they be?

*ISSUE:* (See issue for question 50, except as it applies to temporary indexes.)

**52.** What documentation will there be at the departmental and individual levels? What documentation will there be of the interfaces between the data warehouse environment and the departmental environment? between the departmental and the individual environment? between the data warehouse environment and the individual environment?

*ISSUE:* Given the free-form nature of processing in the departmental and the individual environments, it is unlikely that there will be much in the way of documentation available. However, a documentation of the relationships between the environments is important for the reconcilability of data.

**53.** Will the user be charged for departmental processing? for individual processing? Who will be charged for data warehouse processing?

*ISSUE:* It is important that users have their own budgets and be charged for resources used. The instant that processing becomes "free," it is predictable that there will be massive misuse of resources. A chargeback system instills a sense of responsibility in the usage of resources.

**54.** If the data warehouse environment is to be distributed, have the common parts of the warehouse been identified? How are they to be managed?

*ISSUE:* In a distributed data warehouse environment, some of the data will necessarily be tightly controlled. The data needs to be identified up front by the designer and metadata controls put in place.

## SUMMARY

Design review is an important quality assurance practice that can greatly increase the satisfaction of the user and reduce development and maintenance costs. Thoroughly reviewing the many aspects of a warehouse environment prior to building the warehouse is a sound practice.

# Appendix

## DEVELOPING OPERATIONAL SYSTEMS—METH 1

---

### M1—Initial Project Activities

PRECEDING ACTIVITY: Decision to build an operational system.

FOLLOWING ACTIVITY: Preparing to use existing code/data.

TIME ESTIMATE: Indeterminate, depending on size of project.

NORMALLY EXECUTED ONCE OR MULTIPLE TIMES: Once.

SPECIAL CONSIDERATIONS: Because of the ambiguity of this step, it tends to drag out interminably. As long as 90 percent (or even less) of the system is defined here, the system development should continue into the next phase.

DELIVERABLE: Raw system requirements.

---

- Interviews—The output of interviews is the "softcore" description of what the system is to do, usually reflecting the opinion of middle management. The format of the output is very freeform. As a rule, the territory covered by interviews is not comprehensive.

- Data gathering—The output from this activity may come from many sources. In general, requirements—usually detailed—that are not caught elsewhere are gathered here. This is a freeform, catchall, requirements-gathering activity, the results of which "fill in the gap" for other requirements-gathering activities.
- JAD (Joint Application Design) session output—The output from these activities is the group "brainstorm" synopsis. One of the benefits of requirements formulation in a JAD session is the spontaneity and flow of ideas, and the critical mass that occurs by having different people in the same room focusing on a common objective. The output of one or more JAD sessions is a formalized set of requirements that collectively represent the end users' needs.
- Strategic business plan analysis—If the company has a strategic business plan, it makes sense to reflect on how the plan relates to the requirements of the system being designed. The influence of the strategic business plan can manifest itself in many ways—in setting growth figures, in identifying new lines of business, in describing organizational changes, and so forth. All of these factors, and more, shape the requirements of the system being built.
- Existing systems shape requirements for a new system profoundly. If related existing systems have been built, at the very least the interface between the new set of requirements and existing systems must be identified.

Conversion, replacement, parallel processing, and so forth are all likely topics. The output of this activity is a description of the impact and influence of existing systems on the requirements for the system being developed.

***PARAMETERS OF SUCCESS:*** When done properly, there is a reduction in the ambiguity of the system, the scope of the development effort is reasonably set, and the components of the system are well organized. The political as well as the technical components of the system should be captured and defined.

## M2—Using Existing Code/Data

PRECEDING ACTIVITY: System definition.

FOLLOWING ACTIVITY: Sizing, phasing.

TIME ESTIMATE: Done very quickly, usually in no more than a week in even the largest of designs.

NORMALLY EXECUTED ONCE OR MULTIPLE TIMES: Once.

SPECIAL CONSIDERATIONS: This step is one of the best ways to ensure code reusability and data reusability. This step is crucial to the integration of the environment.

In an architected environment, it is incumbent on every project to:

■ Use as much existing code/data as possible.
■ Prepare for future projects that will use code and data to be developed in the current project. The output from this step is an identification of existing code/data that can be reused and the steps that need to be taken for future processing.

If existing code/data is to be modified, the modifications are identified as a regular part of the system development requirements. If existing code/data is to be deleted, the deletion becomes a part of the specifications. If conversion of code/data is to be done, the conversion becomes a component of the development effort.

***PARAMETERS OF SUCCESS:*** To identify code/data that already exists that can be built upon; to identify what needs to be built to prepare for future efforts.

## M3—Sizing, Phasing

PRECEDING ACTIVITY: Using existing code/data.

FOLLOWING ACTIVITY: Requirements formalization; capacity analysis.

TIME ESTIMATE: This step goes rapidly, usually in a day or two, even for the largest of designs.

NORMALLY EXECUTED ONCE OR MULTIPLE TIMES: Once, then revisited for each continuing phase of development.

DELIVERABLE: Identification of phases of development.

After the general requirements are gathered, the next step is to size them and divide development up into phases. If the system to be developed is large, it makes sense to break it into development phases. In doing so, development is parceled out in small, manageable units. Of course, the different development phases must be organized into a meaningful sequence, so that the second phase builds on the first, the third phase builds on the first and second, and so on.

The output from this step is the breakup of general requirements into doable, manageable phases, if the requirements are large enough to require a breakup at all.

*PARAMETERS OF SUCCESS:* To continue the development process in increments that are both economic and doable (and within the political context of the organization as well).

## M4—Requirements Formalization

PRECEDING ACTIVITY: Sizing, phasing.

FOLLOWING ACTIVITY: ERD specification; functional decomposition.

TIME ESTIMATE: Indeterminate, depending on size of system, how well the scope of the system has been defined, and how ambiguous the design is up to this point.

NORMALLY EXECUTED ONCE OR MULTIPLE TIMES: Once per phase of development.

DELIVERABLE: Formal requirements specification.

Once the requirements have been gathered, sized, and phased (if necessary), the next step is to formalize them. In this step, the developer ensures that:

■ The requirements that have been gathered are complete, as far as it is reasonably possible to gather them.
■ The requirements are organized.
■ The requirements are readable, comprehensible, and at a low enough level of detail to be effective.
■ The requirements are not in conflict with each other.
■ The requirements do not overlap.
■ Operational and DSS requirements have been separated.

The output from this step is a formal requirements definition that is ready to go to detailed design.

***PARAMETERS OF SUCCESS:*** A succinct, organized, readable, doable, quantified, complete, usable set of requirements that is also a document for development.

---

## CA—Capacity Analysis

PRECEDING ACTIVITY: Sizing, phasing.

FOLLOWING ACTIVITY: ERD specification; functional decomposition.

TIME ESTIMATE: Depends on the size of the system being built, but with estimating tools and a focused planner, two or three weeks is a reasonable estimate for a reasonably sized system.

NORMALLY EXECUTED ONCE OR MULTIPLE TIMES: Once per phase of development.

SPECIAL CONSIDERATIONS: The capacity planning function has a history of confusing issues and including extraneous factors that do not merit special attention. It is important to keep the capacity planning portion of the development process focused and to the point. Otherwise, the exercise can become a roadblock to progress.

---

The gross amounts of resources to be consumed by the project being analyzed need to be estimated in this early phase of development. In particular, the following needs to be considered:

- DASD consumption
- Software requirements (including system software, utilities, special custom code, network software, interface software)
- CPU consumption
- I/O utilization
- Main memory requirements
- Network/channel utilization

Not only are raw requirements analyzed, but the arrival rate of transactions, peak-period processing, patterns of processing, response time requirements, availability requirements, and mean time to failure requirements are factored in as well.

In addition, if any hardware/software must be ordered, the lead time and the "burn in" time must be accounted for to ensure that proper resources will be in place in time for the application being reviewed.

The output of this phase of development is the assurance that the resources needed to be in place are, in fact, in place.

***PARAMETERS OF SUCCESS:*** No surprises when it comes to resources being in place when needed, the lead time needed to acquire resources, and the amount of resources needed.

## PREQ1—Technical Environment Definition

PRECEDING ACTIVITY: Establishment of the information processing environment.

FOLLOWING ACTIVITY: Sizing, phasing.

TIME ESTIMATE: NA

NORMALLY EXECUTED ONCE OR MULTIPLE TIMES: NA

SPECIAL CONSIDERATIONS: On occasion, it is necessary to build an application system from scratch, including defining the technical environment. If this is the case, the considerations of technical definition are outside the boundaries of the data-driven development methodology.

---

In order to proceed, it is necessary that the technical environment be defined. If the technical environment is not defined at this point, the result will be much "thrashing." Simply stated, detailed design cannot be meaningfully done until the technical environment is defined.

Certain elements of design beyond this point depend on one or the other of the technical cornerstones previously identified. At the least, the following should be established:

- The hardware platform(s) that will be used
- The operating system(s) that will be used
- The DBMS(s) that will be used
- The network software to be used
- The language(s) to be used for development

In addition to whatever hardware, software, and networking will be used, it is helpful to establish the following as well:

- Node residency definition (for network systems)
- Management of the system of record

***PARAMETERS OF SUCCESS:*** A firm, workable, technical definition that will meet the needs of the system being developed.

---

### D1—ERD (Entity Relationship Diagram)

PRECEDING ACTIVITY: Requirements formalization.

FOLLOWING ACTIVITY: Data item set specification.

TIME ESTIMATE: For even the largest of systems, two weeks suffice if the designers know what they are doing. If they don't, the amount of time required here is indeterminate.

NORMALLY EXECUTED ONCE OR MULTIPLE TIMES: Once.

DELIVERABLE: Identification of major subject areas.

---

From the general set of formal requirements comes the need to identify the major subjects that will make up the system and the relationship of those major subjects. As a rule, the major subject is at the highest level of abstraction.

Typical major subjects are CUSTOMER, PRODUCT, TRANS-ACTION, and so forth. The relationships of the major subjects are identified, as well as the cardinality of the relationship.

The output of this step is the identification of the major subjects that will make up the system, as well as their relationships to each other.

***PARAMETERS OF SUCCESS:*** All major subjects are identified so that there are no conflicts in domain; they are identified at the highest level of abstraction.

One major parameter of success is that only primitive data be modeled. Another parameter of success is that the scope of the model be defined prior to starting the ERD modeling.

---

### D2—DIS (Data Item Sets)

PRECEDING ACTIVITY: ERD definition.

FOLLOWING ACTIVITY: Performance analysis; data store definition.

TIME ESTIMATE: As long as one month per subject area.

NORMALLY EXECUTED ONCE OR MULTIPLE TIMES: Once for each subject area.

---

Each subject is further broken down—in terms of level of detail—into a DIS (data item set). The DIS contains attributes of data, the grouping of attributes, and keys. In addition, "type of" data is identified. Other structures of data here include connectors—representations of relationships—and secondary groupings of data. The output from this step is the fleshing out of the subject areas identified in D1.

***PARAMETERS OF SUCCESS:*** All types of the major subject are identified; all connectors are correctly identified; all relationships are identified by a connector; all attributes are identified; all attributes are grouped with other attributes that share the same relationship to the key of the grouping of data; all multiply occurring groups of attributes are separated from singularly occurring groups of attributes; all recursive relationships are designed in the most general case necessary. Only primitive data is found here. Derived data is identified, stored, and managed elsewhere.

---

## D3—Performance Analysis

PRECEDING ACTIVITY: Data item set development.

FOLLOWING ACTIVITY: Physical database design.

TIME ESTIMATE: One week per subject area, unless the subject area is huge.

NORMALLY EXECUTED ONCE OR MULTIPLE TIMES: Once per subject area.

SPECIAL CONSIDERATIONS: This step does not need to be done in the case of small amounts of data and/or small amounts of processing.

---

This step is performed if the volume of data, the volume of processing, the traffic over the network, the growth of data and processing, or the peak period of processing will produce significant amounts of activity. If none of those factors will occur, this step is not done.

In this step, the issue of physical denormalization of data is addressed. Specifically, the design practices of merging tables, selective introduction of redundancy, creating popular pools of derived data, creating arrays of data, and further separation of data where there is a wide disparity in the probability of its access are considered.

If this activity is done at all, the output reflects a much more streamlined design, with little or no loss of the benefits of normalization of data.

***PARAMETERS OF SUCCESS:*** A design that will be efficient to access and update, in terms of both data and programs that access and update data. Done properly, this step ensures efficient resource utilization.

---

### D4—Physical Database Design

PRECEDING ACTIVITY: Performance analysis.

FOLLOWING ACTIVITY: Pseudocode development.

TIME ESTIMATE: One day per table to be designed.

NORMALLY EXECUTED ONCE OR MULTIPLE TIMES: Once per table.

SPECIAL CONSIDERATIONS: If the input to this step is incorrect or ambiguous, the amount of work required here can be much more than that estimated.

DELIVERABLE: Tables, databases physically designed.

---

Now the output from D3 and/or D4 is used to produce a physical database design. Some of the characteristics of the output include:

■ Indexing
■ Physical attribution of data
■ Partitioning strategies
■ Designation of keys
■ Clustering/interleaving
■ Management of variable-length data
■ NULL/NOT NULL specification
■ Referential integrity

The output of this step is the actual specification of the database to the DBMS, or whatever data management software/conventions are adopted.

***PARAMETERS OF SUCCESS:*** Done properly, this stage of analysis transforms all the considerations of logical design of data, performance, update, access, availability, reorganization, restructuring of data, and so on, into a workable database design.

---

### P1—Functional Decomposition

PRECEDING ACTIVITY: Requirements formalization.

FOLLOWING ACTIVITY: Context level 0 specification.

TIME ESTIMATE: Depends on size of system and degree of ambiguity (and how firmly and unambiguously the scope has been established). As a rule, two weeks for a reasonably sized system is adequate.

NORMALLY EXECUTED ONCE OR MULTIPLE TIMES: Once per phase of development.

---

From the requirements document comes the functional decomposition. The functional decomposition merely takes the broad function accomplished by the system and breaks it down into a series of successively smaller functions (down to a level sometimes called the *primitive* level).

The output of this process is a large functional decomposition describing the different activities to be performed from a high level to a low level.

***PARAMETERS OF SUCCESS:*** Solely reflected in this section and are the functions to be designed. Factored into the step are the considerations of other functions that have served or will serve as building blocks. Done properly, this step produces a document that is comprehensible, organized, readable, and complete.

---

### P2—Context Level 0

PRECEDING ACTIVITY: Functional decomposition.

FOLLOWING ACTIVITY: Context level 1-n specification.

TIME ESTIMATE: Three days.

NORMALLY EXECUTED ONCE OR MULTIPLE TIMES: Once per phase.

---

Context level 0 of the functional decomposition describes, at the highest level of abstraction, the major activities to be developed. Context level 0 for process specification corresponds to the ERD in data modeling.

***PARAMETERS OF SUCCESS:*** Done correctly, *only* the major activities of the system and how they relate are identified in this document.

---

### P3—Context Level 1-*n*

PRECEDING ACTIVITY: Context level 0 specification.

FOLLOWING ACTIVITY: DFD specification.

TIME ESTIMATE: One day per function.

NORMALLY EXECUTED ONCE OR MULTIPLE TIMES: Once per function.

DELIVERABLE: Complete functional decomposition. (Note: Multiple steps contribute to this deliverable.)

---

The remaining levels of the functional decomposition describe the more detailed activities that occur. Context levels 1-n correspond, in terms of process design, to the data item set (DIS) in terms of data design.

***PARAMETERS OF SUCCESS:*** When this step has been done properly, all major activities are broken down to a primitive level. The breakdown is orderly, organized, complete, and in accordance with the flow of activity.

---

### P4—Data Flow Diagram (DFD)

PRECEDING ACTIVITY: Context level 1-*n* specification.

FOLLOWING ACTIVITY: Algorithmic specification.

TIME ESTIMATE: One hour per activity (at a primitive level).

NORMALLY EXECUTED ONCE OR MULTIPLE TIMES: Once per activity.

DELIVERABLE: Data flow diagram for each process.

---

At each context level $n$—the primitive level—a DFD is drawn. The DFD indicates the input to a process, the output of a process, the data stores needed to establish the process, and a brief description of the process. A DFD may be done for context levels higher than $n$ if it turns out that a program or process is likely to be written for that context level.

***PARAMETERS OF SUCCESS:*** The input and output for every primitive activity is identified, and the flow of activity is identified as well. Data stores are outlined, and the work to be done by each activity is specified.

---

**P5—Algorithmic Specification; Performance Analysis**

PRECEDING ACTIVITY: DFD specification.

FOLLOWING ACTIVITY: Pseudocode.

TIME ESTIMATE: Varies from five minutes to two days per activity at the primitive level that must be specified.

NORMALLY EXECUTED ONCE OR MULTIPLE TIMES: Once per activity.

---

The processes that are defined by the DFD for primitives are further broken down into detailed algorithmic specification. In other words, in this step, the actual processing to occur step by step is outlined.

In addition, if performance is to be an issue, the effect of performance on program design is factored in. Such design techniques as the following are considered here:

- Breaking a long-running program into a series of shorter programs
- Requiring a program to access a smaller amount of data
- Shortening the time a unit of data is locked
- Changing a lock from update potential to access only

***PARAMETERS OF SUCCESS:*** Algorithmic specification is done correctly when all details needed for specification are identified, and only details needed for specification are identified, one step at a time, including all possibilities. In addition, conformance to the standard work unit (SWU) is ensured here.

---

### P6—Pseudocode

PRECEDING ACTIVITY: Algorithmic specification; physical database design; data store design.

FOLLOWING ACTIVITY: Coding.

TIME ESTIMATE: Varies (see previous activity).

NORMALLY EXECUTED ONCE OR MULTIPLE TIMES: Once per activity (at the primitive level).

---

The algorithms and program specifications are further refined into pseudocode. The designer ensures that all needed data for processing is available. All variables used in calculations, transformations, updates, and so on, are identified here. Any loose ends are identified. Performance at the design level is considered here. The output of this activity is coding specifications ready for actual code.

***PARAMETERS OF SUCCESS:*** The final pass at programming specification includes:

- Completeness
- Order of execution
- All required cases

- All contingencies, including error handling and exception conditions
- Structure of coding

---

### P7—Coding

PRECEDING ACTIVITY: Pseudocode.

FOLLOWING ACTIVITY: Walkthrough.

TIME ESTIMATE: Depends, from one day per activity to two weeks per activity.

NORMALLY EXECUTED ONCE OR MULTIPLE TIMES: Once per activity.

DELIVERABLE: Source code.

---

The pseudocode is translated into source code. If the data has been designed properly, and if the specification of pseudocode has been thorough, this step goes smoothly. The output of this step is source code.

***PARAMETERS OF SUCCESS:*** The complete and efficient translation of pseudocode into code, including inline documentation. Done properly, all requirements previously identified are satisfied by this point.

---

### P8—Walkthrough

PRECEDING ACTIVITY: Coding.

FOLLOWING ACTIVITY: Compilation.

TIME ESTIMATE: One hour per activity.

NORMALLY EXECUTED ONCE OR MULTIPLE TIMES: Once per activity.

---

The walkthrough is the verbal explanation of code in front of peers. The intent is to find coding errors (or any other kind) before testing. The output of this step is code that has been publicly aired and is as free from error as possible.

***PARAMETERS OF SUCCESS:*** The detection of errors prior to coding. When this step has been done properly, there will be very few errors left to be found by other means.

---

### P9—Compilation

PRECEDING ACTIVITY: Walkthrough.

FOLLOWING ACTIVITY: Unit testing; stress testing.

TIME ESTIMATE: One hour or less per activity.

NORMALLY EXECUTED ONCE OR MULTIPLE TIMES: Until a clean compile is achieved.

---

Source code is run through the compiler. All errors found in compilation are corrected. The output of this step is compiled code, ready to be tested.

***PARAMETERS OF SUCCESS:*** Compiled code that is ready for testing.

---

### P10—Unit Testing

PRECEDING ACTIVITY: Compilation.

FOLLOWING ACTIVITY: Implementation.

TIME ESTIMATE: Varies widely.

NORMALLY EXECUTED ONCE OR MULTIPLE TIMES: Varies.

---

Compiled code is tested. There are several levels of unit testing. The simplest (lowest) level of unit testing occurs when the compiled module is tested by itself, ensuring that the function it

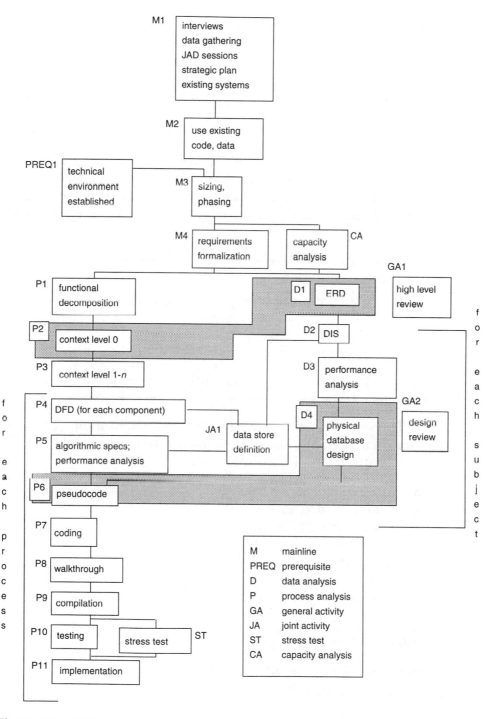

**Figure A.1** METH 1.

does is satisfactory. Next, the compiled code is added to other code with which the compiled code will have to work. New levels of unit testing occur in order to ensure the integration of the compiled code with other modules that will be interfaced. A third level of unit testing occurs when major groups of modules are ready to be tested together.

The output of this step is tested code, ready for execution.

***PARAMETERS OF SUCCESS:*** When executed properly, the code that passes on to the next step has program logic correctly specified. Furthermore, all conditions are tested before code is passed to the next stage, including error and exception conditions.

---

### P11—Implementation

PRECEDING ACTIVITY: Unit test; stress test.

FOLLOWING ACTIVITY: NA

TIME ESTIMATE: NA

DELIVERABLE: A system that satisfies specifications.

---

There are many activities in implementation. To some extent, implementation is an ongoing activity. Some of the typical activities of implementation are:

- Training, indoctrination
- Loading of programs
- Initial loading of data
- Conversions of data, if necessary
- Monitoring utilities established
- Writing documentation
- Recovery, reorg procedures established

The output of this step (if there really is an *end* to the step) is a satisfactorily running system.

***PARAMETERS OF SUCCESS:*** When this step is done, the result is a happy user.

## DATA WAREHOUSE DEVELOPMENT—METH 2

---

### DSS1—Data Model Analysis

PRECEDING ACTIVITY: The commitment to build a data warehouse.

FOLLOWING ACTIVITY: Subject area analysis; breadbox analysis; data warehouse design.

TIME ESTIMATE: Varies widely, depending on the status and quality of the data model.

NORMALLY EXECUTED ONCE OR MULTIPLE TIMES: Once.

---

At the outset, a data model needs to have been defined. The data model needs to have:

■ Identified the major subject areas
■ Clearly defined boundaries of the model
■ Separated primitive from derived data
■ The following identified for each subject area:
   ■ Keys
   ■ Attributes
   ■ Groupings of attributes
   ■ Relationships among groupings of attributes
   ■ Multiply occurring data
   ■ "Type of" data

The output from this step is a confirmation that the organization has built a solid data model. If the model does not meet the criteria specified, then progress should be halted until the model is brought up to standards of quality.

***PARAMETERS OF SUCCESS:*** The data model will have:

■ Major subjects identified
■ Each major subject with its own separate definition of data, including:
   ■ Subtypes of data
   ■ Attributes of data

- Clearly defined relationships of data
- Defined groupings of data
- Defined keys

In addition, each group of data that will go into the data warehouse will have DSS data and operational-only data delineated. All DSS data will have its own time-variant key specified, usually as the lower order of a higher key.

---

## DSS2—Breadbox Analysis

PRECEDING ACTIVITY: Data model analysis.

FOLLOWING ACTIVITY: Data warehouse database design.

TIME ESTIMATE: From one day to two weeks, depending on how well the scope has been defined, how well the data model has been defined, etc.

NORMALLY EXECUTED ONCE OR MULTIPLE TIMES: Once.

DELIVERABLE: Granularity analysis.

---

Once the model has been analyzed and brought up to a level of sufficient quality, the next step is to do breadbox analysis. *Breadbox analysis* is a sizing—in terms of gross estimates—of the DSS environment. If volume of data is going to be a problem, it is important to know at the outset. Breadbox analysis simply projects—in raw terms—how much data the data warehouse will hold.

The output of breadbox analysis is simple—if the data warehouse is to contain large amounts of data, then multiple levels of granularity need to be considered. If the data warehouse is not to contain a massive amount of data, then there is no need to plan the design for multiple levels of granularity.

***PARAMETERS OF SUCCESS:*** An estimate of the amount of data—in terms of number of rows—both on the one-year horizon and on the five-year horizon for the entire data warehouse environment, is the result of the process. Based on the results of the estimate, the issue of whether different levels of granularity are needed is decided. If multiple levels of granularity are needed, defining exactly what those levels are is a part of the output of this step.

---

### DSS3—Technical Assessment

PRECEDING ACTIVITY: The commitment to build a data warehouse.

FOLLOWING ACTIVITY: Technical environment preparation.

TIME ESTIMATE: One week.

NORMALLY EXECUTED ONCE OR MULTIPLE TIMES: Once.

DELIVERABLE: Technical environment assessment.

---

The technical requirements for managing the data warehouse are very different from the technical requirements and consideration for managing data and processing in the operational environment. That is why a separate, central store of DSS data is so popular.

***PARAMETERS OF SUCCESS:*** When executed properly, the technical definition of the data warehouse satisfies the following criteria:

- Ability to manage large amounts of data
- Ability to allow data to be accessed flexibly
- Ability to organize data according to a data model
- Ability both to receive and send data to a wide variety of technologies
- Ability to have data periodically loaded en masse
- Ability to access data a set at a time or a record at a time

---

### DSS4—Technical Environment Preparation

PRECEDING ACTIVITY: Technical assessment.

FOLLOWING ACTIVITY: Data warehouse design; population.

TIME ESTIMATE: One week to one month.

NORMALLY EXECUTED ONCE OR MULTIPLE TIMES: Once.

---

Once the architectural configuration for the data warehouse has been established, the next step is to technically identify how the configuration can be accommodated. Some of the typical issues that must be addressed here are

- The amount of DASD required
- What link—either across the network or into the network—will be required
- The volume of processing anticipated
- How to minimize and/or alleviate conflicts of processing between competing access programs
- The volume of traffic that will be generated from the technology that controls the data warehouse
- The nature of traffic—either short or long bursts—generated from the technology that controls the data warehouse

***PARAMETERS OF SUCCESS:*** When this step has been done properly, there are no technical barriers to success. The technical components that should have been installed, allocated, "burned in," and ready to receive data include:

- The network
- DASD
- The operating system managing DASD
- The interface to and from the warehouse
- The software used to manage the data warehouse
- The data warehouse

---

## DSS5—Subject Area Analysis

PRECEDING ACTIVITY: Data model analysis.

FOLLOWING ACTIVITY: Source system analysis.

TIME ESTIMATE: One day.

NORMALLY EXECUTED ONCE OR MULTIPLE TIMES: Once per population project.

DELIVERABLE: Which subject area to build next.

---

Now the subject area to be populated is selected. The first subject area to be selected must be large enough to be meaningful and small enough to be implemented. If by some chance a subject area is truly large and complex, a subset of the subject area may be chosen for implementation. The output from this step is a scope of effort in terms of a subject.

***PARAMETERS OF SUCCESS:*** The output from this phase when done correctly is a definition of what data is to be populated next. In the first few populations, small subjects are usually selected. In later populations, larger subjects, or even subsets of subjects, are selected. When properly done, the subject selected for population meets the needs of the current stage of development of the data warehouse.

---

### DSS6—Data Warehouse Design

PRECEDING ACTIVITY: Data model analysis; source system analysis; breadbox analysis.

FOLLOWING ACTIVITY: Program specification.

TIME ESTIMATE: One week to three weeks.

NORMALLY EXECUTED ONCE OR MULTIPLE TIMES: Once.

DELIVERABLE: Physical database design for the warehouse.

---

The data warehouse is designed based on the data model. Some of the characteristics of the ultimate design include:

■ An accommodation of the different levels of granularity, if indeed there are multiple levels of granularity

- An orientation of data to the major subjects of the corporation
- The presence of only primitive data and publicly derived data
- The absence of non-DSS data
- Time variancy of every record of data
- Physical denormalization of data where applicable (i.e., where performance warrants)
- Creation of data artifacts where data that once was in the operational environment is brought over to the data warehouse

The output of this step is a physical database design of the data warehouse. Note that not all of the data warehouse needs to be designed in detail at the outset. It is entirely acceptable to design the major structures of the data warehouse initially, then fill in the details at a later point in time.

***PARAMETERS OF SUCCESS:*** When this step is properly done, the result is a data warehouse that has a manageable amount of data that can be loaded, accessed, indexed, and searched in a reasonably efficient fashion.

---

**DSS7—Source System Analysis**

PRECEDING ACTIVITY: Subject area analysis.

FOLLOWING ACTIVITY: Program specification; data warehouse design.

TIME ESTIMATE: One week per subject area.

NORMALLY EXECUTED ONCE OR MULTIPLE TIMES: Once per subject area.

DELIVERABLE: Identification of the system of record.

---

Once the subject to be populated is identified, the next activity is to identify the source data for the subject in the existing systems environment. It is absolutely normal for there to be a variety of sources of data for DSS data. It is at this point that the issues of integration are addressed. The following represents the issues to be addressed here:

- Key structure/key resolution as data passes from the operational environment to the DSS environment
- Attribution
  - What to do when there are multiple sources to choose from
  - What to do when there are no sources to choose from
  - What transformations—encoding/decoding, conversions, etc.—must be made as data is selected for transport to the DSS environment
- How time variancy will be created from current value data
- Structure—how the DSS structure will be created from the operational structure
- Relationships—how operational relationships will appear in the DSS environment

The output of this step is the mapping of data from the operational environment to the DSS environment.

***PARAMETERS OF SUCCESS:*** When done properly, the source system that serves the needs of the data warehouse uses data that is timely, complete, accurate, near to the source and easy to access, and that conforms to the structure of data warehouse needs.

---

### DSS8—Specifications

PRECEDING ACTIVITY: Source system analysis; data warehouse design.

FOLLOWING ACTIVITY: Programming.

TIME ESTIMATE: One week per extract/integration program.

NORMALLY EXECUTED ONCE OR MULTIPLE TIMES: Once for each program that needs to be written.

---

Once the interface between the operational and the DSS environments has been outlined, the next step is to formalize it in terms of program specifications. Some of the major issues here include the following:

- How do I know what operational data to scan?
  - Is the operational data time stamped?
  - Is there a *delta* file?
  - Are there system logs/audit logs that can be used?
  - Can existing source code and data structure be changed to create a delta file?
  - Do *before* and *after* image files have to be rubbed together?
- How do I store the output, once scanned?
  - Is the DSS data preallocated, preformatted?
  - Is data appended?
  - Is data replaced?
  - Are updates in the DSS environment made?

The output from this step is the actual program specifications that will be used to bring data over from the operational environment to the data warehouse.

***PARAMETERS OF SUCCESS:*** When properly done, this step allows the extract and integration of data to be done as efficiently and as simply as possible. (Seldom is this a smooth, simple process.)

## DSS9—Programming

PRECEDING ACTIVITY: Specification.

FOLLOWING ACTIVITY: Population.

TIME ESTIMATE: One week per extract/integration program.

NORMALLY EXECUTED ONCE OR MULTIPLE TIMES: Once per program.

DELIVERABLE: Extract, integration, time-perspective program transformation.

This step includes all the standard activities of programming, such as the following:

- Development of pseudocode
- Coding
- Compilation
- Walkthroughs
- Testing—unit, stress—in its many forms

*PARAMETERS OF SUCCESS:* When done properly, code that is generated out of this step is efficient, documented, able to be changed easily, accurate, and complete.

---

### DSS10—Population

PRECEDING ACTIVITY: Programming; technical environment preparation.

FOLLOWING ACTIVITY: Usage of the data warehouse.

TIME ESTIMATE: NA

NORMALLY EXECUTED ONCE OR MULTIPLE TIMES: NA

DELIVERABLE: Usable data warehouse.

---

This step entails nothing more than the execution of the DSS programs previously developed. The issues addressed here are the following:

- Frequency of population
- Purging populated data
- Aging populated data (i.e., running tallying summary programs)
- Managing multiple levels of granularity
- Refreshing living sample data (if living sample tables have been built)

The output of this step is a populated, functional data warehouse.

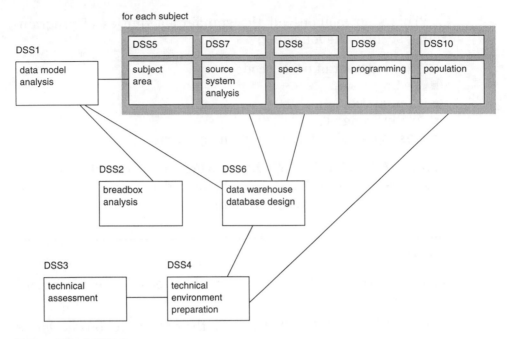

**Figure A.2** METH 2.

***PARAMETERS OF SUCCESS:*** When done properly, the result is an accessible, comprehensible warehouse that serves the needs of the DSS community.

## HEURISTIC PROCESSING—METH 3

The third phase of development in the architected environment is the usage of data warehouse data for the purpose of analysis. Once the data in the data warehouse environment is populated, usage may commence.

There are several essential differences between the development that occurs at this level and development in other parts of the environment. The first major difference is that at this phase the development process always starts with data, that is, the data in the data warehouse. The second difference is that requirements are not known at the start of the development process. The third difference (which is really a byproduct of the first two factors) is that processing is done in a very iterative, heuristic fashion. In other types of development, there is always a certain amount of iteration. But in the DSS component of development that occurs after the data warehouse is developed, the whole nature of iteration changes. Iteration of processing is a normal and essential part of the analytical development process, much more so than it is elsewhere.

The steps taken in the DSS development components can be divided into two categories—the repetitively occurring analysis (sometimes called the "departmental" or "functional" analysis) and the true heuristic processing (the "individual" level).

Figure A.3 shows the steps of development to be taken after the data warehouse has begun to be populated.

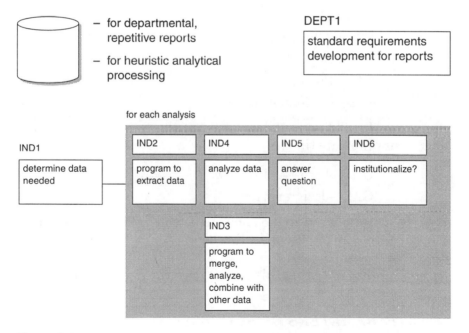

**Figure A.3** METH 3.

## HEURISTIC DSS DEVELOPMENT—METH 4

DEPT1—Repeat Standard Development—For repetitive analytical processing (usually called delivering standard reports), the normal requirements-driven processing occurs. This means that the following steps (described earlier) are repeated:

M1—interviews, data gathering, JAD, strategic plan, existing systems

M2—sizing, phasing

M3—requirements formalization

P1—functional decomposition

P2—context level 0

P3—context level 1-n

P4—DFD for each component

P5—algorithmic specification; performance analysis

P6—pseudocode

P7—coding

P8—walkthrough

P9—compilation

P10—testing

P11—implementation

In addition, at least part of the following will occur at the appropriate time:

GA1—high-level review

GA2—design review

It does not make sense to do the data analysis component of development because the developer is working from the data warehouse.

The output of this activity are reports that are produced on a regular basis.

***PARAMETERS OF SUCCESS:*** When done properly, this step ensures that regular report needs are met. These needs usually include:

- Regulatory reports
- Accounting reports
- Key factor indicator reports
- Marketing reports
- Sales reports

Information needs that are predictable and repetitive are met by this function.

***NOTE:*** For highly iterative processing, there are parameters of success, but they are met collectively by the process. Since requirements are not defined a priori, the parameters of success for each iteration are somewhat subjective.

## IND1—Determine Data Needed

At this point, data in the data warehouse is selected for potential usage in the satisfaction of reporting requirements. While the developer works from an educated guess perspective, it is understood that the first two or three times this activity is initiated, only some of the needed data will be retrieved.

The output from this activity is data selected for further analysis.

## IND2—Program to Extract Data

Once the data for analytical processing is selected, the next step is to write a program to access and strip the data. The program written should be able to be modified easily because it is anticipated that the program will be run, modified, then rerun on numerous occasions.

DELIVERABLE: Data pulled from the warehouse for DSS analysis.

## IND3—Combine, Merge, Analyze

After data has been selected, it is prepared for analysis. Often this means editing the data, combining it with other data, and refining it.

Like all other heuristic processes, it is anticipated that this program be written so that it is easily modifiable and able to be rerun quickly. The output of this activity is data fully usable for analysis.

DELIVERABLE: Analysis with other relevant data.

### IND4—Analyze Data

Once data has been selected and prepared, the question is "Do the results obtained meet the needs of the analyst?" If the results are not met, another iteration occurs. If the results are met, then the final report preparation is begun.

DELIVERABLE: Fulfilled requirements.

### IND5—Answer Question

The final report that is produced is often the result of many iterations of processing. Very seldom is the final conclusion the result of a single iteration of analysis.

### IND6—Institutionalization

The final issue to be decided is whether the final report that has been created should be institutionalized. If there is a need to run the report repetitively, it makes sense to submit the report as a set of requirements and to rebuild the report as a regularly occurring operation.

### SUMMARY

How the different activities relate to each other and to the notion of data architecture are described by the diagram shown in Figure A.4.

## SELECTED TOPICS

The best way to describe the data-driven nature of the development methodology is graphically. Figure A.5 shows that the data model is at the heart of the data-driven methodology.

The data model relates to the design of operational data, to the design of data in the data warehouse, to the development and design process for operational data, and to the development and design process for the data warehouse. Figure A.5 shows how the same data model relates to each of those activities and databases.

The data model is the key to identifying commonality across applications. But one might ask, "Isn't it important to recognize the commonality of processing as well?"

The answer is that of course it is important to recognize the commonality of processing across applications. But there are several problems with trying to focus on the commonality of processes—processes change much more rapidly than data, processes tend to mix common and unique processing so tightly that they are often inseparable, and classical process analysis often places an artificially small boundary on the scope of the design. Data is inherently more stable than processing. The scope of a data analysis is easier to enlarge than the scope of a process model. Therefore, focusing upon data as the keystone for recognizing commonality makes sense. In addition, the assumption is made that if commonality of data is discovered, the discovery will lead to a corresponding commonality of processing.

For these reasons, the data model—which cuts across all applications and reflects the corporate perspective—is the foundation for identifying and unifying commonality of data and processing.

### Deliverables

The steps of the data-driven development methodology include a deliverable. In truth, some steps contribute to a deliverable with other steps. For the most part, however, each step of the methodology has its own unique deliverable.

The deliverables of the process analysis component of the development of operational systems are shown by Figure A.6.

# DATA-DRIVEN DEVELOPMENT METHODOLOGY
## DSS Sector

## Data Warehouse

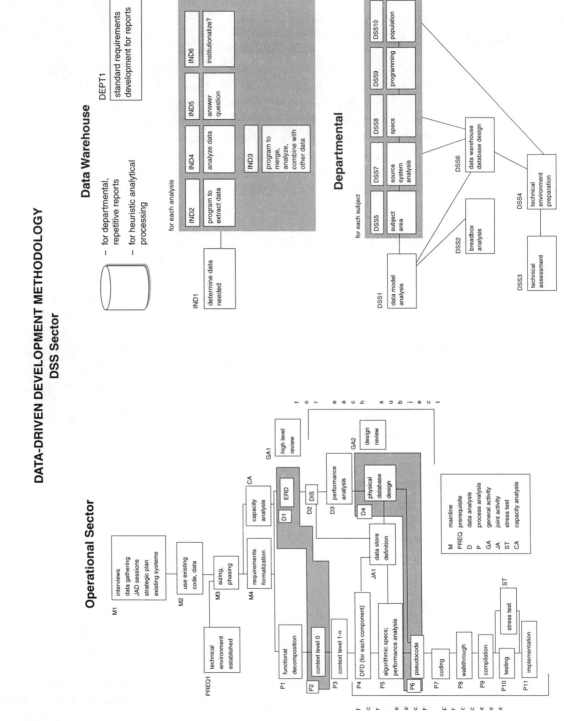

– for departmental, repetitive reports
– for heuristic analytical processing

**DEPT1** standard requirements development for reports

for each analysis

**IND2** program to extract data

**IND4** analyze data

**IND5** answer question

**IND6** institutionalize?

**IND3** program to merge, analyze, combine with other data

**IND1** determine data needed

## Departmental

for each subject

**DSS5** subject area

**DSS7** source system analysis

**DSS8** specs

**DSS9** programming

**DSS10** population

**DSS1** data model analysis

**DSS2** breadbox analysis

**DSS6** data warehouse database design

**DSS4** technical environment preparation

**DSS3** technical assessment

## Operational Sector

**M1** interviews, data gathering, JAD sessions, strategic plan, existing systems

**M2** use existing code, data

**M3** sizing, phasing

**M4** requirements formalization

**CA** capacity analysis

**GA1** high level review

**PREQ1** technical environment established

**P1** functional decomposition

**P2** context level 0

**P3** context level 1-n

**P4** DFD (for each component)

**P5** algorithmic specs; performance analysis

**P6** pseudocode

**P7** coding

**P8** walkthrough

**P9** compilation

**P10** testing

**ST** stress test

**P11** implementation

**D1** ERD

**D2** DIS

**D3** performance analysis

**D4** physical database design

**GA2** design review

**JA1** data store definition

for each process

for each process

| | |
|---|---|
| M | mainline |
| PREQ | prerequisite |
| D | data analysis |
| P | process analysis |
| GA | general activity |
| JA | joint activity |
| ST | stress test |
| CA | capacity analysis |

# DATA ARCHITECTURE

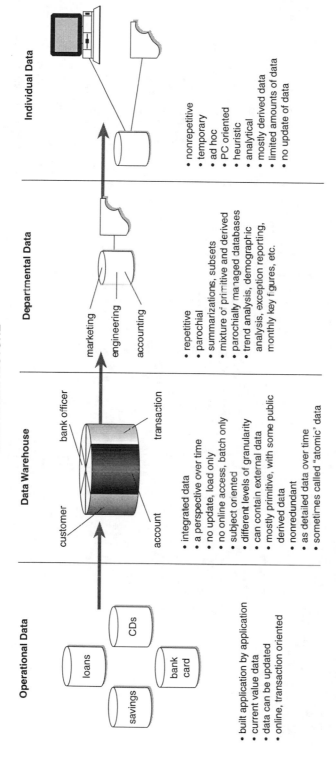

**Operational Data**

- built application by application
- current value data
- data can be updated
- online, transaction oriented

savings | loans | CDs | bank card

**Data Warehouse**

customer | bank officer | account | transaction

- integrated data
- a perspective over time
- no update, load only
- no online access, batch only
- subject oriented
- different levels of granularity
- can contain external data
- mostly primitive, with some public derived data
- nonredundant
- as detailed data over time
- sometimes called "atomic" data

**Departmental Data**

marketing | engineering | accounting

- repetitive
- parochial
- summarizations, subsets
- mixture of primitive and derived
- parochially managed databases
- trend analysis, demographic analysis, exception reporting, monthly key figures, etc.

**Individual Data**

- nonrepetitive
- temporary
- ad hoc
- PC oriented
- heuristic
- analytical
- mostly derived data
- limited amounts of data
- no update of data

**Figure A.4** METH 4. Data-driven development methodology.

351

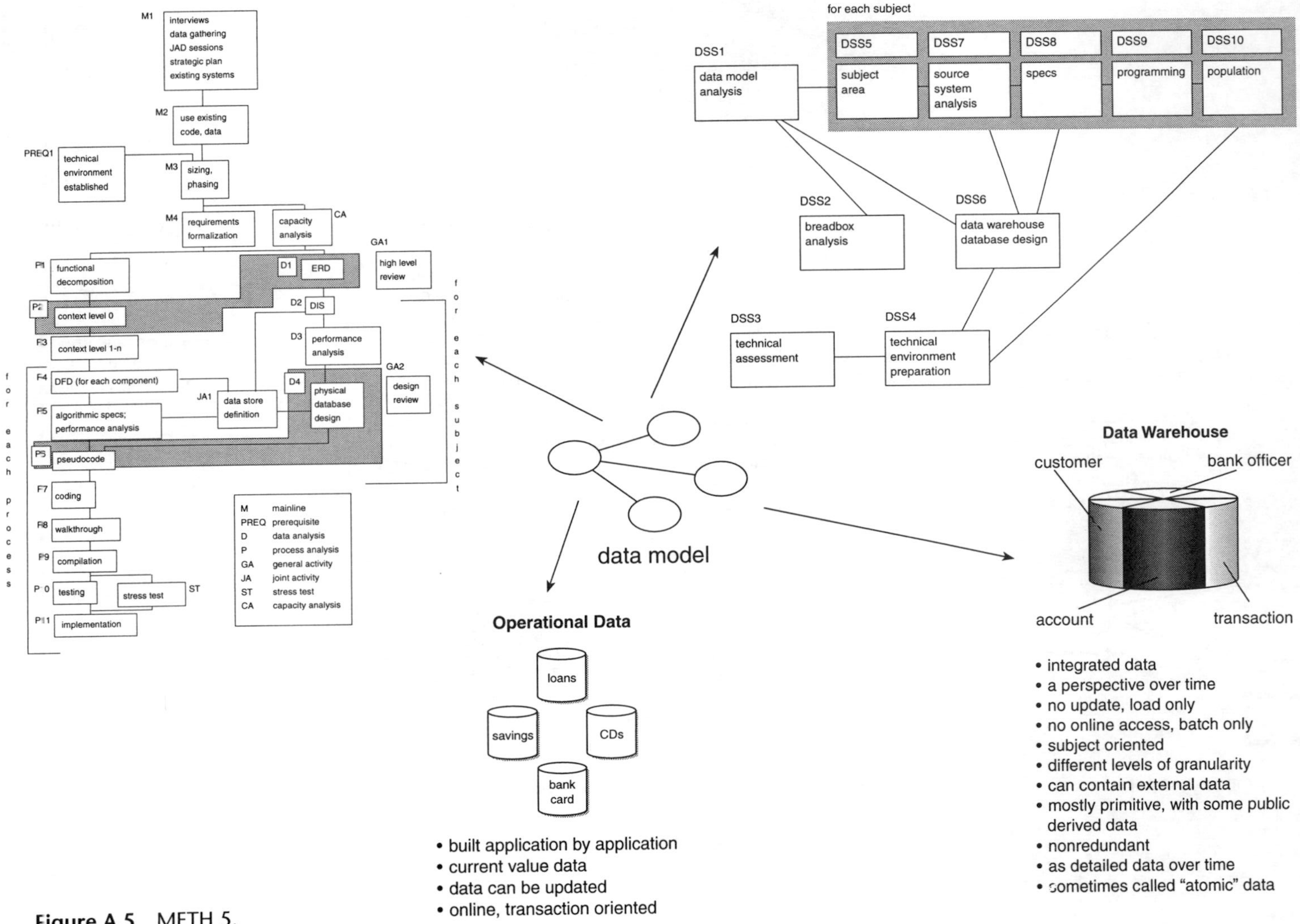

**Figure A.5** METH 5.

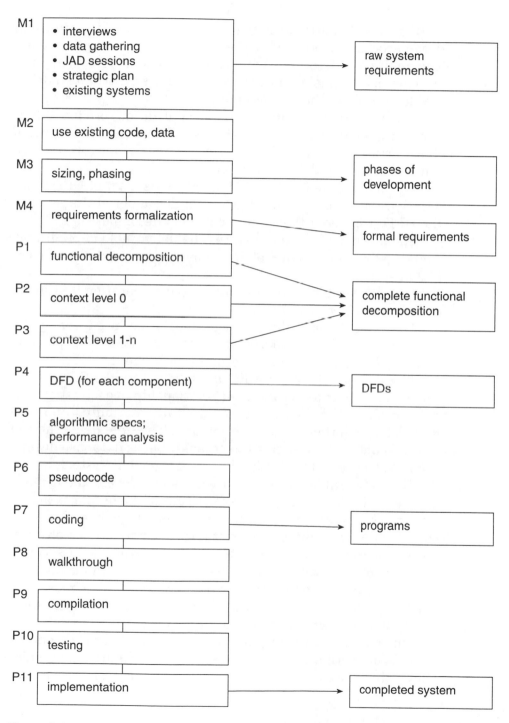

**Figure A.6** METH 6. Deliverables throughout the development lifecycle.

Figure A.6 shows that the deliverable for the interview and data-gathering process is a raw set of systems requirements. The analysis to determine what code/data can be reused and the step for sizing/phasing the raw requirements contribute a deliverable describing the phases of development.

The activity of requirements formalization produces (not surprisingly) a formal set of system specifications. The result of the functional decomposition activities is the deliverable of a complete functional decomposition.

The deliverable for the DFD definition is a set of DFDs that describe the functions that have been decomposed. In general, the DFDs represent the primitive level of decomposition.

The activity of coding produces the deliverable of programs. And finally, the activity of implementation produces a completed system.

The deliverables for data analysis for operational systems are shown in Figure A.7.

The same deliverables discussed earlier are produced by the interview and data gathering process, the sizing and phasing activity, and the definition of formal requirements.

The deliverable of the ERD activity is the identification of the major subject areas and their relationship to each other. The deliverable of the DIS activity is the fully attributed and normalized description of each subject area. The final deliverable of physical database design is the actual table or database design, ready to be defined to the database management system(s).

The deliverables of the data warehouse development effort are shown in Figure A.8, where the result of the breadbox analysis is the granularity and volume analysis. The deliverable associated with data warehouse database design is the physical design of data warehouse tables. The deliverable associated with technical environment preparation is the establishment of the technical environment in which the data warehouse will exist. Note that this environment may or may not be the same environment in which operational systems exist.

On a repetitive basis, the deliverables of data warehouse population activities are represented by Figure A.9, which shows that the deliverable for subject area analysis—each time

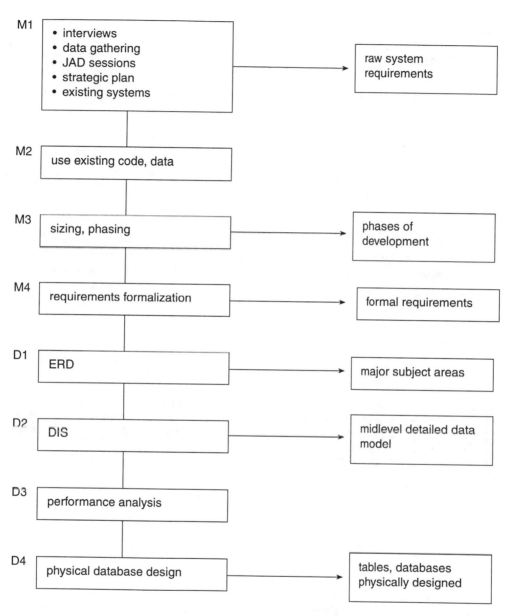

M1
- interviews
- data gathering
- JAD sessions
- strategic plan
- existing systems

raw system requirements

M2 use existing code, data

M3 sizing, phasing

phases of development

M4 requirements formalization

formal requirements

D1 ERD

major subject areas

D2 DIS

midlevel detailed data model

D3 performance analysis

D4 physical database design

tables, databases physically designed

**Figure A.7**   METH 7. Deliverables for operational data analysis.

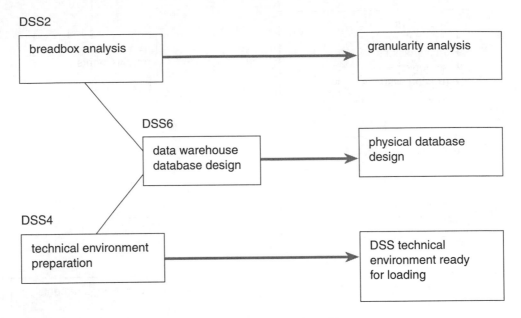

**Figure A.8** METH 8. Preliminary data warehouse deliverables.

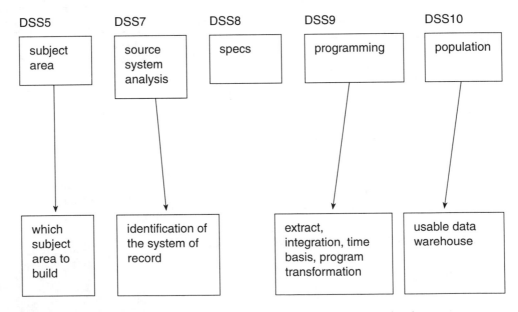

**Figure A.9** METH 9. Deliverables from the steps of data warehouse development.

the data warehouse is to be populated—is the selection of a subject (or possibly a subset of a subject) for population.

The deliverable for source system analysis is the identification of the system of record for the subject area being considered. The deliverable for the programming phase is the programs that will extract, integrate, and change data from current value to time variant.

The final deliverable in the population of the data warehouse is the actual population of the warehouse. It is noted that the population of data into the warehouse is an ongoing activity.

Deliverables for the heuristic levels of processing are not as easy to define as they are for the operational and data warehouse levels of development. The heuristic nature of the analytical processing in this phase is much more informal. However, Figure A.10 shows some of the deliverables associated with heuristic processing based on the data warehouse.

Figure A.10 shows that data pulled from the warehouse is the result of the extraction program. The deliverable of the subsequent analysis step is further analysis based on data already refined. The deliverable of the final analysis of data is the satisfaction (and understanding) of requirements.

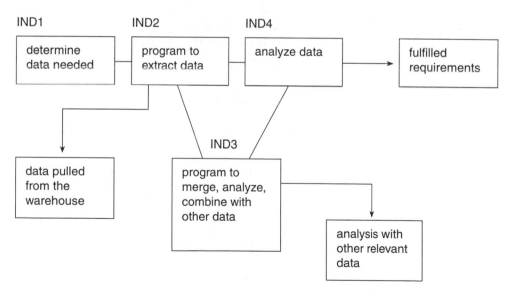

**Figure A.10**  METH 10. Deliverables for the heuristic level of processing.

### A Linear Flow of Deliverables

Except for heuristic processing, a linear flow of deliverables is to be expected. Figure A.11 shows a sample of deliverables that would result from the execution of the process analysis component of the data-driven development methodology.

It is true that within reason there is a linear flow of deliver-

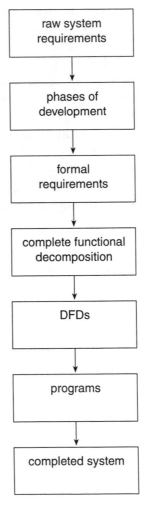

**Figure A.11** METH 11. A linear flow of deliverables for operational process analysis.

ables. However, the linear flow shown glosses over two important aspects:

- The deliverables are usually produced in an iterative fashion.
- There are multiple deliverables at any given level. In other words, deliverables at any one level have the capability of spawning multiple deliverables at the next lower level, as shown by Figure A.12.

Figure A.12 shows that a single requirements definition results in three development phases. Each development phase

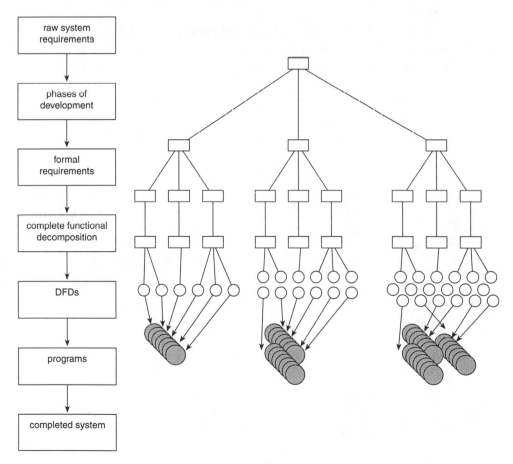

**Figure A.12** METH 12. Deliverables usually spawn multiple deliverables at a lower level.

goes through formal requirements definition and into decomposition. From the decomposition, multiple activities are identified, each of which has a DFD created for it. In turn, each DFD creates one or more programs. Ultimately, the programs form the backbone of the completed system.

### Estimating Resources Required for Development

Looking at the diagram shown in Figure A.12, it becomes apparent that once the specifics of exactly how many deliverables are being spawned are designed, then an estimation of how many resources the development process will take can be rationally done.

Figure A.13 shows a simple technique, in which each level of deliverables first is defined so that the total number of deliverables is known. Then the time required for the building of each

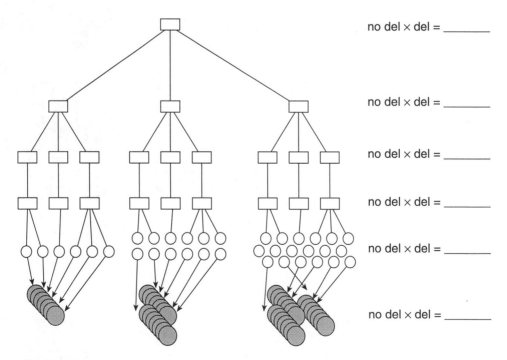

**Figure A.13** METH 13. Estimating system development time.

deliverable is multiplied by each deliverable, yielding an estimate of the employee resources required.

## SDLC/CLDS

Earlier discussions alluded to the fact that operational systems are built under one system development life cycle, and DSS systems are built under another system development life cycle. Figure A.14 shows the development life cycle associated with operational systems, where requirements are at the starting point. The next activities include analysis, design, programming, testing, integration, implementation, and maintenance.

The system development life cycle associated with DSS systems is shown by Figure A.15, where DSS processing begins with data. Once data for analysis is secured (usually by using the data warehouse), programming, analysis, and so forth continue. The development life cycle for DSS data ends with an understanding of the requirements.

## Data Dictionary

The role of the data dictionary is depicted by the graph shown in Figure A.16.

The data dictionary plays a central role in operational processing in the activities of ERD development and documentation, DIS development, physical database design, and coding. The data dictionary plays a heavy role in data model analysis, subject area selection, source system selection (system of record identification), and programming in the world of data warehouse development.

## What About Existing Systems?

In very few cases is development done freshly with no backlog of existing systems. Existing systems certainly present no problem to the DSS component of the data-driven development methodology. Finding the system of record in existing systems to serve as a basis for warehouse data is a normal event.

the classical system development lifecycle

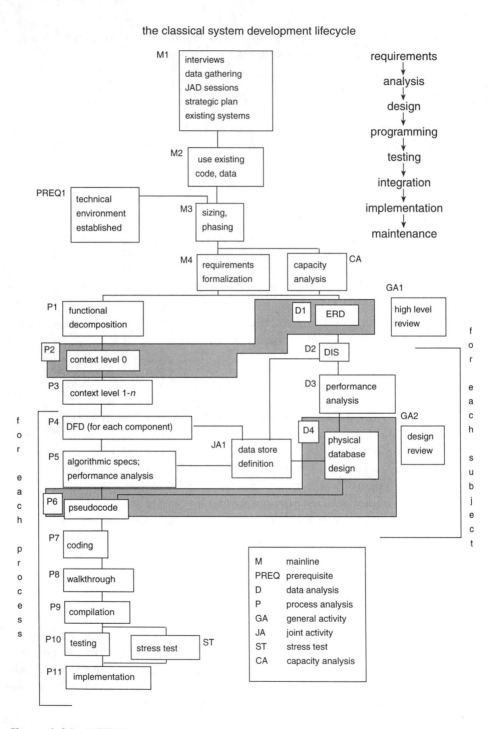

**Figure A.14** METH 14.

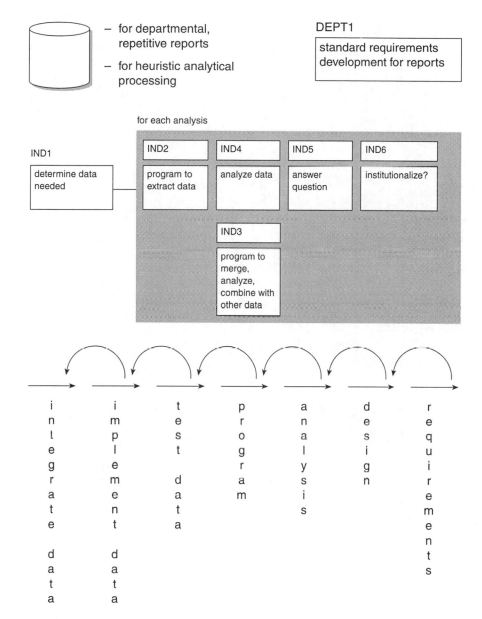

**Figure A.15** METH 15.

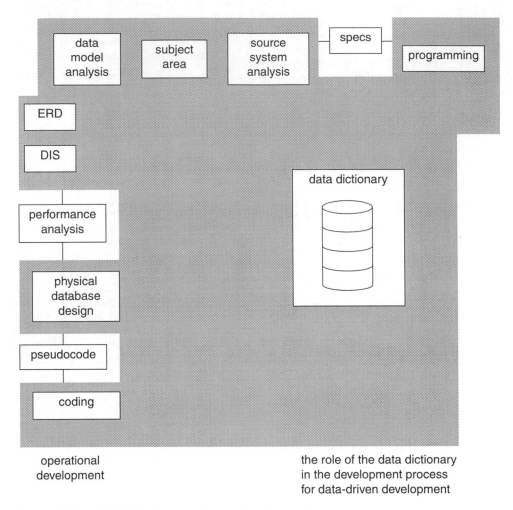

**Figure A.16**   METH 16. Data warehouse development.

However, a word needs to be said about existing systems in the operational environment. The first approach to existing operational systems is to try to build on them. When this is possible, much productivity is the result. But in many cases existing operational systems cannot be built upon.

The second stance is to try to modify existing operational systems. In some cases this is a possibility; in most cases it is not.

The third stance is to do a wholesale replacement and enhancement of existing operational systems. In this case, the existing operational system serves as a basis for gathering requirements, and no more.

A variant of a wholesale replacement is the conversion of some or all of an existing operational system. This approach works on a limited basis, where the existing system is small and simple. The larger and more complex the existing operational system, the less likelihood that the system can be converted.

# Glossary

**access**—the operation of seeking, reading, or writing data on a storage unit.

**access method**—a technique used to transfer a physical record from or to a mass storage device.

**access pattern**—the general sequence in which the data structure is accessed (for example, from tuple to tuple, from record to record, from segment to segment, etc.).

**accuracy**—a qualitative assessment of freedom from error or a quantitative measure of the magnitude of error, expressed as a function of relative error.

**ad hoc processing**—one time only, casual access, and manipulation of data on parameters never before used, usually done in a heuristic, iterative manner.

**after image**—the snapshot of data placed on a log upon the completion of a transaction.

**agent of change**—a motivating force large enough not to be denied, usually aging of systems, changes in technology, radical changes in requirements, etc.

**algorithm**—a set of statements organized to solve a problem in a finite number of steps.

**analytical processing**—using the computer to produce an analysis for management decision, usually involving trend analysis, drill-down analysis, demographic analysis, profiling, etc.

**application**—a group of algorithms and data interlinked to support an organizational requirement.

**application database**—a collection of data organized to support a specific application.

**archival database**—a collection of data containing data of a historical nature. As a rule, archival data cannot be updated. Each unit of archival data is relevant to a moment in time, now passed.

**artifact**—a design technique used to represent referential integrity in the DSS environment.

**atomic**—(1) data stored in a data warehouse; (2) the lowest level of process analysis.

**atomic database**—a database made up of primarily atomic data; a data warehouse; a DSS foundation database.

**atomic-level data**—data with the lowest level of granularity. Atomic-level data sits in a data warehouse and is time variant (i.e., accurate as of some moment in time now passed).

**attribute**—a property that can assume values for entities or relationships. Entities can be assigned several attributes (for example, a tuple in a relationship consists of values). Some systems also allow relationships to have attributes as well.

**audit trail**—data that is available to trace activity, usually update activity.

**backup**—a file serving as a basis for the activity of backing up a database. Usually a snapshot of a database as of some previous moment in time.

**batch**—computer environment in which programs (usually long-running, sequentially oriented) access data exclusively, and user interaction is not allowed while the activity is occurring.

**batch environment**—a sequentially dominated mode of processing; in batch, input is collected and stored for future, later processing. Once collected, the batch input is transacted sequentially against one or more databases.

**before image**—a snapshot of a record prior to update, usually placed on an activity log.

**bitmap**—a specialized form of an index indicating the existence or nonexistence of a condition for a group of blocks or records. Bitmaps are expensive to build and maintain but provide very fast comparison and access facilities.

**blocking**—the combining of two or more physical records so that they are physically located together. The result of their physical colocation is that they can be accessed and fetched by a single execution of a machine instruction.

**cache**—a buffer usually built and maintained at the device level. Retrieving data out of a cache is much quicker than retrieving data out of a cylinder.

**cardinality (of a relation)**—the number of tuples (i.e., rows) in a relation.

**CASE**—computer-aided software engineering.

**checkpoint**—an identified snapshot of the database or a point at which the transactions against the database have been frozen or have been quiesced.

**checkpoint/restart**—a means of restarting a program at some point other than the beginning—for example, when a failure or interruption has occurred. N checkpoints may be used at intervals throughout an application program. At each of those points, sufficient information is stored to permit the program to be restored to the moment in time the checkpoint has been taken.

**"CLDS"**—the facetiously named system development life cycle for analytical, DSS systems. CLDS is so named because in fact it is the reverse of the classical systems development life cycle—SDLC.

**COBOL**—Common Business Oriented Language—a computer language for the business world. A very common language.

**column**—a vertical table in which values are selected from the same domain. A row is made up of one or more columns.

**commonality of data**—similar or identical data that occurs in different applications or systems. The recognition and management of commonality of data is one of the foundations of conceptual and physical database design.

**compaction**—a technique for reducing the number of bits required to represent data without losing the content of the data. With compaction, repetitive data are represented very concisely.

**condensation**—the process of reducing the volume of data managed without reducing the logical consistency of the data. Condensation is essentially different from compaction.

**contention**—the condition that occurs when two or more programs try to access the same data at the same time.

**continuous time span data**—data organized so that a continuous definition of data over a span of time is represented by one or more records.

**CPU**—central processing unit.

**CPU-bound**—the state of processing in which the computer can produce no more output because the CPU portion of the processor is being used at 100 percent capacity. When the computer is CPU-bound, typically the memory and storage processing units are less than 100 percent utilized. With modern DBMS, it is much more likely that the computer be I/O-bound, rather than CPU-bound.

**current value data**—data whose accuracy is valid as of the moment of execution, as opposed to time variant data.

**DASD**—see **direct access storage device**

**data**—a recording of facts, concepts, or instructions on a storage medium for communication, retrieval, and processing by automatic means and presentation as information that is understandable by human beings.

**data administrator (DA)**—the individual or organization responsible for the specification, acquisition, and maintenance of data management software and the design, validation, and security of files or databases. The data model and the data dictionary are classically the charge of the DA.

**database**—a collection of interrelated data stored (often with controlled, limited redundancy) according to a schema. A database can serve single or multiple applications.

**database administrator (DBA)**—the organizational function charged with the day-to-day monitoring and care of the databases. The DBA function is more closely associated with physical database design than the DA is.

**database key**—a unique value that exists for each record in a database. The value is often indexed, although it can be randomized or hashed.

**database management system (DBMS)**—a computer-based software system used to establish and manage data.

**data-driven development**—the approach to development that centers around identifying the commonality of data through a data model and building programs that have a broader scope than the immediate application. Data-driven development differs from classical application-oriented development.

**data element**—(1) an attribute of an entity; (2) a uniquely named and well-defined category of data that consists of data items and that is included in a record of an activity.

**data item set (DIS)**—a grouping of data items, each of which directly relates to the key of the grouping of data in which the data items reside. The data item set is found in the midlevel model.

**data model**—(1) the logical data structures, including operations and constraints provided by a DBMS for effective database processing; (2) the system used for the representation of data (for example, the ERD or relational model).

**data structure**—a logical relationship among data elements that is designed to support specific data manipulation functions (trees, lists, and tables).

**data warehouse**—a collection of integrated, subject-oriented databases designed to support the DSS function, where each unit of data is relevant to some moment in time. The data warehouse contains atomic data and lightly summarized data.

**decision support system (DSS)**—a system used to support managerial decisions. Usually DSS involves the analysis of many units of data in a heuristic fashion. As a rule, DSS processing does not involve the update of data.

**decompaction**—the opposite of compaction; once data is stored in a compacted form, it must be decompacted to be used.

**denormalization**—the technique of placing normalized data in a physical location that optimizes the performance of the system.

**derived data**—data whose existence depends on two or more occurrences of a major subject of the enterprise.

**derived data element**—a data element that is not necessarily stored but that can be generated when needed (age, current date, date of birth).

**design review**—the quality assurance process in which all aspects of a system are reviewed publicly prior to the striking of code.

**direct access**—retrieval or storage of data by reference to its location on a volume. The access mechanism goes directly to the data in question, as is generally required with online use of data. Also called random access or hashed access.

**direct access storage device (DASD)**—a data storage unit on which data can be accessed directly without having to progress through a serial file such as a magnetic tape file. A disk unit is a direct access storage device.

**download**—the stripping of data from one database to another based on the content of data found in the first database.

**drill-down analysis**—the type of analysis where examination of a summary number leads to the exploration of the components of the sum.

**dual database**—the practice of separating high-performance, transaction-oriented data from decision support data.

**dual database management systems**—the practice of using multiple database management systems to control different aspects of the database environment.

**dumb terminal**—a device used to interact directly with the end user where all processing is done on a remote computer. A dumb terminal acts as a device that gathers data and displays data only.

**EIS (Executive Information Systems)**—systems designed for the top executive, featuring drill-down analysis and trend analysis.

**encoding**—a shortening or abbreviation of the physical representation of a data value (e.g., male = "M," female = "F").

**entity**—a person, place, or thing of interest to the data modeler at the highest level of abstraction.

**entity-relationship diagram (ERD)**—a high-level data model—the schematic showing all the entities within the scope of integration and the direct relationship between those entities.

**event**—a signal that an activity of significance has occurred. An event is noted by the information system.

**external data**—(1) data originating from other than the operational systems of a corporation; (2) data residing outside the central processing complex.

**extract**—the process of selecting data from one environment and transporting it to another environment.

**flat file**—a collection of records containing no data aggregates, nested repeated data items, or groups of data items.

**foreign key**—an attribute that is not a primary key in a relational system but whose values are the values of the primary key of another relation.

**fourth-generation language**—language or technology designed to allow the end user unfettered access to data.

**functional decomposition**—the division of operations into hierarchical functions (activities) that form the basis for procedures.

**granularity**—the level of detail contained in a unit of data. The more detail there is, the lower the level of granularity. The less detail there is, the higher the level of granularity.

**heuristic**—the mode of analysis in which the next step is determined by the results of the current step of analysis. Used for decision support processing.

**image copy**—a procedure in which a database is physically copied to another medium for the purposes of backup.

**index**—the portion of the storage structure maintained to provide efficient access to a record when its index key item is known.

**information**—data that human beings assimilate and evaluate to solve a problem or make a decision.

**integrity**—the property of a database that ensures that the data contained in the database is as accurate and consistent as possible.

**interactive**—a mode of processing that combines some of the characteristics of online transaction processing and batch processing. In interactive processing, the end user interacts with data over which he or she has exclusive control. In addition, the end user can initiate background activity to be run against the data.

**"is a type of"**—an analytical tool used in abstracting data during the process of conceptual database design (for example, a cocker spaniel is a type of dog).

**iterative analysis**—the mode of processing in which the next step of processing depends on the results obtained by the existing step in execution; heuristic processing.

**JAD (joint application design)**—an organization of people—usually end users—who create and refine application system requirements.

**judgment sample**—a sample of data where data is accepted or rejected for the sample based on one or more parameters.

**key**—a data item or combination of data items used to identify or locate a record instance (or other similar data groupings).

**key, primary**—a unique attribute used to identify a single record in a database.

**key, secondary**—a nonunique attribute used to identify a class of records in a database.

**living sample**—a representative database typically used for heuristic, statistical, analytical processing in place of a large database. Periodically, the very large database is selectively stripped of data so that the resulting living sample database represents a cross-section of the very large database as of some moment in time.

**load**—to insert data values into a database that was previously empty.

**log**—a journal of activity.

**logging**—the automatic recording of data with regard to the access of the data, the updates to the data, etc.

**loss of identity**—when data is brought in from an external source and the identity of the external source is discarded, loss of identity occurs. A common practice with microprocessor data.

**magnetic tape**—(1) the storage medium most closely associated with sequential processing; (2) a large ribbon on which magnetic images are stored and retrieved.

**master file**—a file that holds the system of record for a given set of data (usually bound by an application).

**metadata**—(1) data about data; (2) the description of the structure, content, keys, indexes, etc., of data.

**microprocessor**—a small processor serving the needs of a single user.

**migration**—the process by which frequently used items of data are moved to more readily accessible areas of storage and infrequently used items of data are moved to less readily accessible areas of storage.

**mips (million instructions per second)**—the standard measurement of processor speed for minicomputers and mainframe computers.

**online storage**—storage devices and storage media where data can be accessed in a direct fashion.

**operational data**—data used to support the daily processing a company does.

**operations**—the department charged with the running of the computer.

**optical disk**—a storage medium using lasers as opposed to magnetic devices. Optical disk is typically write only, is much less expensive per byte than magnetic storage, and is highly reliable.

**overflow**—(1) the condition in which a record or a segment cannot be stored in its home address because the address is already occupied. In this case, the data is placed in another location referred to as overflow; (2) the area of DASD where data is sent when the overflow condition is triggered.

**ownership**—the responsibility for updating operational data.

**page**—(1) a basic unit of data on DASD; (2) a basic unit of storage in main memory.

**parameter**—an elementary data value used as a criterion for qualification, usually of data searches or in the control of modules.

**partition**—a segmentation technique in which data is divided into physically different units. Partitioning can be done at the application or the system level.

**populate**—to place occurrences of data values in a previously empty database. See **load**.

**primary key**—an attribute that contains values that uniquely identify the record in which the key exists.

**primitive data**—data whose existence depends on only a single occurrence of a major subject area of the enterprise.

**processor**—the hardware at the center of execution of computer programs. Generally speaking, processors are divided into three categories—mainframes, minicomputers, and microcomputers.

**processor cycles**—the hardware's internal cycles that drive the computer (e.g., initiate I/O, perform logic, move data, perform arithmetic functions).

**production environment**—the environment where operational, high-performance processing is run.

**punched cards**—an early storage medium on which data and input were stored. Today punched cards are rare.

**query language**—a language that enables an end user to interact directly with a DBMS to retrieve and possibly modify data held under the DBMS.

**record**—an aggregation of values of data organized by their relation to a common key.

**record-at-a-time processing**—the access of data a record at a time, a tuple at a time, etc.

**recovery**—the restoration of the database to an original position or condition, often after major damage to the physical medium.

**redundancy**—the practice of storing more than one occurrence of data. In the case where data can be updated, redundancy poses serious problems. In the case where data is not updated, redundancy is often a valuable and necessary design technique.

**referential integrity**—the facility of a DBMS to ensure the validity of predefined relationships.

**reorganization**—the process of unloading data in a poorly organized state and reloading the data in a well-organized state. Reorganization in some DBMSs is used to restructure data. Reorganization is often called "reorg," or an "unload/reload" process.

**repeating groups**—a collection of data that can occur several times within a given record occurrence.

**rolling summary**—a form of storing archival data where the most recent data has the most details stored, and data that is older has fewer details stored.

**scope of integration**—the formal definition of the boundaries of the system being modeled.

**SDLC**—system development life cycle—the classical operational system development life cycle that typically includes requirements gathering, analysis, design, programming, testing, integration, and implementation.

**sequential file**—a file in which records are ordered according to the values of one or more key fields. The records can be processed in this sequence starting from the first record in the file, continuing to the last record in the file.

**serial file**—a sequential file in which the records are physically adjacent, in sequential order.

**set-at-a-time processing**—access of data by groups, each member of which satisfies a selection criterion.

**snapshot**—a database dump or the archiving of data out of a database as of some moment in time.

**solutions database**—the component of a DSS environment where the results of previous decisions are stored. Solutions databases are consulted to help determine the proper course of action in a current decision-making situation.

**storage hierarchy**—storage units linked to form a storage subsystem, in which some units are fast but small and expensive, and other units are large but slower and less expensive.

**subject database**—a database organized around a major subject of the corporation. Classical subject databases are for customer, transaction, product, part, vendor.

**system log**—an audit trail of relevant system events (for example, transaction entries, database changes, etc.)

**system of record**—the definitive and singular source of operational data. If data element abc has a value of 25 in a database record but a value of 45 in the system of record, by definition the first value is incorrect and must be reconciled. The system of record is useful for managing redundancy of data.

**table**—a relation that consists of a set of columns with a heading and a set of rows (i.e., tuples).

**time stamping**—the practice of tagging each record with some moment in time, usually when the record was created or when the record was passed from one environment to another.

**time variant data**—data whose accuracy is relevant to some moment in time. The three forms of time variant data are continuous time span, event discrete, and periodic discrete data. See **current value data.**

**transition data**—data possessing both primitive and derived characteristics; usually very sensitive to the running of the business. Typical transition data are interest rates for a bank, policy rates for an insurance company, retail sale rates for a manufacturer/distributor, etc.

**trend analysis**—the process of looking at homogeneous data over a spectrum of time. See **EIS**.

**true archival data**—data at the lowest level in the atomic database, usually stored on bulk storage media.

**update**—to change, add, delete, or replace values in all or selected entries, groups, or attributes stored in a database.

**user**—a person or process issuing commands and messages to the information system.

# References

Boehm, B. *Software Engineering Economics*, Prentice-Hall, Englewood Cliffs, NJ, 1981.

Brooks, F. P., Jr. *The Mythical Manmonth: Essays on Software Engineering*, Addison-Wesley, Reading, MA, 1974.

Chen, P. P. "The Entity Relationship Model—Toward a Unified View Of Data," in *Transactions on Database Systems*, Vol. 1, No. 1, March 1976.

———. *The Entity Relationship Approach to Logical Database Design*, QED Info Sciences, Wellesley, MA, 1977.

Date, C. J. *An Introduction to Database Systems*, Addison-Wesley, Reading, MA, 1975.

Davis, A. M. "Automating the Requirements Phase: Benefits to Later Phases of Software Life Cycle," in *COMPSAC 80, Proceedings IEEE*, Computer Society, Los Alamitos, CA, October 1980.

Davis, G. B., and M. H. Olson. *Developing a Long-Range Information Systems Plan in Management Information Systems*, McGraw Hill, New York, 1985.

DeMarco, T. *Structured Analysis and Systems Specification*, Yourdon Press, New York, 1978.

Digital Equipment Corporation manual, *Information Systems Technical Strategy and Architecture*, DEC, Marlboro, MA, June 1989.

Gane, C., and T. Sarson. *Structured Systems Analysis: Tools and Techniques*, Prentice-Hall, Englewood Cliffs, NJ, 1979.

Inmon, W. H. *Information Engineering for the Practitioner*, Yourdon Press, New York, 1988.

————. *Using DB2 for Decision Support Systems*, QED, Wellesley, MA, 1989.

————. *Using Oracle for Decision Support Systems*, QED, Wellesley, MA, 1989.

————. *Third Wave Processing: Data Base Machines and Decision Support Systems*, QED, Wellesley, MA, 1991.

————. *Understanding Data Pattern Processing*, QED, Wellesley, MA, 1991 (with S. Osterfelt).

————. *Using Rdb for Decision Support Systems*, QED, Wellesley, MA, 1992.

————. *Practical Information Engineering*, QED, Wellesley, MA, 1992.

————. *Building the Data Warehouse,* John Wiley & Sons, Inc., New York, 1993.

————. *Information Systems Architecture: Development in the 90's,* John Wiley & Sons, Inc., New York, 1993.

————. *Rdb/VMS: Developing the Data Warehouse,* John Wiley & Sons, Inc., New York, 1993.

————. *Using the Data Warehouse,* John Wiley & Sons, Inc., New York, 1994.

————. *Building the Operational Data Store,* John Wiley & Sons, Inc., New York, 1995.

Jackson, M. A. *Principles of Program Design*, Academic Press, New York, 1975.

Karimi, J. "Computer Aided Process Organization in Software Design," Dept. of MIS, University of Arizona, 1983.

Kelly, Sean. *Data Warehousing—The Key to Mass Customization,* John Wiley & Sons, Inc., New York, 1994.

Kerr, M. J. *The IRM Imperative*, John Wiley & Sons, Inc., New York, 1990.

Konsynski, B. R., and R. J. Nunamaker. *Decision Support in Enterprise Analysis*, Plenum Publishing, New York, 1984.

Loper, M., and W. H. Inmon. "A Unified Data Architecture for Systems Integration," *ISEC Conference,* Washington, DC (Feb).

Love, Bruce. *Enterprise Information Technologies,* New York.

Martin, J. *Strategic Data Planning Methodologies*, Prentice-Hall, Englewood Cliffs, NJ, 1982.

Martin, J., and C. Finklestein. *Information Engineering*, Savant Institute, Cornforth, Lancashire, England, 1981.

Meyer, D., and M. Boone. *The Information Edge*, Dow Jones Irwin, Homewood, IL, 1988.

Orr, K. T. *Structured Systems Development*, Yourdon Press, New York, 1977.

Parker, M., R. Benson, and E. Trainor. *Information Economics: Linking Business Performance to Information Technology,* Prentice-Hall, Englewood Cliffs, NJ, 1989.

Parsaye, K., and M. Chignell. *Intelligent Database Tools & Applications,* John Wiley & Sons, Inc., New York, 1995.

Perkinson, R. *Data Analysis: The Key to Database Design*, QED, Wellesley, MA, 1984.

Rousopolous, N. "The Logical Access Path Schema of a Database Design," *ACM Transactions in Software Engineering,* Vol. SE-8, No. 6, November 1982.

Smith, J. M., and D. C. P. Smith. "Database Abstraction Aggregation," *Communications of the ACM,* Vol. 20, No. 6, June 1977.

———. "Conceptual Database Design," *INFOTECH, State of the Art Report on Database Design,* June 1978.

Teichrow, D., and E. A. Hershey. "PSL/PSA: A Computer Aided Technique for Structured Documentation and Analysis of Information Processing Systems," in *IEEE Transactions on Software Engineering*, Vol. SE-3, No. 1, 1977.

Tschritzis, D. C., and F. H. Lochovsky. *Data Models*, Prentice-Hall, Englewood Cliffs, NJ, 1981.

Yourdon, E. *Techniques of Program Structure and Design*, Prentice-Hall, Englewood Cliffs, NJ, 1975.

Zachman, J. "A Framework for Information Systems Architecture," *IBM Systems Journal*, Vol. 26, No. 3, White Plains, New York, 1986.

## ARTICLES OF INTEREST

Ashbrook, J. "Information Preservation" (an executive's view of the data warehouse), *CIO Magazine,* July 1993.

*Data Management Review.* "ChargeBack In the Information Warehouse" (chargeback in the datawarehouse can be both a blessing and a curse. This article addresses both sides of the issue.) March 1993.

*Database Programming Design.* "Now Hich is Data, Which is Information" (the difference between data and information). May 1993.

Devlin, B. A., and P. T. Murphy. "An Architecture for a Business and Information System" (the first mention of information warehouse in the IBM environment), *IBM Systems Journal*, Vol. 27, No. 1, 1988.

*Discount Store News.* "Retail Technology Charges Up at KMart" (a description of the technology employed by KMart for their data warehouse, ODS environment), Feb. 17, 1992.

Geiger, J. "Information Management for Competitive Advantage" (a discussion of how the data warehouse and the Zachman framework have advanced the state of the art), *Strategic Systems Journal, ACR,* June 1993.

Gilbreath, R., MD. "Health Care Data Repositories: Components and a Model" (an excellent description of information architecture as it relates to health care), *Journal of the Healthcare Information and Management Systems Society,* Vol. 9, No. 1, Spring 1995.

———. "Informational Processing Architecture for Outcomes Management" (a description of data warehouse as it applies to health care and outcomes analysis; under review—214-682-0113).

Goldberg, P., Lambert, R. and Powell, K. "Guidelines for Defining Requirements for Decision Support Systems" (a good description of how to define end user requirements before building the data warehouse), *Data Resource Management Journal*, Spring 1991.

Hufford, D. "Data Administration Support for Business Process Improvement" (data warehouse and data administration), *AMS*.

Inmon, W. H. *IBM Systems Journal.* "An Architecture for a Business and Information System" (a description of IBM's understanding of the data warehouse), vol 17, no. 1, 1088.

———. "A Conceptual Model for Documenting Data Synchronization Requirements" (data synchronization and data warehouse), *AMS*.

———. "At the Heart of the Matter" (primitive and derived data and what the differences are), *Data Base Programming / Design*, June 1990.

————. "Going Against the Grain" (a description of the granularity issue and how it relates to the data warehouse), *Data Base Programming/Design*, July 1990.

————. "The Atomic Database" (the prediction that a split database environment is the direction of database), *Enterprise Systems Journal*, Nov. 1990.

————. "The Cabinet Effect" (a description of why the data warehouse–centered architecture does not degenerate into the spider web environment), *Data Base Programming/Design*, May 1991.

————. "A Tale of Two Cycles" (the development life cycles of the operational and the data warehouse, DSS environment are diametrically opposed. This is a discussion of the difference), *Data Base Programming/Design*, Dec. 1991.

————. "Data Structures in the Information Warehouse" (a description of the common data structures found in the data warehouse), *Enterprise Systems Journal*, Jan. 1992.

————. "Winds of Change" (data administration and the data warehouse—a description of how data administration evolved to where it is today), *Data Base Programming/Design*, Jan. 1992.

————. "Data Warehouse—A Perspective of Data Over Time" (a description of the relationship of data warehouse and the management of data over time), *370/390 Data Base Management*, Feb. 1992.

————. "Building the Data Bridge" (ten critical success factors in building the data warehouse), *Data Base Programming/Design*, April 1992.

————. "Metadata: A Checkered Past, A Bright Future" (a conversation about metadata and how metadata relates to data warehouse), *370/390 Data Base Management*, July 1992.

————. "The Need for Reporting" (the different kinds of reports found throughout the different parts of the architecture), *Data Base Programming/Design*, July 1992.

————. "Neat Little Packages" (a description of how data relationships are treated in the data warehouse), *Data Base Programming/Design*, Aug. 1992.

————. "EIS and the Data Warehouse" (the relationship between EIS and data warehouse), *Data Base Programming/Design*, Nov. 1992.

———. "Untangling the Web" (exploring the factors that turn data into information), *Data Base Programming Design,* May 1993.

———. "The Structure of the Data Warehouse" (addresses the different levels of data found in the data warehouse), *Data Management Review,* Aug. 1993.

———. "Data Warehouse Lays Foundation for Bringing Data Investment Forward" (a description of data warehouse and the relation to legacy systems), *Application Development Trends,* Jan. 1994.

———. "The Data Warehouse—All Your Data at Your Fingertips" (an overview of data warehouse), *Communications Week,* Aug. 29, 1994.

———. "The Data Warehouse: Managing the Infrastructure" (a description of the data warehouse infrastructure and the budget associated with it), *Data Management Review,* Dec. 1994.

———. "EIS and Detail" (a description of how much detail is needed to support EIS and the role of summarized data in the data warehouse environment), *Data Management Review,* Jan. 1995.

———. "Multidimensional Data Bases and Data Warehousing" (a description of how current detailed data in the data warehouse fits with multidimensional DBMS), *Data Management Review,* Feb. 1995.

———. "The Operational Data Store" (a description of the ODS), *INFODB,* Vol. 9, No. 1, Feb. 1995.

———. "Profiling the DSS Analyst" (a description of DSS analysts as farmers and explorers), *Data Management Review,* March 1995.

———. "The Anatomy of a Data Warehouse Record" (a description of the internal structure of a data warehouse record), *Data Management Review,* July 1995.

———. "Profile/Aggregate Records in the Data Warehouse" (a description of how profile/aggregate records are created and used in the data warehouse environment), *Data Management Review,* July 1995.

———. "Date Warehouse and Contextual Data: Pioneering a New Dimension" (a description of the need for contextual data over time as found in the data warehouse), *Data Base Newsletter,* Vol. 23, No. 4, July/August 1995.

———. "Transformation Complexity" (why automating the transformation process is a superior idea to manually programming the transformations that are required in order to build the data warehouse), *Data Management Review,* Sept. 1995.

————. "The Ladder of Success" (Building and managing the data warehouse environment entails more than selecting a platform. This article outlines the many necessary steps required to achieve a successful data warehouse environment.), *Data Management Review,* Nov. 1995.

————. "Growth in the Data Warehouse" (a description of why the data warehouse grows so fast and the phenomenon of increasing amounts of storage while decreasing the percent utilization of storage), *Data Management Review,* Dec. 1995.

Inmon, W. H., and C. Kelly. "The 12 Rules of Data Warehouse" (a description of the defining characteristics of data warehouse), *Data Management Review,* May 1994.

Inmon, W. H., and P. Koslow. "Commandeering Mainframe Database for Data Warehouse Use" (a discussion of optimal data warehouse use inside the mainframe), *Application Development Trends,* Aug. 1994.

Inmon, W. H., and M. Loper. "The Unified Data Architecture: A Systems Integration Solution" [the original paper (republished in a revised state) suggesting that a data architecture was in order for future systems development], Auerbach, 1992.

Inmon, W. H., and S. Osterfelt. "Data Patterns Say the Darndest Things" (a description of the usage of the data warehouse in the DSS community and how informational processing can be derived from a warehouse), *Computerworld,* Feb. 3, 1992.

Kador, J. "One on One—Interview with Bill Inmon" (a discussion about the data warehouse with Bill, including some of the history of how it came to be), *Midrange Systems,* Oct. 27, 1995.

Kimball, R., and K. Strehlo. "Why Decision Support Fails and How to Fix It" (a good description of fact tables and star joins, with a lengthy discussion about Ralph's approach to data warehouse and decision support), *Datamation,* June 1994.

Konrad, W. "Smoking Out the Elusive Smoker" (a description of database marketing in the advertising restricted marketing environment), *BusinessWeek,* March 16, 1992.

Lambert, B. "Breaking Old Habits to Define Data Warehousing Requirements" (a description of how the end user should be approached to determine DSS requirements), *Data Management Review.*

O'Mahoney, M. "Revolutionary Breakthrough in Client/Server Data Warehouse Development" (a description of older legacy development methodologies versus modern iterative methodologies), *Data Management Review,* July 1995.

Sloan, R., and H. Green. "An Information Architecture for the Global Manufacturing Enterprise" (a description of information architecture in the large-scale manufacturing environment), Auerbach, 1993.

Thiessen, M. "Proving the Data Warehouse to Management and Customers: Where Are the Savings?" (presentation by Mark Thiessen, Hughes Aircraft, 1994 *Data Warehouse Conference,* foils and handouts, 714-732-9059).

Wahl, D., and D. Hufford. "A Case Study: Implementing and Operating an Atomic Data Base" (based on the US Army DSS data architecture), *Data Resource Management*, Auerbach, Spring 1992.

Welch, J. D. "Providing Customized Decision Support Capabilities: Defining Architectures" (decision support systems and architecture, based on the PacTel Cellular DSS architecture), *Data Resource Management*, Auerbach, 1990.

## PRISM SOLUTIONS TECH TOPICS ON DATA WAREHOUSE

*Accessing Data Warehouse Data from the Operational Environment.* Most flow of data is from the operational environment to the data warehouse environment, but not all. This Tech Topic discusses the "backward" flow of data.

*Capacity Planning for the Data Warehouse.* This Tech Topic discusses the issue of capacity planning and projection for both disk storage and processor resources for the data warehouse environment.

*Changed Data Capture.* The resources required for repeatedly scanning the operational environment for the purpose of refreshing the data warehouse can be enormous. This briefing addresses an alternative way to accomplish the same thing.

*Client / Server and Data Warehouse.* Client/server processing is quite able to support data warehouse processing. This Tech Topic addresses the issues of architecture and design.

*Creating the Data Warehouse Data Model from the Corporate Data Model*—The steps you need to take to create the data warehouse data model from the corporate data model.

*Data Warehouse and Cost Justification.* A priori cost justification is a difficult thing to do for a data warehouse. This Tech Topic discusses the issues.

*The Data Warehouse Budget.* This Tech Topic addresses the different patterns of spending and the rate at which funds are spent. Some suggestions for minimizing expenses are included.

*Defining the System of Record*—The design considerations of identifying and defining the system of record.

*EIS and Data Warehouse.* EIS under a foundation of legacy systems is very shaky, but EIS under a data warehouse foundation is very solid, as detailed in this Tech Topic.

*Explaining Metadata to the End User.* When a user first encounters metadata, the initial reaction usually is "What in the world is metadata and why would I ever need it?" This Tech Topic addresses metadata in very plain, straightforward terms.

*Getting Started.* The data warehouse is built iteratively. This Tech Topic describes, in a detailed manner, the first steps you need to take.

*Information Architecture for the Nineties: Legacy Systems, Operational Data Stores, Data Warehouses*—Describes the role of operational data stores, along with a description of the architecture that results when you mix an operational data store and data warehouse.

*Information Engineering and the Data Warehouse.* The data warehouse architecture is extremely compatible with the design and modeling practices of information engineering. This Tech Topic describes that relationship.

*Loading the Data Warehouse.* At first glance, loading data into the data warehouse seems to be an easy task. It is not. This discussion is on the many different considerations of loading data from the operational environment into the data warehouse.

*Managing Multiple Data Warehouse Development Efforts.* When the organization starts to build multiple data warehouse efforts simultaneously, a new set of design and development issues arise. This Tech Topic identifies and addresses those issues.

*Metadata in the Data Warehouse.* Metadata is an important component of the data warehouse. This Tech Topic discusses why, and what the different components of metadata are for the data warehouse.

*OLAP and Data Warehouse.* Lightly summarized data has always been an integral part of the data warehouse architecture. Today this construct is known as OLAP, or a datamart. This Tech Topic addresses the relationship of OLAP to the detailed data found in the data warehouse.

*Operational and DSS Processing from a Single Data Base: Separating Fact and Fiction.* An early notion was that a single database should serve as the basis for both operational processing and DSS analytical processing. This Tech Topic explores the issues and describes why the data warehouse is the appropriate foundation for DSS informational processing.

*The Operational Data Store.* The operational counterpoint of the data warehouse is the operational data store (ODS). The ODS is defined and described in detail in this Tech Topic.

*Parallel Processing in the Data Warehouse.* The management of volumes of data is the first and major challenge facing the data architect. Parallel technology offers the possibility of managing much data. This Tech Topic is on the issues of parallel technology in the data warehouse environment.

*Performance in the Data Warehouse Environment.* Performance is as important in the DSS data warehouse environment as it is in the OLTP environment. This Tech Topic is all about performance in the DSS data warehouse environment.

*Reengineering and the Data Warehouse.* Many organizations are not aware of the very strong and very positive relationship between reengineering and the data warehouse. This Tech Topic identifies the relationship and discusses the ramifications.

*Representing Data Relationships in the Data Warehouse: Artifacts of Data*—Design issues for the building of data relationships in the data warehouse.

*Security in the Data Warehouse.* Security takes on a very different dimension in the data warehouse. This Tech Topic describes the issues.

*Service-Level Agreements in the Data Warehouse Environment.* One of the cornerstones of online operations is the service-level agreement. Service-level agreements are applicable to the data warehouse but are implemented quite differently.

*Snapshots of Data in the Warehouse*—A description of the different types of snapshots and the advantages and disadvantages of each.

*Summary Data in the Data Warehouse/Operational Data Store.* Summary data has its own set of unique considerations. There is, for example, dynamic summary data and static summary data. Each type of summary data requires very different treatment from the designer and the end user. This Tech Topic creates a taxonomy for summary data and relates the different types of summary data to the data warehouse and the operational data store.

*Telling the Difference Between Operational and DSS.* In every shop the issue arises—what is operational and what is DSS? This Tech Topic tells you how to tell the difference.

*Time Dependent Data Structures*—A discussion of the different types of data structures and their advantages and disadvantages.

*Using the Generic Data Model.* Some corporations have a data model as a point of departure for the design of their data warehouse; others do not. The generic data model jump starts the data warehouse design and development effort.

*What Is a Data Warehouse?* This Tech Topic defines what a data warehouse is and what its structure looks like. This is a basic discussion appropriate to anyone investigating the world of the data warehouse.

PRISM Solutions
1000 Hamlin Court
Sunnyvale, CA 94089
1-800-995-2928

# Index